Baseball: Never Too Old To Play "The" Game is about a love affair between Al and baseball, a fond recollection, and an entertaining description of his life-long connection with the game. A perfect companion to the summer game we all love.

The book captures the essence of baseball in general and senior baseball specifically. It will take you to the joy of baseball in your youth and reveal that you never lost it. Al's respect for and love of the game shines through.

Greg Rhodes
Executive Director, Cincinnati Reds Hall of Fame and Museum,
Author, Six Books about the Cincinnati Reds

Sometime during our teen years, most of us face the reality that we aren't headed for the major leagues and pack away our baseball gloves (and our dreams). We retreat to the stands, figuring, "That's the end of playing hardball." But wait! Alan Spector brings good news—senior baseball can keep you playing, well, nearly forever. There is no excuse. Got an artificial hip? Parkinson's disease? Ninety-four years old? Spector details the passion that keeps such players on the field. Along the way, he reflects on the purity of the essential game as opposed to MLB's branded product, the science of groundskeeping, and an essential section on conditioning and treating injuries (ice is good).

Jean Hastings Ardell
Author, *Breaking into Baseball: Women and the National Pastime*

...you've really poured your heart into it and should make true baseball fans like ourselves reflect on the human side of baseball.

I met Al at a Cincinnati Reds fantasy camp where he showed his love of baseball far outshone his talent for playing. This book is a warm read of his love affair with the game.

Chris W
Former Major League Pitcher, Cincinnati Re
Publisher, *The Thi*

D1042466

BASEBALL

NEVER TOO OLD
TO PLAY THE GAME

AL SPECTOR

KC —
You will too old
[never] be too [to play the game.]
to play the [game]
Al Spector

Cincinnati Book Publishers
Jarndyce & Jarndyce Press
www.cincybooks.com

Baseball: Never Too Old To Play "The" Game
Al Spector

Copyright © by Al Spector

Cover and text design: Brent Beck
Photo credits: Ann Spector, cover by Jan Miller (Jan Miller Photography, Ft Myers, Florida)

Published by Cincinnati Book Publishers
Anthony W. Brunsman, President
Cincinnati Book Publishers World Wide Web address is http://www.cincybooks.com

ISBN: 978-0-9772720-4-4

Printed by John S. Swift Co., Inc.
Printed in the United States of America
First Edition, 2007

DEDICATIONS

This book is dedicated to three special people in my life.

To my mother, Jeanette Friedman Spector, who provided me a balance of freedom and support to be the best that I could be, regardless of what I chose to do. I only hope that her wisdom lives well beyond her all too brief 54 years.

To my father, Herman Spector, who established fair play, team play, and baseball as cornerstones of my life. "Oh you're Herm Spector's boy. Wow, can your dad ever hit the ball!"

To my wife, Ann, who is my life, family, and baseball partner—in that order. She is the glue that holds the family, the team, and me together.

This book is also dedicated to Roy "Yoke" Yocum, dearest of baseball friends, who was killed in a motorcycle accident during the writing of this book. Yoke loved life and baseball and played them both hard.

TABLE OF CONTENTS

Pre-Game	ACKNOWLEDGMENTS	1
	INTRODUCTION	3
	PROLOGUE	7
First Inning	NEVER TOO YOUNG; NEVER TOO OLD	9
Second Inning	WHO ARE THESE GUYS?	31
Third Inning	RESPECT THE GAME	55
Fourth Inning	CRACK OF THE BAT	75
Fifth Inning	ATHLETIC SUPPORTERS	99
Sixth Inning	PLAYING CATCH WITH DAD	133
Seventh Inning	CHARACTERS	153
Eighth Inning	LOSING A STEP	169
Ninth Inning	FUTURE OF SENIOR BASEBALL	201
Extra Innings	FITNESS GUIDELINES	223
	BIBLIOGRAPHY	229
	WEB SITE RESOURCES	231

PRE-GAME

ACKNOWLEDGMENTS

Thank you to those who shared their time, energy, and knowledge to help this first time author survive the process. First and foremost, thank you to Ann—you gave your full support, patience, good humor, and editing capability.

To Dr. Alan A. Halpern and Dr. Douglas Magenheim, thank you for lending your expertise to the medical and fitness aspects of the book. Dr. Halpern is an orthopedic surgeon in Kalamazoo, Michigan and author of *Runner's World Knee Book: What Every Athlete Needs to Know About the Prevention and Treatment of Knee Problems* (Simon & Schuster) and *The Kalamazoo Arthritis Book.* Dr. Magenheim is a doctor of internal medicine whose practice in Cincinnati is named "My Doctor."

To Peter Schiff Ph.D., Associate Professor of English at Northern Kentucky University, you combined your love of the English language and of baseball to provide me with invaluable editing insights. Thank you.

Thank you to Sue Ann Painter and Tony Brunsman at Cincinnati Book Publishers for making the potentially intimidating process of book editing, publishing, and marketing so friendly and comfortable. And thanks to Judge Mark Painter for editing the text.

To all of you in the senior baseball community who, without exception, were so encouraging and helpful. I am especially grateful to those of you who helped by filling out questionnaires and subjecting yourselves to interviews. You brought diverse insight to the book.

Finally, thank you to my parents, aunts, and uncles, who passed along their love of reading, discourse, and the power of ideas.

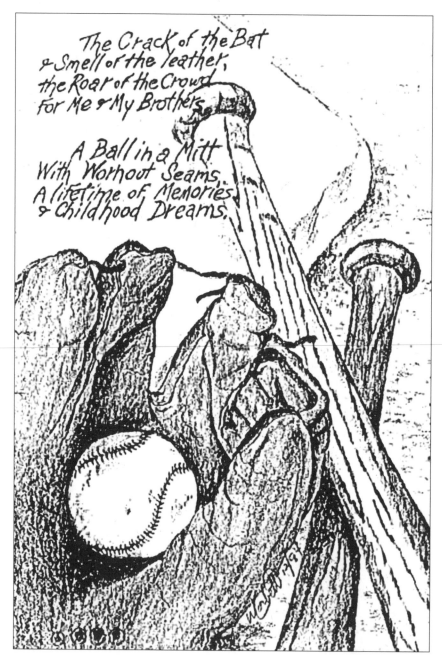

Written and illustrated in September 1994, by Willy Corbett, baseball coach at McNicholas High School, Cincinnati, Ohio, to thank his older brothers for supporting him as he grew up and as he took up coaching.

INTRODUCTION

There was a classic and recurring character who appeared in the "Weekend Update" segment during the 1975-1977 seasons of *Saturday Night Live*. Garrett Morris acted the part of Chico Escuela, a retired Hispanic All-Star second baseman for the New York Mets. During interviews, regardless of the question that Chico was asked by the "Weekend Update" news anchors, Chevy Chase and Jane Curtin, he included in his response, "Base-ball bin berry, berry good to me."

Despite the show's intent to draw humor from Chico's English shortcomings, his line is profound and millions of former and current baseball players and fans can relate to his deep connection to the game. I am among the fortunate who can say that baseball has been very, very good to me.

Through my 60 years, baseball helped provide me with a growthful childhood, deep friendships, ongoing camaraderie, life lessons, and an escape from the routine of the everyday. It also helped provide me with self-confidence, self-respect, and everlasting cross-generational relationships with my father, my son, and my grandsons. The game is a significant building block for who I am and, fortunately, who I continue to become.

This all may sound like this book is personal and specifically about me. Well, it is. But it is also about all of us who have either played the game or, in some other way, been closely connected with it. For over 100,000 players in the United States, the meaningfulness and attraction of baseball remains vital because they are still playing even though they are over 30 years old—and a significant number are into their 40s, 50s, 60s, and beyond. It is in large part for and about these senior amateur baseball players that this book is written.

In November 2004, I was sitting in the dugout between innings on a prototypically brilliant fall day at the City of Palms Stadium in Fort Myers, Florida. Given time by the leisurely pace of the game, I had the opportunity to reflect on where I was and why I was there. I was fortunate to be actively playing baseball at the age of 58. I was in Florida with Ann, my wife, who avidly and actively supports me in this baseball diversion. I was surrounded by teammates and friends all of whom had committed to the game and each other. Life was good and baseball had a significant impact on making it so. At that moment, a lifelong love of books and my appreciation of my baseball circumstances came together. I knew then that I needed to write about what baseball means to my teammates, to our families, to the senior baseball community, and to me. Importantly, I needed to capture what it means to continue to play the game and grow older simultaneously.

The book is written as though its audience is only current senior baseball players, referring to "you" and "we." But there are two other groups that I also hope will appreciate the book. One group is those who played the game in their youth, left it for other sports or life priorities, would love to get back into baseball, and are capable of doing so, but are not fully informed of their opportunity. You have the opportunity to play again and make baseball a life-long sport.

The other audience for the book is baseball fans in general. Most fans follow their favorite major league team or their local semi-pro or amateur team. They love the game for its purity, traditions, and any number of other reasons. These baseball fans will enjoy learning more about senior amateur baseball and its players, who play for the purest joy of the game itself.

Many things must come together to enable seniors to continue to play ball as we get older. We must have been introduced to the game in our youth and learned to play it and love it. We need to either have continued to play throughout our lives or, as is true for most of us, be reintroduced to the game in later years. We must continue to love and respect the game and have respect for ourselves and others who play. Critically, we need to be healthy and fit enough to play and have the personal resources to do so. And we need the support of our families and those who create the leagues, tournaments, fantasy camps, and other opportunities for us to play.

This book is about all of those components, which come together every season for the senior baseball family. The original outline for the book had eight chapters, but I could not resist converting that into nine chapters called "innings" to tell the story. The first inning, "Never Too Young; Never Too Old," introduces senior baseball and how its roots are firmly established in the playing fields of our youth. It traces the story of our passion for baseball from eight-year-old Scott Perkins playing youth baseball in 1981 to 92-year-old George Goodall playing senior baseball in Beijing, China. George's baseball career runs throughout the book as he exemplifies the senior baseball player.

On the surface, one could conclude that what baseball offers us is a recreational activity. While that in itself would be a gift, baseball provides us with so much more. The second and third innings, "Who Are These Guys?" and "Respect the Game," respectively, characterize senior players, describe the playing opportunities available, and relate what baseball means to us and why we love and respect the game so much.

Baseball is alluring, in part, because of its traditions, which become more important to us as we grow older and continue to play the game. The fourth inning, "Crack of the Bat," reflects on the game's traditions as they manifest themselves in senior baseball— some positively, some negatively.

Inning five, "Athletic Supporters," characterizes the support of our families and all of the league administrators, tournament directors, fantasy camp staff, umpires, and others who create the opportunities for us to play. We, the players, are thankfully not alone in this experience.

Baseball is a game of intergenerational relationships. It is a special experience, shared by only a few, to play catch with your son in the front yard when he is four and then to be able to play with him when he turns 30 and joins you in senior baseball. In the sixth inning, "Playing Catch with Dad," we will examine baseball's role in our relationships with both sons and daughters.

As with any life experience, senior baseball is defined more by those who participate than by the game itself. Regardless of their skill or age, it is the "Characters" who have contributed to the creation, continuity, and culture of senior baseball. The seventh inning shares only a small but representative sampling of the entire community.

Reality for all senior players is that aging affects our ability to play as we did in our youth. We are not as strong, flexible, nor fast as we were then or even as we were five years ago. But these truths do not detract from our enjoyment. Rather they serve to enhance it. The eighth inning, "Losing a Step," details how aging affects our play and how we may best compensate for that reality.

Senior baseball has grown significantly in the past 25 years with the advent of national organizations, fantasy camps, and tournaments being played nationwide—it is thriving. But it will be interesting to see what its future holds. The ninth inning, "Future of Senior Baseball," is an attempt to project where our game is heading. Will senior baseball grow at double-digit rates per year? Will the rules change to accommodate both the traditions of baseball and the unique needs of older players? Will more women be playing the game? Will you? Will I?

This book will refer to major league baseball and some of its players because they are important to how we think about the game. Yet baseball is about so much more than the big leagues. Both baseball and this book are about the game itself and those who play it as amateurs, both in our youth and as we grow older. The book is about who we are, where we play, why we play, and what it takes to keep playing. It is about those who support us and those who make the playing opportunities available. It is about how we were passionate about the game when we were young and about how we love and respect it now.

This book is a love letter to baseball, an ode to George Goodall, and a memoir. Baseball has been and continues to be very, very good to me.

PROLOGUE

> *"What's past is prologue."*
> William Shakespeare

> *"Baseball presents a living heritage, a game poised
> between the powerful undertow of seasons past and the
> hope of next day, next week, next year."*
> John Thorn

The months following the injury were both physically and emotionally draining. For the first few weeks, I was unable to stand or walk for more than a minute or two without having to sit down to allow the nerves in my right hip and leg to calm down. The three corticosteroid shots in my spine, spaced over four weeks, helped relieve the pain, and months of physical therapy helped me to begin to retrain my body.

Over those months I vividly recalled my senior year in high school more than 40 years earlier. I see the defensive end breaking free from our blockers and charging as I look downfield for an open receiver. I feel the jolt to my midsection as he gets to me just as I am releasing the ball. I smell the clump of dirt and grass stuck in my helmet face mask as I lay on the field trying to turn my head to see whether my pass is complete. I taste the short-lived joy of seeing our wide receiver, Jim Cohen, jumping up and down in the end zone having just scored the touchdown. And I feel the pain radiate down my right leg.

I was to miss the rest of that game and a full game a week later, which hurt more than the injury as we were playing our archrivals, Ladue High School. They told me I had sciatic neuritis caused by a muscle spasm in my lower back brought on by the hit I took. My body was 17 years old and healed quickly. I went on with my life, virtually forgetting about the injury to my back. That is, until now.

In that fall of 1963, I missed a game and a half with a relatively minor, albeit painful, back injury. In 2006, the year of my 60th birthday, I was at risk of missing an entire season with what the MRI showed were multiple problems with my lower back. In fact, depending on the pace of recovery and the risk of recurrence, this back injury was threatening the end of my playing career.

No, I am not still playing tackle football. That experience was over in 1963, at the end of that high school season. While I loved football, my lifelong passion has been baseball. Since my father put a ball and bat in my hands as soon as I could grip them, I have been on a 60-year baseball journey. I am a senior baseball player and hope to continue to be so.

Baseball has helped define who I am. From the game and those who taught it to me, I learned important lessons, which held me in good stead as I built a family, a career, and a life. The game has been the basis of many long-term friendships and the source of many new ones. There have been periods in my life when I was not playing baseball, periods filled with softball and other life priorities. But baseball always drew me back.

I know there will be a time when I can no longer play and perhaps, because of the back injury, that time is now. But the experience of playing baseball and growing older simultaneously has taught me something important. The senior baseball experience has surrounded me with those who are playing into their 40s, 50s, 60s and beyond, some even playing with serious infirmities. But senior baseball has shown it can accommodate all of these players regardless of skill level, fitness, or age. The experience has taught me that if you love baseball, have the support of family, can learn to compensate for the physical and emotional reality of aging, and have sufficient resources, you are never too old to play the game.

NEVER TOO YOUNG; NEVER TOO OLD

"You try to git that game out your mind, but it never leaves ya. Something about it never leaves ya."

James Thomas "Cool Papa" Bell

"Baseball fever, catch it? Baseball is not a fever, it's a disease, and even old age can't cure it."

George Goodall

We are in the third base dugout at City of Palms Stadium in Fort Myers, Florida, the spring training home ballpark of the Boston Red Sox. We are playing in the Masters Division (for those 48 years and older) of the Roy Hobbs amateur senior baseball World Series. Having won our morning game against a good team from Seattle, Washington, we have warmed up, shaken off the soreness that has been accumulating through the tournament week, and are awaiting the opening pitch of the afternoon game of our doubleheader. The New Jersey team, which we have played in previous tournaments, is in the other dugout and about to take the field.

Four of us, all well into our 50s, are settled into a shady corner of the dugout. Jack Herbert, our third baseman, works as a financial manager for the Hamilton County Commissioners in Cincinnati, Ohio. Jack, who has a lot of smile and not much hair, is as solid a player as there is in senior baseball. He just loves to see a fastball coming his way.

Ken Schug plays first base and is in the computer software business in Dayton, Ohio. Ken is a true gentleman who brought a lack of natural talent with him into his senior baseball career but has been relentlessly improving his game year by year.

John "JR" Reed runs a landscaping business in Loxahatchee, Florida, plays center field, and pitches. He is the most laid-back person we know.

I am retired from a 33-year managerial career with Procter & Gamble in Cincinnati and am an infielder with periodic stints as a catcher and pitcher.

Jack: "Can you believe we're in Florida playing baseball in the middle of November and back home they're shoveling snow. It just doesn't get any better than this."

JR: "Well, I live down here. So I'm used to the warmth and the palm trees. But, this is about the game. As long as the wheels stay on, I'm planning to play."

Ken: "I love this game; I have since as long as I can remember."

Jack: "My dad put a ball in my hand as soon as I could grip it and I haven't been far from one since."

Al: "When I was growing up in St. Louis, we started playing organized ball when we were seven. And I thought my baseball career was over when I finished playing college ball. But now that I'm back in it, I want to keep on playing forever."

Scott Perkins—Never Too Young

In 1981, the boys on my team, including my son, Kevin, were eight years old and just beginning to establish their baseball bearings. On a steamy Cincinnati Saturday summer afternoon we were scheduled to play the last baseball game of our season. The league schedule and the standings brought together the two strongest teams, the winner to emerge as the league champion. While we were playing in a recreational league and the rivalry was friendly, you would have thought, based on the energy level of the players and parents, that we were entering game seven of the major league World Series.

To get to the field we needed to climb from the parking lot up an inclined asphalt path, which had softened in the heat of the day. But the equipment bags, full of bats, bases, and balls, felt light as we hurried in anticipation of the game ahead. At any level and age of amateur baseball, there is the ritual of the pregame and postgame walks with equipment bags in hand from and to the parking lot or locker room. The ritual starts with the choice of what to take in your bag and finishes with trying to determine whether you ended up with everything with which you started. This day was no exception.

Players and parents arrived early and helped set up the fields and dugouts. Parents surrounded the field with aluminum folding chairs, coolers, and an occasional umbrella to ward off the Midwestern summer sun. These loyalists had been supportive all year long and were geared up for the championship game.

The clumpy infield and outfield grass was turning from green to brown as it did most years in July and August in the unwatered public parks in our area. The infield had not been dragged, it seemed, since Pete Rose was an eight-year-old playing ball in Cincinnati more than 40 years earlier. There were holes at the bottom of the screen behind home plate that required a ground rule for balls that would likely roll through during the game. On this and on most of the fields we played on, each dugout was merely a metal bench behind a chain-link fence, so close to the field that there was no room for on-deck batters. And any semblance of marked foul lines was long gone. But it was a baseball field. And to us that day, it might as well have been Wrigley or Fenway or Crosley or Sportsman's Park.

The boys were excited to be at the park as they always were when it was game time. Actually, they were pretty excited at practices as well. They just loved to play. There was a high sky but the boys were not old enough to know what that meant until there was to be a pop-up in their direction. Then they would look up to find only the glare of the clear blue sky but no ball.

From the beginning the game had that feel of a close one. Our best pitcher and most developed player, Scott Perkins, a strong, curly haired left-hander, was on the mound. Later that day he would remind me of a life lesson from my youth.

We were the home team, a good feeling when the game was what I sensed would be one in which the team that batted last would win. Every time they scored, we scored. The parents screamed their support. The boys stayed energetic throughout. As befitting an important game between two strong teams, we were tied after the regulation seven innings and went tensely into extra innings.

In the eighth, they scored a run and we matched them. In the ninth, they scored two and we came up with the same in our half to keep the game going. In the tenth, they scored another run and we came up in the bottom of the inning. If measured by the look on the faces of the parents, we were out of emotional energy. Happily, however, it was the boys who were playing the game. We found a way to score two runs. The parents erupted. The coaches were jumping for joy. The boys were hollering and throwing hats in the air.

We congratulated the other team on a truly great game and our celebration continued. After about five minutes of backslapping, hugging, and general revelry, things were starting to wind down. It was then I was reminded of that life lesson. Scott Perkins, who had a great game at the plate, on the mound, and later at first base, was to be my teacher. Scott, both physically and emotionally mature for an eight-year-old, was at my side, incessantly tugging on my pants leg to get my attention. I finally realized this was more than part of the celebration and crouched down to see what he wanted.

"Coach Spector," he said, "did we win?"

I looked down at him in disbelief. My first instinct was to ask him if he had been paying attention to the game and to the postgame celebration. But before I could, it hit me. He had played the game for the passion of it and was celebrating for the pure joy of it. To him it was not about winning or even keeping score; it was about the passion and the joy. It was about being on a baseball field with his teammates and being part of something pure and simple and energetic and fulfilling. My response was, "Yes we did, Scott. Wasn't it fun?"

Scott's lesson for me was that while playing to win is an important part of the game, in the end, it is all about the game itself. He reminded me about why we compete and about what is truly important. And he taught me that we are never too young to love the game.

George Goodall—Never Too Old

Fast forward 20 years from my graduation from the Scott Perkins School of Life and Baseball. I had returned to playing the game myself several years before and, at 55, was fortunate enough to hear about John Gilmore's Baseball International trips. For a decade, Gilmore had been organizing trips to myriad countries to play ball against the locals and do extensive sightseeing. My wife, Ann, and I decided to join Gilmore on one of his memorable baseball adventures to Beijing, China.

While the trip was postponed because we were originally scheduled to leave the Friday after September 11, 2001, we eventually went in May 2002. With one exception, we had not previously met any of the players or their family members who were making the China trip from all over the United States. The experience was spectacular, both from a baseball and sight-seeing perspective.

On the 2002 trip, we played against five different Chinese teams and one team of Japanese expatriates, who were living and working in Beijing. Playing against college teams, a Chinese minor-league team, and the Japanese team, we had a balanced four and two record for these goodwill games.

The sightseeing was exciting and playing baseball in China was a special experience. But perhaps the highlight of the trip was meeting George Goodall. George traveled to China on his own to play and sightsee with the Gilmore group. At the time of the trip, George was 92. Playing in a vintage White Sox uniform and with a 60-year-old glove, George was an inspiration to all. In one game, when George came to bat for the first time, the Chinese players in the field put down their gloves before the first pitch to George and gave him a round of applause. The Chinese revere senior citizens and these players, who love baseball, appreciated George for who he was and what he was doing.

Late in the trip, one of our sight-seeing excursions was to a Chinese pearl factory. It was interesting to see how they "farmed" the pearls. But when it came time to shop in the company store, I lost interest and sought out George to see if I could learn more about him. Having grown up in St. Louis, I had many memories in common with George, who lived his whole life just across the Mississippi River in Belleville, Illinois. While we were from different generations, he shared my personal Cardinal memories and I shared many of his indirectly through stories my dad had told me. I was an amateur storyteller compared to George. For a half hour, this short, thin, quiet, and proper gentleman did not stop talking about his baseball heroes and experiences, keeping me enthralled the whole time.

While twenty years earlier Scott Perkins had reaffirmed for me that we are never too young to love baseball, George Goodall taught me we are never too old to love and to play the game.

George Goodall (right), with his 60 year-old glove, and me in China in 2002

Lifetime of Baseball Achievement

We next saw George at the August 2004 Legends of Baseball Cooperstown tournament. At the closing banquet of that tournament week, Thom Lach, who runs the Legends of Baseball program, announced the establishment of the "George Goodall Life-Time Achievement Award" to "honor George and recognize other players who share George's enthusiasm and love for the game and are positive role models for the younger generations that follow." The inaugural award recipients were George, Ralph Hazelbaker, Ed Berkich, Bob Wagner, Bill Brockway, Bob "Chief" Kehrbaum, John Aquilla, Chet Collin (umpire), Jim Delaney (umpire), and Ralph Lach (Thom's father).

The following May, Ann and I visited George at his home in Belleville, Illinois, on the way home from seeing relatives in St. Louis. We were excited to see George again and have a chance to talk baseball and life with him.

He was 95 yet still looking forward to flying to Columbus, Ohio, where he would reconnect with Thom Lach and drive to Cooperstown for the August tournament. George was no longer expecting to play, but he felt a need to continue to be near the game and the people that have meant so much to him all of his life.

We used the opportunity at his home to learn more about his long and exciting baseball history. From 1927 to 1930, George played high school ball in Belleville. He recalled working out with the team from 3:00–6:00pm every day, going home for dinner, and then rushing back to the field to practice until it was too dark to see.

When George was only several years out of high school, the town of Belleville built a lighted stadium to attract barnstorming teams to the community. George played on Belleville's town team, giving him the opportunity to play against the St. Louis Browns and Cardinals, the House of David, and many Negro League and American Association teams. It is from that era that George related what he called the "greatest thrill of my baseball life." In 1934, his team played an exhibition game against the St. Louis Cardinal Gashouse Gang, who were in fourth place in the National League when they came to play against Belleville. The Gashouse Gang was made up of, among others, Joe "Ducky" Medwick, Dizzy and Paul "Daffy" Dean, Frankie Frisch (The Fordham Flash), Leo "The Lip" Durocher, and Pepper Martin.

George's memory was impeccable. In the seventh inning, Belleville was down 6–4, but had the bases loaded and George at bat. He came through with a single to drive in two runs to tie the score. The game went 11 innings before the Gashouse Gang won on Pat Crawford's home run. Following the game in Belleville, the Cardinals returned to their major league schedule and went on to win the National League pennant and the World Series, beating Detroit in seven games.

George continued to play ball every chance he got, including in the army. When he was stationed at Camp Claiborne in Louisiana, he was asked to go to the baseball equipment room to pick up the bases, bats, and balls for a practice. He found some gloves in the room, used one of them that day, and continued to use it throughout his army career, including playing two years in Europe and six months in the Philippines, where he played with Early Wynn and Dom DiMaggio. It is the same glove he still uses today, more than 60 years later. The pocket has been sewn and hand strap has been duct taped, but the leather still smells the way a baseball glove should. The glove and George have both stood the test of time.

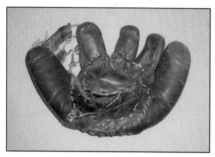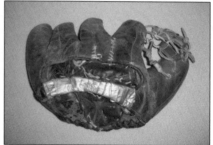

The pocket and back of George Goodall's 60-plus year old glove

When George was 42, he quit the game and thought he would never play again. But when he was 60, he found an opportunity to do just that. George heard about the Chicago Cubs fantasy camp, billed as "The Originators of Fantasy Baseball Camps." He called Randy Hundley, longtime Cubs catcher, who initiated the camp and was still running it. George describes his first conversation with Hundley.

"I called him and asked for information, saying I played a lot of ball. He stated he had to ask a few questions. 'Are you 30 years old?' 'Thirty! How far do you go?' I asked for the upper age. When I told him I was 60, he said, 'Wow!' and asked, 'What kind of shape are you in?' My answer was, 'Quit wasting your time—I am in great condition.' I signed the papers, sent bucks, and ventured into twenty years of paradise."

George went on to attend two decades of fantasy camps, played ten years at the Legends of Baseball Cooperstown tournament, met Bob Wagner and played in his Wooden Bat Classic in Fort Myers, Florida, played in a 1991 "Field of Dreams Game," and joined a number of John Gilmore's Baseball International trips, including the 2002 China trip at age 92. George had a room in his home that could easily be described as a baseball shrine. One of the many memory-laden baseballs in the room reads, "Played ball on the Great Wall of China, 14 May 02."

But to best represent his playing career and love of the game, George proudly recalls a speech by Hall of Famer Ernie Banks during a closing banquet at one of the Cubs fantasy camps. Banks was the keynote speaker and used each letter of the word B-A-S-E-B-A-L-L to help describe what the game meant to him. He finished his speech by giving George a plaque as the recipient of the Chicago Cubs Fantasy Camp Ernie Banks Award and said, "I played 19 years in the big leagues and never saw anyone who loved the game more; I dedicate this speech and plaque to George Goodall."

There is an obvious, yet subtle, connection between our love for the game, which we developed early in our lives, and our desire to continue to play. Scott Perkins epitomized a youthful love of the game. George Goodall is the global ambassador of the message that we are never too old to play the game. All of us who continue to play have a lot of Scott and George in us.

"You're Herm Spector's boy."

I feel fortunate that, as I am writing this, I am in my 53rd year of organized ball (albeit some of those were softball years). Like many senior players, I started playing organized baseball as young as league rules would allow. I was seven in the Atom division of the Khoury League in St. Louis. But even before starting to play in Khoury League, baseball was a significant part of my life. I was handed a bat and ball just after I was born and have not been far from either since.

While baseball was never forced on me, it was all around me. My dad was a great ballplayer, although his sport was fast pitch softball. He played in the Army and then in the elite leagues in St. Louis. The pitchers were dominant in high-level fast pitch—one season Dad led the league with a .188 batting average. He played third base, although that is not what they called the position. It was called "bunt-short" because the fielder would play almost halfway between third base and home to guard against the bunt. Often, bunting was the only way for a batter to get on base against the top pitchers—to try to create that one run that could win the game. Dad took me to his games and introduced me to his teammates. It felt great when one of them said something I will never forget, "Oh, you're Herm Spector's boy. Wow, can your dad ever hit the ball!" I was proud then and throughout my life to be Herm Spector's boy.

Dad in his "Army uniform" playing for the Snipers

Dad, my uncles, and even my grandmother would have me outside playing catch or batting from as early as I can remember or as pictures document.

Batting and playing catch at ages two and three in 1948 and 1949, respectively

But I was not only introduced to the game by playing it. We were also pleasantly barraged with baseball through radio and the sports pages. The Cardinal games were on the radio on KMOX, "the voice of St. Louis."

At the time, the Cardinals were the major league team that was farthest west and had, therefore, developed a broad geographic fan base. KMOX was a strong clear channel 50,000 watt station that could be picked up around much of the country. In his book, *Field of Dreamers—Tales from Baseball Fantasy Camp*, Vince Gennaro talks about growing up with baseball in New York City. Not only does he refer to the joy of having the Yankees, Dodgers, and Giants in the same city, but also listening to the Cardinal games on KMOX. While Vince grew up in New York and I grew up in St. Louis, we were bonded by listening to Cardinal games, perhaps some of the same games, in our bedrooms at night. About 50 years later, we would be likewise bonded by enjoying the experience of playing and writing about senior baseball.

As my generation was growing up, watching baseball on television was limited to the "Game of the Week," as cable television and ESPN's SportsCenter were still 30 years away. Our hunger for sports news was fed by listening to the radio and reading the sports pages. My dad casually mentioned to me when I was in high school that he had listened to KMOX and kept score of every game of the 1946 Cardinal season. That was a year the Cardinals won the pennant, beating the Red Sox in a seven-game World Series. I saw the score book once but, regrettably, have been unable to locate it in any family storage place.

Not only was KMOX a powerful station, but over the course of my early years, KMOX had a team of all-star announcers who helped us appreciate the game of baseball. In that era, Harry Carey, Jack Buck, and Joe Garagiola were each in the radio booth announcing Cardinal games for KMOX. In fact, for awhile, they were in the booth together. That is not bad considering each is in the broadcaster's wing of the Baseball Hall of Fame as Ford Frick Award winners. They won the award in 1987, 1989, and 1991, respectively. The Ford C. Frick Award is presented annually at the Hall of Fame Induction Ceremony to a broadcaster for "major contributions to baseball." It is a prestigious award—its first two recipients in 1978 were Mel Allen and Red Barber.

So, even before I began playing organized baseball at age seven, I was already exposed to baseball tradition, which was passed on by family and community. We played catch. We followed our teams and players. We were never too young to love the game.

Organized Ball and Not-So Organized Ball

Organized youth baseball in St. Louis was Khoury League, founded by George Khoury, a local printer, in 1936. The league eventually spread throughout Missouri, Illinois, and parts of Florida. Divisions were organized in two-year age groups, starting with Atoms at age seven and eight. There was some controversy at the time about whether seven was too young to begin playing organized baseball. A prominent physical education leader in the St. Louis area, Ms. Helen Manley, contended that it was dangerous and seven-year-olds were not mature enough to play team sports.

Something Ms. Manley probably did not know or consider was that whether we were playing organized ball or not, we were already playing baseball and other similar team games. Being happily within walking distance of school playgrounds and parks with baseball diamonds, even before age seven we were beginning to meet friends to play. Throughout our youth, the neighborhood boys and I spent all day, every possible day, when weather permitted and sometimes when it did not, playing some game with a bat and ball. Sometimes we made it home for lunch; we were typically late for dinner. Regrettably, it is different today but, thankfully, our parents were not concerned for our safety when we left the house in the morning with a bat over our shoulder, our glove dangling from our bike or belt, and a ball stuffed into a pocket or the bike's saddle bags (yes, we really did have saddle bags).

On the way to the playground or park, we stopped at the homes of the usual suspects and accumulated players on the way. When we got to the park, we would discover who else came from other neighborhoods and count noses. Depending on the number of players, we would decide what game to play. Seldom did we have enough for two full nine-man teams. But if we were close, say seven on seven, we could adjust and play a full game of baseball. Two outfielders versus three and the at-bat team providing the catcher would suffice.

If we did not have enough for two "full" teams, we would start playing Indian ball, rounds, hit the bat, step ball, wall ball, run-down, bottle cap ball, cork ball, or other games. Then, on no particular schedule, we would change games throughout the day just for variety or because the number of players changed as kids came and went. It did not matter because we were playing baseball or its adequate substitute. All that mattered was that we got to simulate Stan "The Man" Musial's stance and pre-pitch wiggle or Wilmer "Vinegar Bend" Mizell's extra high leg kick while pitching or just have fun saying the names of Cardinals Rip Repulski (outfielder) and Ray Jablonski (third baseman). We were learning how to play, learning to be teammates, and learning to love the game. Ms. Manley just did not understand.

The poem and drawing on the page before the introduction were created in 1994 by Willy Corbett, who, since 1998, has been the varsity baseball coach at McNicholas High School in Cincinnati. Corbett says he did the poem and sketch as a gift to his brothers, "who always supported me and my coaching." He also made copies and gave them to his "coaching brothers." As he recalled his baseball beginnings, Corbett wrote, "I numbered five of six kids and the youngest of four boys. I remember as a real young kid, probably 4 or 5, playing all the 'big' kids who were no more than 8, 9, or 10...there were 17 houses and about 50 kids on our street. At the top of the street was an open lot that was converted into a ball field. I would get to bat, miss the ball, but one of the older guys playing catcher would kick the ball so I could run the bases."

He continued, "In the same neighborhood, I remember playing make believe games of home run derby in the backyards of different kids. Being left handed, I loved Vada Pinson. Having the name Willy, I loved Willie Mays and Willie McCovey and fell in love with baseball. At the age of six, we moved to another neighborhood with a bunch of kids my age, another open lot, and a couple of ball fields within walking distance. Everything in the 60s was within walking distance. We played stick ball, wiffle ball, strike out, home run derby, houseball, squirrel or pickle, and any type of game we could imagine. On rainy days we even played sock ball on the front porch."

I believe it is a significant loss to our society that today, for many reasons, our youth generally do not have the freedom and opportunity to gather, unsupervised, to form and play group games as Willy Corbett, many of the current generation of senior players, and I did when we were young.

Baseball-Like Games

Two examples of games we played in my neighborhood when we had fewer than the requisite number of players for two full teams were Indian ball and rounds. Indian Ball can be played comfortably with anywhere from four to 12 players. A field is laid out with a home plate and two foul lines, the angle of which is determined by the number of players; the fewer players, the closer the foul lines to each other. Defensively, an infielder (or two, if enough players) is positioned from 60 to 90 feet from the plate, depending on whether you are playing with a hard ball (preferred) or softball. The outfielders then populate the area behind the infielder with the intent of being able to catch any ball hit in the air. The batter is pitched to by a teammate (slow and underhanded; easy to hit but requiring good hand-eye coordination to hit squarely).

Any ball hit foul is an out and any ball caught in the air is an out. If a ground ball is caught cleanly by an infielder, it is an out. There is no base running in Indian Ball. Rather, any ball not caught for an out is a single. Sometimes it is played that a ball hit over the deepest outfielder's head is a home run. The teams keep track of base runners, runs, and outs. Typically, to save time, the team at bat stays in for two innings and just "clears the bases" when there are three outs in the first of the two innings. Games can be played for any number of innings, typically nine. Sometimes we would play all day keeping score through hundreds of innings. I also recall that if the scores were lopsided, we would make trades between games to seek parity. Even then, and without supervision, we knew that we should play to win, but also that the real thrill was in the competition.

Since beginning to play Indian Ball, I was under the impression that it was a St. Louis-specific game. I had mentioned it to non-St. Louisians over the years but no one had heard of the game. Almost 50 years later, I was to learn differently. In the summer of 2004, Ann and I joined a John Gilmore Baseball International trip to Italy. The group played games against Italian teams in Rome and Florence and did extensive sightseeing in those historic and magnificent cities. One day in Florence, Ann and I were sitting at an outdoor restaurant having lunch with my late teammate Roy Yocum and his wife, Chris, friends from Cincinnati. "Yoke," a retired firefighter, and I played on a league team together as well as in a number of tournaments around the country each year. Chris and Ann have spent many a game together in the stands.

Chris and Roy "Yoke" Yocum on the Baseball International Italy trip

During lunch Yoke and I were talking about the games we played when we were young. I mentioned Indian Ball and he asked me what the rules were. When I described it, Yoke sat speechless—definitely not his normal condition. He was finally able to tell me that he grew up in an Appalachian area of Kentucky and had played a game called Indian Ball with exactly the same rules. Until that moment, he thought it was only played in his area as he had mentioned it to people from around the country and had found no one who had ever played it. We agreed it was a small world as two friends and teammates, one from Appalachian Kentucky and the other from St. Louis, learned of our shared Indian Ball game at a pleasant outdoor café on a baseball trip in Florence, Italy.

The second example of games we played when we did not have enough players was rounds. The game could be played with as few as ten players, but 12 to 14 were better. We played the rules of baseball but rotated through the positions and batting. We would fill the nine fielding positions and everyone left over was at bat. If we had too few players, we would play with two outfielders or one of the batters would act as catcher. We were luckier than smart in that we played the catching position without equipment without anyone ever getting hurt.

The catcher called balls and strikes and the first, second, and third basemen umpired plays at their bases and the foul lines. I do not recall any umpiring arguments—but they must have occurred. Because of the nature of the game, with everyone rotating through the positions, we made every attempt to call a fair game because we would soon be at the mercy of someone else's calls.

The batters would pick an order and start batting. When an out was made, the person who was out went to right field. The right fielder would move to center, center to left, left to third base, around the infield to pitcher to catcher, and the catcher became last in the batting order.

At each of the fantasy camps and several senior tournaments in which I have played, I made it a point to play each of the nine defensive positions during the course of the week. I am convinced that my flexibility to help a team by playing many positions—and my wanting to do so—goes back to the hours and hours of playing rounds at our local park.

There was another wonderful aspect to the game of rounds—no scoring. Certainly, we felt we were rewarded if we could stay at bat for a long time. But, in general, we were playing a game for the pure enjoyment of playing. It was baseball for the sake of baseball.

"Not That You Won Or Lost..."

I am not trying to say that winning is not important. It is. But in senior men's amateur baseball, like in my earlier games of rounds, it is the playing and competing that is preeminent. As I am writing this section of the book, I am playing on a team whose record is anything but spectacular. After another loss a few weeks ago, as we were gathering our equipment for the walk to the car and ride to the bar, someone said, "We're having such a great time. Imagine how much fun it would be if we were winning."

And he was right. Perhaps for professional teams, the win-loss statistics are the most important thing. But most of us measure our worth not in our winning percentage but, rather, in the fact that we are still competing. We value what we bring to the game and those with whom we play.

In 1941, the "dean of American sports writers," Grantland Rice, wrote a poem entitled "Alumnus Football." The last two lines of that poem have been the basis for an oft-quoted adage: "For when the One Great Scorer comes to mark against your name, He writes—not that you won or lost but how you played the game."

While Rice was certainly not thinking about senior baseball players of the 21st century, his words are applicable. As senior players, we know that if we prepare ourselves as best we can, play the game to the best of our abilities, help our teammates do the same, and, yes, play to win, the outcome of the game is what it will be. If we do these things, whether we win or lose by the counting of runs, we win in the ledger of baseball and life. As senior players, we know this because we have seen enough of life to make the comparison.

On that same Baseball International trip to Italy in the summer of 2004, we came from behind late in the game to win a game we were playing in Nettuno, a town about thirty-five kilometers south of Rome. It was the only game we won of the five games we played on the trip. Would we have preferred to have won more often? Yes. Did we play to win every day? Yes. Did it fundamentally matter that we lost? No.

The town of Nettuno is the birthplace of baseball in Italy. On the way to the game, the bus took us to the American cemetery where the servicemen were buried after losing their lives during the invasion at Anzio Beach. It is a beautiful setting but a sobering experience to walk amid the endless rows of grave markers and try to relate to the tragedy of the lives lost during World War II or any other war.

The Americans who were establishing the cemetery at the end of the war often ended their work day by playing catch and pitching batting practice to one another to help take their minds off the terrible task they had been asked to do. The local Italians in nearby Nettuno were fascinated by the game and asked the Americans what they were doing. The Americans began explaining and teaching baseball to the locals. Sixty years later, Nettuno has a full baseball program from youth through seniors, having supplied many players to the Italian National Team. Their baseball complex is impressive and well maintained. But mostly, their love of the game and appreciation for the Americans liberating their country are evident through their actions.

It did not fundamentally matter to the locals who won or lost our games in Nettuno. What mattered to them was that we had come to their community to play the game they love with them. Regardless of the game's outcome, the locals still prepared an aromatic and wonderfully tasty pasta dinner that we shared under a pavilion at their baseball complex. We ate, drank local wine, and struggled with language. But the Italian players, their families, and the townspeople made it clear that they were thankful for our having come to play. And it was easy for us to communicate how much we appreciated their hospitality and their love for the game.

One of the Italian players spoke English fairly well. He told us that he fell in love with baseball the first time he saw it and was thrilled to be playing. He chose to find a job near Nettuno because he wanted to be a part of the baseball family there. The one issue he had was that his own family was disappointed in him because, like most Italians, soccer was their favorite sport. He decided to live with his family's disappointment and play the game he loves.

I have played baseball in China, Russia, and Italy and have bonded with these international players by a love of a game that has the same allure, rules, dimensions, and language around the world. While we played to win our international games, it did not matter who won. Nor did the score matter. What did matter was the game and how it brought us together to follow our passion with those who share it.

Boundless Enthusiasm

One dictionary definition of the word "passion" is "boundless enthusiasm." I would argue that senior baseball players have a passion for the game. We know we are going to be sore and the soreness will take longer each year to wear off. We know it will cost us money, time away from the family, and energy to play in our leagues and to travel as extensively as many of us do. We play the game with everything we have and some things we think we used to have. Would anyone do this if he did not have boundless enthusiasm for the game? It is passion, pure and simple.

There is another view about how playing baseball and passion relate. I had the opportunity to retire from the Procter & Gamble Company in May 2002, at age 55, after working there for more than 33 years. I thoroughly enjoyed the work and the working environment and had no regrets about either my career or my decision to retire. But I only half-jokingly tell people that work was getting in the way of playing baseball—so I quit.

Periodically, I get together with Keith Lawrence, a friend and former Procter & Gamble colleague. As we recently compared notes, he asked me how I was spending my time and if I was still playing baseball. I told him yes, and he said that he had discovered why. He had read a book in which one premise was that to have a happy, successful retirement, each of us should be doing what we were passionate about when we were ten years old. The idea is that when we are ten, or thereabouts, we are old enough to choose to do what we really love to do, but not yet old enough to have been burdened by inhibitions, peer pressure, and all the other things that guide us away from our passions. Doing what we are passionate about should help make us happy, whether we are ten or 60. As simply put in the lyrics of Irene Cara's song "What a Feeling" in the 1983 movie *Flashdance*, "Take your passion and make it happen; what a feeling."

I recently ran into Marty Satz, whose father coached our ten-year-old youth baseball team. I had not seen Marty since then, so we had a lot to catch up on and shared many memories. I told him that I still had a team picture from the end-of-the-year banquet our sponsor had for us when we had played together. Excitedly, Marty asked if I could send him a copy. As I pulled out the picture to scan and send, I realized I could still recognize and name virtually every player even though I had not seen about 70% of them since that banquet, 50 years before. Only a love of what we were doing together could have emblazoned those names in my memory. It should not be surprising, therefore, that I rediscovered baseball and began playing again later in life; it was and is a passion.

Logan Franklin is a retired publisher who maintains a web site for seniors called "Gray Iron Fitness." In an article entitled, "Rediscover Your Passion in Retirement," Franklin writes, "Your interests probably are very different from mine. But somewhere in each of us the interests are there, only waiting to be rediscovered and released. One good way to uncover them is by looking backward to your childhood and adolescence. Recall the thoughts, activities and dreams that sent your imagination and spirit soaring. Those are your clues. Develop interests related to them and most people will experience a personal renaissance."

Jim Brosnan finished a nine-year major league pitching career in 1963. His teammates, recognizing his love of books and classical music, nicknamed him "Professor." During and following his baseball career, Brosnan was an author, penning such books as *The*

Long Season, Pennant Race, and *Ron Santo, 3rd Baseman.* As a reflection of the quality of his work, Brosnan was chosen by Mike Shannon as one of the writers highlighted in his book, *Baseball: The Writer's Game.*

During an interview for Shannon's book, Brosnan told him, "I have always loved books and been fascinated by them. From the time I was eight or nine years old, I spent as much time in the library reading as I did playing sports." Brosnan went on to say, "So my ambitions as a kid were to write a book...and way off in the distance, maybe be a major league baseball player."

Whether our youthful passion was baseball, writing, cooking, skiing, or whatever, we do not have to wait for retirement to pursue that passion. Those of us playing senior baseball have already made the connection to the boundless enthusiasm of our youth, whether consciously or subconsciously, whether before or during retirement. Perhaps one reason the growth of senior baseball has been strong is that many are taking advantage of the opportunity to return to the game that was our youthful passion.

In 1990, I played on a Cincinnati Men's Senior Baseball League (MSBL) team. While I was 44 at the time, most of the league's players were in their 30s. The oldest and, perhaps, most energetic player in the league, however, was Don Johnson, who, at the time, was in his early 60s. Johnson was a Negro League veteran, having played for several teams from 1947 to 1953. He had signed with both the Cincinnati Reds and Cleveland Indians, but never made it to the major leagues.

Johnson played with obvious ability and boundless enthusiasm. He played every inning of every game and hit for high average. At the time, we were in awe of his performance because he was "so old." We were convinced it was his love of and passion for the game that kept him going. As it turned out, Don Johnson was ahead of his time because many 60-year olds are playing the game today and, like him, are doing it with youthful energy. Now that I am 60 and looking back, I do not think that he was so old.

I played the game when I was young because I loved it; the sight of it, the sound of it, the smell of it, the feel of it. I loved the field, the equipment, the competition, and the teammates. And, if there were not a game scheduled as part of our organized leagues, I would go from house to house until I found enough boys, go to the local playground, choose up sides, and play until it was too dark to keep going. I had a passion for the game then and I still do. And while I know intellectually that there will come a time when I cannot do so, I will never be too old to play the game.

SECOND INNING

WHO ARE THESE GUYS?

"The older they get, the better they were when they were younger."
Jim Bouton, on Old Timers' Days

"How old would you be if you didn't know how old you was?"
Satchel Paige

Ken: *"We barely got out of that mess in the first. The double play we turned with the bases loaded and one out reminds me of that league game at Kettering Park. Remember, we needed the DP in the last inning to hold our lead and that's what we got."*

Jack: *"The league schedule and other tournaments we were in got us in pretty good playing shape for this week."*

JR: *"You know; we're pretty fortunate. There is no lack of places for us old farts to play ball."*

Jack: *"I was thinking about playing in Palm Beach in that Play at the Plate tournament and Sheryl and I are considering a Baseball International trip to China next year. Al, you've done both; what do you think?"*

Al: *"I'd jump on the opportunity to do both. Ann and I had a great time in China and how can you beat Palm Beach and playing at the Cardinal-Marlins complex?"*

Ken: "JR, you're leading off. Get something started. We need some runs."

40 Years Between Games of Catch

In October, 2004, I attended the 40th-year reunion of my graduating class from University City High School in St. Louis, a city in which one is identified by his or her high school. Here is a typical conversation between two people who meet and discover they both grew up in St. Louis.

"Where are you from?"

"I live in Boston now, but I grew up in St. Louis."

"Me too, but I live in Cincinnati now."

"That's great, where did you go to high school?"

University City was a special place to be in the early 1960s. We had a lot going for us. But we also dealt with some difficult issues because of what was facing the country. Made constantly aware of the threat of nuclear devastation, we endured the Cuban Missile Crisis as it brought us to the brink of war. And we watched Viet Nam escalate as we approached military draft age. Tragically, everyone in my graduating class is still burdened by knowing the answer to the question, "Where were you when President Kennedy was shot?" The answer only differs by the class we were in on November 22, 1963, when the announcement came over the public-address system. For me, the answer is Mr. Fendleman's English Literature class.

University City's athletic program was solid during our tenure. Within those few high school years, U City won state championships in swimming, track, and wrestling and conference championships in water polo, cross-country, and golf. And I had the privilege of playing varsity baseball, being the first baseman my junior year on the 1963 Missouri High School Baseball State Championship team.

Another highlight of my high school baseball years was catching Kenny Holtzman, who went on to a very productive major league pitching career. For high school games, I played first base while Myron Kinberg, also a state-champion wrestler, was our catcher. But Myron did not play American Legion ball during the summer, so I was Kenny's primary catcher for Jerome L. Goldman Post 96.

Kenny was joy to catch. He had a live fastball, pinpoint control, and a wicked 12:00 to 6:00 curveball. His curve broke so sharply I had to move even closer than normal to the plate to keep from losing strikes that crossed the plate in the zone but bounced in front of me. Although I was in constant jeopardy of a catcher's interference call, I do not remember ever having had one.

Kenny's major-league career was exemplary. He started with the Cubs in 1965 and pitched two no-hitters while in Chicago. His trade to the Oakland Athletics in 1972 made him a member of the "Catfish" Hunter, Vida Blue, "Blue Moon" Odom, Rollie Fingers pitching staff. Yet with all of those great pitchers, Kenny was chosen to pitch many of the A's key World Series games. In 1973, for example, he started games one, four, and seven. That was the second consecutive year Kenny started and won game seven of the World Series. From 1972-1974, he won 19, 21, and 19 games, respectively.

At our 40th-year high school reunion, I was able to reminisce about Kenny and our championship team with several of my teammates. One was Steve Novack, who was our second baseman and is a founding partner of a successful Chicago law firm. We remembered that one day in our junior year, Steve and I were walking to practice and needed to cross the school's running track to do so. The track team had left the hurdles on the track and Steve thought it would be a good idea to show me how much of a hurdler he was—which he was not. Steve caught the first hurdle with his knee and went down on the track face first. As if it were not bad enough to have fallen, those were the days when track surfaces were cinders. It took weeks for Steve to get all the cinders out of his body. Coach Buffa, who, to our delight was also at the reunion, did not remember the incident. But Steve and I remembered that he was not pleased.

Coach Buffa was upset with Steve and me more than once during our high school years. One day before practice, we thought it would be fun to warm up by playing catch over a huge old oak tree beyond the outfield. Coach was not thrilled that his starting first and second basemen played the next several games with sore arms.

Friday night of the reunion weekend was held in the high school gym. After a couple hours of reconnecting with people, I told Steve, Ronnie Neeter, and Ira Bergman, also former teammates, that I had brought two gloves and a baseball to the reunion for the express purpose of playing catch with them in the gym. Without hesitation, they nodded their heads. I went to my car and brought back my fielder's mitt, my catcher's mitt, and a new ball. We took turns and played catch with each other for the first time in 40 years. What a thrill it was!

With more than 300 people milling around, you can imagine the attention we drew. After a few minutes, one of our classmates came over to some of those who were watching and said, "Who are these guys?" Oh, he knew our names, but he was astonished that we were playing catch. His reaction was like many of my classmates and others when they find out that I am still playing baseball. Typical reactions are:

"You mean softball, don't you?"

"What about your knees?"

"I wish I were doing that. I still love the game."

"How do you find the time?"

"If I were only in shape..."

"I'm proud of you."

Leagues Big and Small

My classmate asked a good question, "Who are these guys?" The same question can be applied to senior baseball players in general. There are as many as 125,000 of us during any given year in the United States. The greatest number play in leagues and tournaments run by three broad geographical senior baseball organizations, the Men's Senior Baseball League (MSBL), the National Adult Baseball Association (NABA), and Roy Hobbs. In addition, there are many independent local leagues, as well as fantasy camps, vintage baseball games, one-time events, and numerous other tournaments.

Before I go on, I will explain the pronoun gender protocol used throughout the book. Women are avid baseball fans and many are strong supporters of senior baseball. Sections of this book address women's relationship to baseball in general and senior baseball specifically. But all but a few senior players are men. For simplicity in the book, therefore, I have chosen to use masculine pronouns when referring to senior players and only use the feminine pronouns when they are specifically warranted.

MSBL, the largest national organization, boasts "325 local affiliates, 3,200 teams and 45,000 members who play organized amateur baseball in local leagues." Along with providing many opportunities to play in leagues, MSBL runs tournaments throughout the year. Leagues are organized by age group, up to 38-and-over divisions. The MSBL World Series and Fall Classic tournaments, played in Arizona and Florida, respectively, every October-November, extend the age divisions to include 48-and-over, 58-and-over, and 65-and-over groups, as well as a father/son division.

MSBL is a success story by any measure. From its modest beginning with 60 players in 1986, it has grown under the leadership of Steve Sigler, who projects that in the next few years, the national organization will surpass 50,000 members. MSBL's members take to heart the organization slogan, "Don't Go Soft—Play Hardball!"

NABA reports "competitive and recreational baseball...in more than thirty-four states...over 42,000 player-members who have played America's favorite pastime every week." NABA not only runs leagues and tournaments through the range of age groups up through 48-and-over, but also attempts to have divisions established based on player experience level. The advanced level (AAA) is for those who have had three to four years of college or professional experience. The intermediate level (AA) is for those players who have had high school or some college experience. The recreational level (A) is for those "players whose love of the game exceeds their level of experience."

NABA supplements league play with a full slate of regional and national tournaments played in Philadelphia, San Francisco, Tucson, San Juan, Los Angeles, Palm Beach, Las Vegas, Atlantic City, Cooperstown, Denver, and their World Championship Series in Phoenix.

Roy Hobbs has, according to Tom Giffen, the organization's Director, about 7,000 players on 450 teams in 25 separate leagues nationwide and in some international sites. There are Roy Hobbs members in Russia, Holland, Italy, Canada, Puerto Rico, and the Virgin Islands.

Roy Hobbs was founded in 1988 by Ron Monks, with the first league being in Woodland, California. The organization name comes from the character in the movie and Bernard Malamud book, The *Natural*. The name is fitting because in the story, Hobbs returns to the game he loves later in life and revels in playing and competing. Having started their own unaffiliated amateur adult league in

Akron, Ohio, in 1989, Ellen and Tom Giffen purchased the rights to Roy Hobbs baseball in 1992 when it had 150 teams nationwide and a 62-team World Series in Kissimmee, Florida. Since then, both the national organization and World Series have grown. The tournament, now held annually in Fort Myers, features about 200 teams and 3,500 players.

One of the distinguishing characteristics of the Roy Hobbs organization under Tom Giffen's leadership is its commitment to supporting Challenger Baseball, a special division of Little League that was established in 1989 to "enable boys and girls with physical and mental disabilities, ages 5-18...to enjoy the game of baseball..." During the Roy Hobbs World Series weeks (and during the Bob Wagner Wooden Bat Classic), there are Challenger exhibition games and opportunities to raise money for the program. The Challenger program has grown as advocates such as Giffen and the Wagners have stepped forward to lead the way.

These three national organizations total nearly 95,000 players. Each has grown dramatically from the early days less than 20 years ago. And they continue to grow as a testament to the increasing awareness and popularity of senior baseball.

The remaining number of senior players is more difficult to estimate. There are a multitude of large and small independent leagues as well as other venues for seniors to play ball. For example, Mike LoBosco, a 44-year-old pitcher-outfielder, who lives in Summit, New Jersey, plays in the independent United States Over Thirty Baseball League (USOTB), which has "more than 200 teams and 3,000 players" in the New York/New Jersey area. The related United States Over Forty Baseball League (USOFB) adds another 30 teams.

I met Mike at a joint Cincinnati Reds/New York Mets Baseball Heaven fantasy camp in 2000. He is one of the most easygoing, yet fiercely competitive men I know. We have played both with and against each other at many fantasy camps and tournaments since then.

My dad once told me that no matter where I go, all I ever need to do is find a baseball game, step across the white lines, and I would immediately be surrounded by friends. Mike LoBosco specifically— and senior baseball in general—validates what Dad told me. It is so easy for baseball teammates and even opponents to become friends.

The league Mike plays in is only one of many independent senior baseball leagues around the country. There is, for example, the Ponce De Leon Baseball League in Maryland (leagues in Baltimore, Fredrick, Howard, Carroll, and Anne Arundel), which has two age divisions, 30-and-over and 48-and-over. The league has 40 teams and 600 players, having started with four teams and 40 players in 1986. The league refers to itself as the "Fountain of Youth" and their web site notes, "Most men lead very busy lives. There are many business, social, and family matters and obligations to deal with. At the same time, the desire to once again play the game they grew up with and still love remains strong."

In southern New Hampshire is a 14-team senior league called the Granite State Over 30 Baseball League, which has been in existence since 1992. There is the 12-team Virginia Baseball Congress, which was founded in 1990 both to provide an organized baseball league for senior players (average age of league is 37) and create a civic fundraising foundation to benefit local charities. Lowell, Massachusetts, hosts a 16-team league (up from four teams in 1993), which "welcomes players of all abilities to join the fun, fairness, and camaraderie that reminds them of the game they played as kids." The Poco Men's Over Thirty Baseball League has nine teams playing in British Columbia. Playing in Canada, they even keep their standings as do hockey leagues, with points (two points for a win, one point for a tie, no points for a loss). I am not sure what a tie means in baseball, but it could fit if there are time limits to games because of field availability.

It is hard to tell how many players are taking advantage of these active, independent leagues. Just these few leagues noted above add another 320 teams or about 4,800 players.

And there are likely a significant number of other large and small leagues. Where I live in Cincinnati, for example, there is a small league in the quaint community of White Oak, played at beautiful and well-maintained Haubner Field. The league began in 1994 for players over 35. It calls itself the "Dream Season" League and has only four teams of about 16 players each. There are more players who want to play, but access to the field is limited.

If the leagues noted above account for only one-third to one-half of those that exist, there may be as many as 10,000-15,000 players across the country (and Canada) who are playing in independent leagues of four to 50 teams.

Baseball Heaven

There are more senior players than those who make up the large affiliated and smaller independent leagues. These are the players who attend fantasy camps, play international baseball, attend one-time events, play vintage baseball, or who are playing pick-up games in the absence of a formal league.

Most baseball fantasy camps are associated with major league teams. And there are some camps that use the fantasy format but are not directly associated with teams. For example, there is a Hall of Fame Fantasy Camp in Cooperstown, "The Path of Legends" at Dodgertown in Vero Beach, Dave Henderson's "The Old School Baseball Wood Bat Tournament," the "Heroes in Pinstripes" Fantasy Camp built around Yankee greats, and the Ripken Baseball Minor League Experience.

There is also, if you want to spend even more than the cost of a traditional fantasy camp, the Ultimate Experience Baseball Tour. For a mere $12,995, you too can spend ten days touring a section of the country playing at major league parks. For example, from November 4–13, 2005, the West Coast Tour included games at Chase Field (Diamondbacks), PETCO Park (Padres), SBC Park (Giants), Dodger Stadium, Angel Stadium, and Safeco Field (Mariners), as well as all of the travel and fantasy camp amenities.

Fantasy camps are a win–win situation for all involved. For the major league teams, the camps further establish the loyalty of their most ardent fans. For the camp operators, they are business ventures that also allow them to stay close to the game they love. For the campers, they provide a glimpse of what it would be like to me a big leaguer and, albeit for only one week, live out a boyhood dream.

While fantasy camps are expensive, generally in the range of $4,000, compared to other senior-baseball playing opportunities, the camps are a great way to get involved and, if desired, open the door to the entire senior-baseball experience. The camps are run for players 30-and-over—players at the Cincinnati Reds fantasy camp average over 47.

At fantasy camp, I have played with a just-turned-30-year-old who received the camp as a birthday gift and could fly around the bases and with a man in his 60s, who had Parkinson's disease. I have played with a former minor leaguer and a guy who had not played baseball since the fourth grade. I have played with a 70-year old who had been disabled from birth and his daughter who was an excellent athlete but had never played baseball. Each of this diverse group had a wonderful baseball experience and each of them enriched mine. Somehow, the fantasy camp format allows everyone, regardless of age, skill, or fitness level, to feel special and get deeply dipped in baseball, the love of which they all have in common.

To get a more in-depth view of how a camp progresses through the course of the week, read Vince Gennaro's book, *Field of Dreamers; Tales from Baseball Fantasy Camp.* In his introduction, Gennaro writes, "I decided to relive my youth, if only for one week, at baseball fantasy camp, known as Indians' Baseball Heaven. And with it I experienced a paradox. On the one hand, I learned that one week was a painfully *short* time to revisit one's childhood. It was tantamount to playing with a new toy for three minutes, before putting it in the closet, uncertain as to when you would be permitted to retrieve it again. On the other hand, one week was a painfully *long* time for a 43-year-old with five knee operations to his credit. When I returned home from fantasy camp, I put away the baseball. But, a strange thing happened...the baseball wouldn't let me go. It had a grip on me once again..."

Gennaro's experience is also captured in a statement by Jim Bouton, "You spend a good piece of your life gripping a baseball and in the end it turns out that it was the other way around all the time."

Like Vince Gennaro, I was reintroduced to the game through a fantasy camp. My senior baseball experience began in my 40s when I was playing softball in leagues around Cincinnati. A couple of guys with whom I was playing mentioned to me that they had started playing baseball and their team needed a catcher. I jumped at the chance and played in an MSBL league.

After playing for several years, I had to hang up my spikes for what I thought would be forever because I was having some serious foot problems. It turned out the foot issues were related more to soccer, which I was also playing. After giving up both soccer and baseball to keep from having to go through painful surgery, I went a long time only playing occasional softball games, working out at the gym, and learning to live with soreness every step of every day.

In 1998 at the age of 52, a St. Louis high school classmate and friend, Ron Unell, told me he was interested in going to a fantasy camp with the Cardinals, but he did not think they had one going at the time. The conversation energized me enough to consider trying to find a camp despite the foot problems, which had been improving because I had found effective anti-inflammatories. After searching for a Cardinal camp and confirming that they were not running one, I found a joint Cincinnati Reds/New York Mets program called Baseball Heaven.

The camp was held on the lush green fields of the Reds spring training facilities in Sarasota, Florida, in February 2000. Despite the soreness of returning to baseball after a long layoff and of playing ten games during the week, catching six of them, I had been dipped once again in the holy waters of the game. At the end of the week I was not thinking of making it other than a one-time experience, except perhaps for the possibility of returning to camp the following year.

That all changed in August of the same year. As part of the Baseball Heaven program, they hold a reunion game each year at the Reds major-league park in Cincinnati, which in 2000 was Riverfront Stadium, the successor to Crosley Field and predecessor of the Great American Ballpark. I had a number of lasting impressions that day. First among them was just the fun of playing in a big league facility. I had that opportunity on only one other occasion. Having been selected for a Khoury League All-Star Game in 1955, I played in St. Louis at the original Busch Stadium, nee Sportsman's Park.

The most memorable impression playing at Riverfront was that, while it was special playing where the professionals do, it was familiar and routine at the same time. After the first inning or two, it was like any other game of baseball; the bases were 90 feet apart and the mound was 60 feet, six inches from the back point of home plate. The fences were the same distance as those when I played high school, college, American Legion, MSBL, and fantasy camp ball. The familiarity of the field allowed me to settle in and play the game, irrespective of my surroundings. Of course, it was still fun to stop every once in awhile and just look around and remind myself where I was.

As I was walking off the field, I was approached by two other fantasy campers, Bob Hawkins and Denny Ehrhardt, neither of whom I got to know at the camp in Florida in February nor on whose team I played that day. They introduced themselves and Hawkins asked me how old I was. When I told him 53, he asked me if I would like to play with his team in a tournament in Fort Myers, Florida, that November. While I was ready to say yes right then, I thought it would be best to check first with Ann, who was quickly supportive, as she always has been

To get ready for the November Fort Myers tournament, I played a couple of games with Hawkins and the Cincinnati Colts in their Dayton, Ohio, Roy Hobbs league. The Colts also practiced as often as they could either indoor or outdoors leading up to what I soon learned was the Roy Hobbs World Series.

Having played in the league games and the tournament in Fort Myers, I found that I had joined the sub-culture of senior baseball and quickly ramped up to be playing in the range of 75 games a year in leagues, in tournaments, and on international baseball trips. I went on to play three more years at Reds Baseball Heaven. The last year I played, my son, Kevin, had turned 30 and joined me.

My 2003 fantasy camp baseball card with Kevin

My experience of being reintroduced to baseball as a senior player through a fantasy camp is by no means unique. Recall that George Goodall returned to the game by attending Randy Hundley's Cubs camp. Many of the senior tournaments are played in what is called the "all-star format," meaning that each player wears his own uniform. It is not uncommon for players to show up in their fantasy camp uniforms, indicative of the number of them who have attended camps.

There are about 30 camps associated with major league teams and a number of other independent camps using the fantasy format. Attendance varies from camp to camp, but the average number is about 100. Every year, therefore, over 3,000 seniors play baseball at a fantasy camp. While many of these campers play in other venues as well, some are once-a-year, fantasy camp only players.

"Thanks Mr. Jimmy"

There are other once-a-year baseball experiences that add to the senior-player ranks, albeit in smaller numbers than leagues and fantasy camps. One example is the "No Bats Baseball Club." While you can check out the web site, perhaps the best way to understand the club is to read club founder Ted Simendinger's book, *Critters, Fish & Other Troublemakers*. The entire book of essays is a treat, but the ultimate story from a great storyteller is "Thanks Mr. Jimmy." The story is a reflection of Simendinger and his "No Bats Baseball Club" compatriots, who have raised hundreds of thousands for baseball-related charities and manage to play some ball once a year as well.

Another example of a one-time annual event is the "Roy McMillan Memorial Game," played each year at the Roosters Stadium in Richmond, Indiana. The event, which also includes golf and a banquet, was initiated and is planned each year by Ray James. Ray is a classic senior player, who despite being slowed by Parkinson's disease, stays deeply involved in the game. He runs the annual game to honor his friend Roy McMillan's, memory. He also created an award that is given each year at Reds Baseball Heaven to the ex-professional who best exemplifies Roy McMillan's spirit of giving back to the game he loved.

McMillan was a Cincinnati Red from 1951 through 1960. He then went on to complete a 16-season career by playing with the Milwaukee Braves and New York Mets. He was a smooth fielding All-Star shortstop who, in 1957 when *The Sporting News* began awarding Gold Gloves for fielding excellence, won the first three trophies at his position.

Each year, James provides a venue for 30 to 40 players to celebrate his friend and baseball by simply playing the game.

Safe or Out in Any Language

Another alternative senior baseball venue that involves a very small number of players, many of whom also play in leagues, other tournaments, and fantasy camps, is international baseball. The preeminent organizer of such trips is John Gilmore, who created and manages Baseball International. Gilmore has been organizing baseball trips overseas since 1994. At the time he was focused on trips to Russia, where he had played for a three-week period in 1990, where he was frequently traveling on business, and which was his lovely wife, Olga's, home country.

Since then, Baseball International has offered trips to Mexico, France, Switzerland, Italy, Denmark, China, Brazil, Argentina, Holland, Cuba, and other countries, including a Caribbean cruise on which a baseball game was played in each port (i.e. Aruba, Curacao, St. Maarten, St. Thomas, and San Juan). Ann and I have had the opportunity to join trips to China (Beijing), Russia (Moscow and St. Petersburg), and Italy (Rome and Florence). Each trip has been packed with baseball, sightseeing, and great eating.

There is another important component of Gilmore's trips that demonstrates his love of the game and his understanding of what baseball does and can mean to others. In an interview with SABR's (Society for American Baseball Research) Ryan Chamberlain, Gilmore said, "Beyond playing a game each day in the country we visit, we also do extensive sightseeing... But the most gratifying aspect is that we donate thousands of dollars of new baseball equipment to the teams and leagues we play against. As an example, last year we went to Russia and donated over 150 gloves, 50 bats, and 50 batting helmets plus six sets of catcher's equipment. Over the years we have donated more than $100,000 of equipment to countries and teams who would otherwise not have the equipment to grow their baseball programs. In addition, many of our players also leave behind their personal equipment (gloves, bats, spikes, etc) when they see how little some teams have."

Gilmore also runs a tournament every January at a different major-league spring-training facility in Florida. He does his best to attract international players to the tournament, something he was more successful doing before September 11, 2001. The timing of the tournament is excellent as it always just precedes the Bob Wagner Wooden Bat Classic, played each January in Fort Myers.

This scheduling allows players to make one trip to Florida to play two tournaments over a week and a half.

Gilmore does much more than organize international baseball and sightseeing trips, run January tournaments, and donate equipment. He strives to deeply involve himself with the baseball programs in the countries he visits, whether on baseball or business trips. He has become so knowledgeable of the baseball programs internationally that he has been hired as a scout by the Cincinnati Reds—with a focus on finding potential major league talent across Asia.

The United States teams that are formed to play internationally are not always the most competitive. They are comprised of players who can afford the cost of the trip (typically under $2,000), airfare, and the local beer; and who can free up the time for the trip. This means that the average age of the teams is significantly higher than you would find at most other senior-baseball events. And since Gilmore takes whoever wants to go, there is not always an adequate "pitching staff," nor are players always in their normal positions. All that being said, the baseball experience is unparalleled.

Imagine playing under the mammoth "wedding cake" structure of Moscow State University on the equivalent of indoor–outdoor carpeting at the only field in Moscow. Or picture playing outside Moscow at a Red Army Base, the best Russian field we saw. I watched Ed Berkich, Robert Siciliano, and George Goodall play catch on the Great Wall of China. We played a team of Japanese expatriates, who organized and were playing in a small Japanese league in Beijing. Imagine playing on a converted dirt soccer field at a university in China. We played at a marvelous multi-field complex in Nettuno, the birthplace of baseball in Italy. We played an afternoon game on the only field in St. Petersburg, Russia, and could have played the game without lights at 10:00 p.m. because the city is so far north it is daylight virtually all day during the summer.

While Ann and I decided not to go, by far the most ambitious Baseball International trip was from May 1–24, 2005. In 1913–1914, Charles Comiskey and John McGraw took their White Sox and Giants teams, supplemented by other teams' players, on a world tour to play baseball in the off season. The trip started with a trek across America from October 18, 1913, in Cincinnati to November 19, in Seattle. From December 6 in Tokyo to February 26, 1914, in London, the teams traveled across the world before returning to the United States on the Lusitania on March 7. With the exception of one game against a Japanese team and four against Australian teams, the White Sox and Giants played each other in exhibition games.

Through much of May 2005, John Gilmore recreated this trip, albeit with modern transportation, as the Baseball International World Tour. At each stop, his American team played a local team and did as much sightseeing as they could fit in. The trip took them to play ball, as did the White Sox and Giants, in Tokyo, Japan; Shanghai and Hong Kong, China; Manila, Philippines; Brisbane, Sydney, and Melbourne, Australia; Colombo, Sri Lanka (Ceylon in 1914); Cairo, Egypt; Rome, Italy; Nice and Paris, France; and London, England. To learn more about the 1913–1914 trip, read *The Tour to End All Tours: The Story of Major League Baseball's 1913–1914 World Tour* by James E. Elfers.

The allure of international baseball is that each foreign team, regardless of the country, loves the game as much as we do. Regardless of whether you can understand the umpire's language, it is clear whether you are out or safe, whether it is a ball or strike, or whether the ball is fair or foul. The bases are still 90 feet (or 27.43 meters) apart and the mound is still 60 feet, six inches (or 18.44 meters) from home. The game is the same and enjoyed worldwide, regardless of the location, language, field conditions, or measurement system.

Who Needs a Glove?

While there is a language of baseball that is understandable worldwide, that language, along with the rules of the game, has developed over time. How would you like to be a "hand out" if the "ball (that is) being struck or tipped...(is) caught either flying or on the first bound?" That's right, you are out if the ball is caught on one bounce, even by a catcher on a foul tip. That was one of only 14 of "The Original Knickerbocker Base Ball Rules of 1845," written by Alexander Cartwright and other club members. Here are two other rules from that era as examples.

"A player, running the bases, shall be out, if the ball is in the hands of the adversary on the base, as the runner is touched by it before he makes his base-it being under-stood, however that in no instance is a ball to be thrown at him."

"If two hands are already out, a player running home at the time the ball is struck, can not make an ace if the striker is caught out."

The language is different, but we can recognize the basis of the game we play today. The Knickerbocker Rules were to be transformed by Henry Chadwick in 1860 to 38, more sophisticated rules, which were adopted by the National Association of Base-Ball Players. By 1866, there were 43 rules.

In 1997, Ann and I attended a presentation at the Cincinnati Museum Center given by Greg Rhodes and John Erardi, who had collaborated on a book entitled *Big Red Dynasty; How Bob Howsom and Sparky Anderson Built the Big Red Machine.* Rhodes is the Cincinnati Reds team historian and the Executive Director of the Cincinnati Reds Hall of Fame and Museum. He has authored numerous books on Reds history. Erardi is a sports reporter for the *Cincinnati Enquirer* and has authored other books about the Reds and Cincinnati.

During the presentation Rhodes shared some of the history of the 1869 Cincinnati Red Stockings, the first openly announced professional team. In doing so, he spent time talking about the rules of the time and mentioned his involvement organizing and playing vintage baseball. After the discussion I cornered him to learn more. He invited me to join his vintage team, which was fashioned after the Red Stockings. They played in an open field at Heritage Village in Sharon Woods, a local county park.

As I first approached the field, I found it to be somewhat different than I had expected. While I was not anticipating a modern groomed field, I had assumed it would at least be flat with some resemblance to what a baseball field should look like. What I found was nothing more than a hay-mowed, irregularly inclined cow pasture surrounded by woods at about the distance of an outfield fence. I quickly learned that I should not have been surprised because, like the rules and equipment we used to simulate mid-nineteenth century baseball, the field, too, was typical of the period.

Rhodes told me I would not need to bring a glove or a bat or a ball. The bats (or perhaps logs would be a better name for the weapons that weighed up to 50 ounces) and the balls would be provided as they were specially made to replicate the equipment of the time. A glove was not necessary because players in the 1860s did not use them. It was not that the ball was soft nor that it was hit softly. Gloves had just not yet been invented. I felt fortunate to have gotten through the day with all of my fingers intact. The game, the language, the pace of the game, and the rules were fun and appealing. And yes, it was clearly baseball. I returned several times and was beginning to get interested enough to buy the vintage uniform when I got deeply involved in playing modern senior baseball.

While I did not continue, there are many dedicated vintage baseball players. The Association has more than 60 teams playing in 19 states and provinces. These vintage teams add nearly 1,000 more players to the ranks of senior baseball as, while younger players are welcomed, vintage players tend to be older. Every summer, they play local games and hold vintage baseball festivals. While not today's modern game, this is definitely baseball, perhaps in its purest form.

"It just doesn't get any better than this"

From leagues and tournaments sanctioned by the major national organizations to vintage baseball festivals; from major league fantasy camps to international baseball experiences; from small independent leagues to special fantasy camps; there are numerous opportunities available for senior players to participate in the game they love and have loved since they were young.

Yet there is even an additional opportunity to play baseball that is made available by those who have developed businesses that run independent tournaments around the country. Compared to fantasy camps, these tournaments provide as much baseball in a week, generally of higher quality competition, at a much lower cost.

I have had the pleasure to play at a number of tournaments run by some of these organizations and find them to be a great value. For the cost of the tournament, travel, food, and lodging, we: 1) get the opportunity to play a lot of baseball, 2) revel in the camaraderie of friends old and new, 3) visit warm places in the middle of winter, and 4) play on fields that are groomed to meet major-league standards. What can be better than playing a doubleheader a day for five days on great fields on sunny days with close friends? It is not uncommon to hear someone at one of these tournaments sigh deeply, slowly look around to take stock of his surroundings, and say, "It just doesn't get any better than this."

The four tournament organizations with which I have played are Baseball International, Legends of Baseball, the Bob Wagner

Wooden Bat Classic, and Play at the Plate. While each has its particular features, there are some things they all have in common. They provide easy registration as an individual or as a group of players, excellent fields, a tournament schedule, umpires, necessary equipment, tournament mementos, and tournament-organized social gatherings. In short, all one needs to do is make the time available, travel to the area, find a place to stay, pay the money, bring personal equipment and uniforms, and play.

Before I go on, I need to provide a caveat. Throughout the book, I will refer to my personal experiences (e.g. teams and teammates with whom I have played, leagues and tournaments in which I have played, the people from around the country with whom I have been involved) and perspectives that I have learned from reading about and talking to others involved in senior baseball. While I recognize this may limit the book to less than the full scope of senior baseball, I am confident it substantially represents the essence of the experience. To those who may have had different and, perhaps, even more diverse senior baseball experiences, I hope you can find a reflection of your personal story in this book.

Legends of Baseball and the Bob Wagner's Wooden Bat Classic grew out of the same history. In July 1992, there was an event scheduled with a fantasy camp format to be played in Cooperstown. Shortly before the camp was to take place, the company running it went out of business. A few of the players who were expecting to play found out that Cooperstown's Doubleday Field was not only still reserved but had already been paid for. Despite the absence of camp organizers and ex-professionals who were to have been there, the campers organized themselves to play and did not miss the opportunity to enjoy baseball in the historic setting. Ed Berkich and Ralph Lach were instrumental in rescuing the 1992 camp. With Ralph's son, Thom, they went on to build on the experience, establish Legends of Baseball, and put on their first Cooperstown event a year later.

The centerpiece of the Legends of Baseball program is their Cooperstown tournament schedule. Each summer, they conduct three one-week events, one each in July, August, and September. Each team plays about half its games at Doubleday Field, the proverbial (albeit not historically accurate) birthplace of baseball and the site of the annual major league Hall of Fame game. The Legends of Baseball organization, now led by Thom and Ralph Lach, uses Doubleday for their tournaments—and they are giving back to the field. The Lachs are at the forefront of Friends of Doubleday, "dedicated to the restoration and preservation of the birthplace of baseball, Abner Doubleday Field." The non-profit foundation is raising funds for an ambitious restoration project.

When not being played at Doubleday Field, tournament games are located at Beaver Valley Field, a short ride south of Cooperstown. The setting is idyllic and has the feel of the *Field of Dreams* site. It is in a campground area owned by the Sharratt family, who even plant rows of corn behind the chain-link outfield fence from foul line to foul line. The dugouts are roomy and nicer than those at Doubleday Field. Legends of Baseball also holds its welcome and farewell parties at the recreation hall at the Beaver Valley site.

I played in Legends' Cooperstown tournaments for several years. Ann joined me each year and we have stayed at the Cooperstown Bed & Breakfast, a wonderful three-story Victorian home owned by Linda and John Smirk. There is something very relaxing about being in the quaint town, which functions at a leisurely pace and offers plenty of baseball, friendliness, and history. Just stroll down Main Street, visit the Hall of Fame, sit in the stands at Doubleday to take in the ambiance, and check out the baseball memorabilia shops. As a fellow B&B lodger said to us once, "If you are looking for something that has to do with baseball in Cooperstown and you can't find it, you're not looking hard enough."

The only time we found Cooperstown to be hectic was the weekend we went to see Ozzie Smith inducted into the Hall of Fame. It was hard to find a place to stay (we ended up in a motel in Herkimer, New York, about a half hour away) and the streets were filled with thousands of baseball fans. Yet, with all of that, we plan to go back to enjoy the excitement of another induction weekend. You can feel the love of baseball in the air and smell the scent of money being spent on memorabilia and Hall of Famers' autographs.

Legends occasionally runs tournaments in other locations as well. In 2002 and 2003, I played in their Coney Island tournament. These weeks were special for a number of reasons. First, they were played in Keyspan Park, where the Brooklyn Cyclones, a Class A affiliate of the New York Mets, play. The Cyclones are the first professional team to play in Brooklyn since the Dodgers abruptly left town in 1957, leaving their rabid fans without professional baseball. Secondly, I had the chance to play ball with many of the New Yorkers who I befriended at my first fantasy camp. I enjoy their passion for the game and for life. Seeing them once or twice a year at a tournament is energizing. But mostly, I enjoyed the event because in 2003, my son, Kevin was able to come down from Boston, where he now lives, and played in the tournament with me.

Bob Wagner, who deeply loved the game, had attended his first senior baseball event in 1985 at Randy Hundley's Chicago Cubs fantasy camp in Mesa, Arizona. (Sound familiar? Yes, Bob and George Goodall met there.) Bob was an active supporter of the Legends of Baseball program, but found himself asking some questions. "What if summer baseball in historic Cooperstown isn't enough baseball for a guy? What if you want to play ball during the winter and not have to deal with snow all over home plate or a $3,000 (cost at the time) fantasy camp payment?"

The answers to those questions led to the first Wooden Bat Classic in 1997 with four teams of 12 players per team. The tournament grew steadily but lost its founder when Bob passed away in 2001. The event was renamed the Bob Wagner Wooden Bat Classic, and Bob's son, Greg, ably took over the labor of love. Greg's stated goal has been to add one team to the tournament each year. In 2005, the tournament exceeded Greg's goal by fielding 17 teams with 230 players.

2005 Bob Wagner Wooden Bat Classic team at Terry Park

The tournament is played at Terry Park, which had been the spring training site for the Philadelphia Athletics, Cleveland Indians, Pittsburgh Pirates, and Kansas City Royals. Since the Royals left in 1987, the park has been administered and maintained by Lee County. In 2004, it was determined that there were structural issues with the stadium's historic grandstand. While the county has redesigned and rebuilt the grandstand, the historic field, which has hosted countless Hall of Famers, remains the same. The combination of the ambiance of Terry Park and the warmth that Greg Wagner brings to the event makes the Bob Wagner Wooden Bat Classic a special tournament.

The newest tournament organization with which I have played is Scott Green's Play at the Plate. He started the organization because he loves baseball and wanted to be as closely associated with the game as possible.

Green has added a couple of special features to the senior baseball tournament experience. First, while he has established a permanent April event at the Cardinals-Marlins spring training facility in Jupiter, Florida, he works to find a wide variety of locations for his three other yearly tournaments. He has run tournaments at Labatt Field in London, Ontario (in proximity to the Canadian Baseball Hall of Fame), New Orleans Zephyr Field (run only one year and cancelled as a result of the 2005 hurricane Katrina damage), and the Nelson Wolff Stadium in San Antonio. To his credit, but mostly because of efforts in New Orleans, before this book was completed, Green announced the rebirth of The Cajun Classic, the return to Zephyr Field.

Green also has committed to enhance the senior baseball experience by making the locker room at each tournament site available to players. When we show up at a Play at the Plate event, we have assigned lockers and access to all the facilities, including a locker-room attendant, who launders uniforms every night. Green has virtually duplicated the fantasy camp experience from a locker-room perspective, minus the ex-professionals and trainers.

If a player wanted to and had the time and resources, he could play the following senior tournament schedule, using 2006 as the example.

2006 Date	Tournament
January 19-22	Baseball International Spring Training
January 23-29	Bob Wagner Wooden Bat Classic
March 2-5	Play at the Plate Cactus Classic
April 6-9	Play at the Plate Palm Beach Classic
July 6-9	Play at the Plate Canadian Classic
August 13-17	Legends of Baseball Cooperstown Classic
October 5-10	Play at the Plate Roy Yocum Memorial Classic

Add this to a player's league games and post-season tournament schedule, and he could play 75 to 100 games a year. This major commitment by both the player and his family will be addressed in more detail in the fifth inning, "Athletic Supporters."

So, who are these guys? They are the up to 125,000 senior players who commit their time and resources to play the game they were passionate about when they were young and continue to love now that they are older. They are over 30 and many are in their 40s, 50s, 60s, and beyond. They play in nationally sanctioned and independent leagues and end-of-season league tournaments, at fantasy camps, on international trips, in one-time annual events, in vintage baseball festivals, and in tournaments. They may play 75 games per year or only a few. They are players who have had professional baseball experience, those who played high school and some college ball, and those with relatively little experience. Regardless of the range of age and experience, the senior baseball circuit provides plentiful opportunities for anyone who wants to play and enjoy. Who are these guys? They are baseball players. As Chris Chambliss, the 17-season major league player, all-star, and gold glove winner, once said, "If you're not having fun in baseball, you miss the point of everything."

"We had some merry times…"

While the major leagues contribute greatly to the establishment of baseball as our national game, baseball is not just about the professional leagues. It is about the game itself. Baseball started out as an amateur endeavor and continues to be largely that. The percentage of baseball players who are in the professional ranks is miniscule.

Seniors do not play the game because we want some day to play professional ball. We are well beyond that. In fact, I do not think that youth, high school, or even college players are in it mainly for a shot at the big leagues. Sure, there are times in our lives when we may harbor aspirations of making it. But it does not take long to have more realistic expectations of our baseball futures. We know that we are playing the game for enjoyment and satisfaction, not as a steppingstone to a professional career.

In 1966, I was a sophomore at the University of Missouri at Rolla. We had just completed an away game in the middle of our varsity season, and I was walking to the bus when a man, with clipboard in hand, approached me and asked if we could talk.

He said his name was Elvin Tappe and he was a scout for the Chicago Cubs. I recognized the name and recalled that he had also been a catcher, manager, and coach for the Cubs. Tappe told me that he had been impressed by what he saw of my play at first base and my swing at the plate. He asked me if I would mind if he stayed in touch because the Cubs might be interested in talking to me further.

Well, you can imagine what that felt like, being noticed by a major league scout. I was hitting just under .300 at the time but got hot shortly thereafter and finished my sophomore year closer to .360. I went on to finish my college baseball career as a 4-year letterman, hit over .350, and was the first baseman on our conference championship team my senior year. Yet, with all of that, I never heard from Elvin Tappe, the Cubs, or any other major league scout again.

Despite enjoying the major league contact, I never played the game because of the prospect of playing professionally. And I never regret that I did not play at even the minor league level—well OK, maybe just a little. The reason I played baseball in Khoury League from age seven, in high school, American Legion, and college, and now at age 60, is because I love to play it.

In his book, *Baseball; A History of America's Game*, Benjamin Rader describes the early days of baseball, before the advent of professional ball. The players were referred to as the ball-playing fraternity. One of the early teams was the Brooklyn Eckfords, a club made up of shipbuilding artisans. Mr. Rader quotes Frank Pidgeon, captain of the Eckfords, who offered two reasons for playing ball.

"First, '...such sport as this brightens a man up, and improves him, both in mind and body...'"

"Second, Pidgeon stressed the sheer pleasure of the experience itself: 'We had some merry times among ourselves; we would forget business and everything else on Tuesday afternoons, go out in the green fields, don our ball suits, and go at it with a perfect rush. At such times, we were boys again.'"

Who are these guys? We are the guys who would have gladly played for the Brooklyn Eckfords. We are the amateur senior baseball fraternity.

RESPECT THE GAME

"It's perfectly legitimate on occasions for the game to make fools of the players, but it's never legitimate for the players to make a fool of the game."

Bob Wagner

"It was the time of my life when I felt most like part of a team."

Ila Borders

Al: "Hey, we're up 2-1. We won the second inning. Nice shot, JR. That double was just what we needed."

Jack: "I can't keep track of all of the places I'm sore. It takes longer every game and tournament to recover, but I can't imagine ever not playing."

Ken: "Yeah, it gets both harder but better every year. Even with the soreness, I love being here. I can't put my finger on it, but part of it is I'm proud of still being able to play a game that most guys I know haven't touched since they were 15. I don't know; it just feels good."

JR: "You're right on. Hey, Al, that home run you gave up last inning—I don't think the ball has come down yet. Do you think you could put have put that pitch any closer to his hitting zone?"

Al: "It's a good thing I have some self respect, or I just might take *that personally. You guys are tough, but in spite of you, I love this game."*

Jack: *"What do you mean? It's because of us you love this game."*

The Doctor and a Tee-Shirt

In 2003, I was winding down the week of my fourth and final Reds Baseball Heaven. My first camp had reintroduced me to playing baseball, and by 2003, I was playing about 75 games a year. More importantly, I had made a host of new friends from all over the country with whom I was staying in touch and seeing at tournaments.

We were sitting in the locker room at the Reds spring training facilities in Sarasota. Some New York friends, my son, Kevin, and I were talking baseball, reviewing the week, and generally horsing around at the end of another great day in baseball paradise. The New Yorkers were Mets fans, who continued to come to the camp even after it had been converted to a Reds-only format two years earlier. Although they realized they would have to wear the uniform of the team to which the Mets traded their beloved Tom Seaver, they sucked it up and stayed the course.

John Geraffo, a transplanted New Yorker, lives in Fayetteville, North Carolina, where he owns a successful pizza business, which it seems has the primary business objective of funding his persistent baseball habit. Mike LoBosco was on a high because he had just earned another pitching victory. Rounding out the New York locker room contingent was David "Doc" Kaufman.

Doc is a prominent cosmetic surgeon from Long Island and among the most generous people I know. He does not get the time to play as much as he would like, but when he does, he's a fierce competitor and willing to catch every inning of every game if that is what his team needs to win. In the midst of our locker room chatter, each of our little group found a gift that Doc had placed in our lockers. David had arranged to get a number of tee-shirts made with a profound message printed in red wrapped around a stark-white baseball at the top back of the black shirt. The message simply read, "Respect the Game."

David Kaufman catching at Reds Baseball Heaven in 2003
and his "Respect the Game" logo

The message said a lot about David and his love for the game. It also said a lot about how we all felt about baseball and why we were playing at every opportunity we could muster. I wear the shirt often, and when I do, I feel good about myself, am reminded how fortunate I am to still be playing, and think about David Kaufman, a true gentleman of the game.

Boys Will be Boys—Not

As a way of understanding what respecting the game really means, there is a great example of how a player chose to respect neither the game nor himself. On July 29, 1996, Chris Sabo was the third baseman for the Cincinnati Reds. In the second inning of a game against the Houston Astros, he hit a ball and shattered "his bat...strewing pieces of cork over the field" (described by BaseballLibrary.com). Sabo was suspended for seven games for the incident, which was consistent with the penalty for the others who, since 1970, have been caught using illegally modified bats: Graig Nettles, Billy Hatcher, Albert Belle, Wilton Guerrero, and Sammy Sosa. Nettles had six super balls in the bat, while the others used cork.

While respect for the game is a serious subject, it never hurts to use humor to keep things in perspective. The late all-star Vada Pinson played his last game in the 1975 season and, years later, was invited to an Old-Timers game, which prompted him to say, "I'm going to get myself a corked bat and blast one out of here. What's the suspension for Old-Timers games, 10 years?"

I was listening to the Sabo corked-bat game on the radio and heard

Marty Brennaman and Joe Nuxhall describe the incident. Much to my dismay, they made light of the situation by taking a "boys will be boys" attitude. Their tones of voice further disparaged the game and the integrity of its rules to the listeners—especially, in my judgment, affecting the many young people who were listening.

I have never met Marty Brennaman, but I have had the real pleasure of spending time with "Nuxie." He is a genuinely gracious and engaging gentleman who loves the game and loves to talk about it. Joe was one of the ex-professionals at the four Reds Baseball Heaven camps I attended. Not having grown up in Cincinnati, I did not have the same deep feelings about Joe that the local Cincinnati guys did. They legitimately love and respect him and his contributions to the game and community. Joe Nuxhall is a class act. But that day in 1996 he and Marty Brennaman got it wrong.

I was so upset by the combined disrespect shown to the game by Chris Sabo and the broadcasting team that, for one of only a few times in my life, I felt compelled to write an opinion article to my local newspaper. The op-ed piece ran in the Opinion Page of the August 17, 1996, *Cincinnati Enquirer*:

> *Reds third baseman Chris Sabo was ejected from the July 29 game for having used an illegal bat. His offense was a deliberate attempt to break the rules. He cheated the rules of the game, the team, the city, the game of baseball, and himself. When the incident occurred, Reds announcers, Marty Brennaman and Joe Nuxhall, treated it lightly, referring to it as if it were a childish prank. Mr. Nuxhall seemed to fondly refer to a previous incident in which he was involved in a similar situation.*
>
> *Mr. Brennaman and Mr. Nuxhall are quick to comment when the Reds play poorly, and this is as it should be—it is part of their jobs as commentators and reporters. For them to miss the opportunity to report the bat incident for what it was—blatant, deliberate cheating and wrong—is unacceptable.*
>
> *The game of baseball (and its rules) is one of the stable and visible values in our society. For Mr. Sabo to have cheated diminishes the game and its values. For Mr. Brennaman and Mr. Nuxhall to make light of the incident diminishes them.*

Thank You, Father Cartwright

Concerns about professional baseball go well beyond cork and super balls. I am writing this paragraph the day after Rafael Palmeiro was suspended for ten games for testing positive in violation of the major league steroid use policy. Palmeiro, at the time of the suspension, had already exceeded 3,000 hits and 500 home runs, only the fourth player in the history of the game to do so (the others are Hank Aaron, Willie Mays, and Eddie Murray). At congressional hearings earlier in the year, Palmeiro was adamant when he said, "I have never used steroids. Period."

Subsequently, Bud Selig, the Commissioner of Major League Baseball, announced the formation of an independent investigation into the issue of steroid use in major league baseball. It is not clear where this investigation will lead, but it is clear that the integrity of major league baseball is at risk. How can we trust the statistics and records that are such a deep tradition of the game? Who cheated the game and who did not? Which records are real and which are not? This is not just about career home run records; it is about the win-loss records of teams. Are the first-place teams there because they are the better teams or because they have the most players on steroids? Hopefully, by the time this book is published, we will have seen how professional baseball will have dealt with the problem, because that is what they must do. Regardless of their actions, however, they will never be able to erase the fact that there were those who disrespected the game.

Notice I said that it is major-league baseball that is the issue, not the game of baseball itself. The purity of the game has not changed. I will get dressed for and drive to my game tonight with no qualms about the fairness of the game. It is the game I played more than 50 years ago and hope to play for many years to come. And it is the game that has been played for more than 150 years.

It is now widely accepted that modern baseball was invented by Alexander Cartwright in 1845, when he published the set of rules for his Knickerbocker Club of New York. Cartwright's Baseball Hall of Fame plaque reads, "FATHER OF MODERN BASE BALL." The Knickerbocker Club rules were adopted, and in 1846, the Knickerbockers lost to the New York Baseball Club at Elysian Fields in Hoboken, New Jersey, in what is believed to be the first modern baseball game. 12 years later, the first organized baseball league, the

National Association of Base Ball Players, was formed.

Baseball grew across the nation as an amateur sport. Not until 1869 did the Cincinnati Red Stockings become the first professional team. Cartwright said in the early years before the professional era, and it is true today, "The game was meant to be played by men like us, men who love the game, who want to compete, who play for camaraderie and merriment, and who uphold the standards of honest, gentlemanly play."

Alexander Cartwright clearly believed that respect for the game was implicit. For amateur players that seems to be sufficient. For major league baseball, the rules should be modified to simply include, "Respect the game."

No Big Deal

Since baseball's inception, players, authors, lyricists, poets, screenwriters, sports columnists, and the general public have been trying to articulate why people are attracted to the game, whether as a player or a fan. For most, the love of the game is instilled early in our lives and then nurtured throughout. This is no less true for senior baseball players. However, as we have been able to continue to play the game as we grow older, we have a unique perspective that seems to magnify what baseball means to us. What makes senior players respect the game, love the game, and want to keep playing?

Continuing to play is not a trivial matter. The effects of aging and some infirmities can threaten to prevent us from playing ball as long as we would like. Yet the compelling nature of the sport combined with the opportunity to play, modifications of some rules, age-group tournament divisions, and open acceptance by fellow players allows even those with apparently serious physiological limitations and those who are much older to play and enjoy the game they love.

In 2002, I played on a fantasy camp team with Jerry Wuest. At the time, he was 63 and had contracted Parkinson's disease. When off the field, he used a cane and frequently had difficulty taking a first step to begin walking. It was not uncommon for him to fall and wait good naturedly for help to get up. Yet, during camp Jerry always took his turn at bat, albeit having a pinch runner assigned to him. During each at bat that week, he would hit the ball, which he did frequently and squarely, and, with absolutely no hesitation or indication of his illness, would take off from the batter's box for a few steps toward first base as the pinch runner took over.

During one at bat, Jerry did not stop after a few steps. His baseball instincts overcame his infirmity. He put his head down and he ran all the way to first base. That night at the fantasy camp kangaroo court, Jerry's pinch runner was fined for almost allowing Jerry to beat him to first base. There was no doubt at the end of the week who our team's MVP selection would be. Jerry's love of the game, his persistence, and his good humor inspired us throughout the week and beyond. Jerry is quoted on the Reds Baseball Heaven web site, "What a week to remember. The baseball was good enough, but the interaction among everyone involved was unbelievable." That summer, while he did not play, Jerry attended Ray James' annual Roy McMillan Memorial Weekend in Richmond, Indiana. At that event, Ray presented a special gift to Jerry, a cane made from a baseball bat similar to the one that Ray had been using for a long time.

Tom Cretella is another example of how physiological limitations are not sufficient barriers to keep dedicated seniors from playing baseball. During my years at the Bob Wagner Wooden Bat Classic, I have had the privilege of playing with Tom. He runs and walks with a limp because of an artificial hip. Yet he is one of our catchers and first basemen and has a formidable on-base percentage. He asks for a pinch runner once he got on base. The Wooden Bat tournament rules, unlike those at fantasy camp, preclude having a substitute runner from home. Tom is never deterred from running hard until on base or, when not playing baseball, from being a serious hiker with a special interest in steep-hill climbing.

Dick Irvin is a 75-year-old player from St. George, Utah. I met Dick at John Gilmore's Baseball International Spring Training Tournament. I asked Dick if he had ever had any injuries while playing senior baseball that have kept him from playing. His response not only said a lot about him but also captured the spirit of senior baseball players who truly believe they are never too old to play. Dick said, "I have a replaced hip and at times it gives me trouble. Many other bumps and strains that come along. No big deal."

"90 feet...perfection"

Wuest, Cretella, and Irvin, by continuing to play through infirmity and age, exhibit the respect and love senior players have for their game. Certainly not all senior players need to overcome physiological issues. But all of us need to find ways to compensate for the effects of aging. What is it about baseball that makes us want to do so? Each of us has his own reasons, but I find there are consistent themes that draw players to and keep them in the game.

One of these common reasons that attract us to sports in general and to baseball specifically is the predictable structure of the game. In our daily lives, it is often difficult to determine how well we are doing. It is sometimes hard to know what the rules are. There are frequently more shades of grey than stark black or white.

But sports are different. There are scores, rules, boundaries, and statistics. During a game, things are clear; a pitch is either a ball or strike, a batted ball is either fair or foul, the runner is either safe or out. As we leave a game, whether we were players or spectators, we know who won and lost and how each player did. There is a comfort in the certainty of this. Sandy Koufax said, "The game has a cleanness. If you do a good job, the numbers say so. You don't have to ask anyone or play politics. You don't have to wait for reviews."

Baseball does not only provide certainty on any given day—it also does so over time, a testament to its long tradition. Bowie Kuhn, the Commissioner of Baseball from 1969 to 1984 said, "I believe in the Rip Van Winkle Theory: that a man from 1910 must be able to wake up after being asleep 70 years, walk into a ballpark and understand perfectly."

I would propose a corollary to Commissioner Kuhn's theory. It is the Man Without A Country Corollary: that a man can travel to any country in the world and, without knowing the language, put on his spikes and glove, take the field, and play a baseball game. This has been one of the wonderful aspects of having the opportunity to join John Gilmore's Baseball International trips. Whether we were playing on a converted dirt soccer field in Beijing, or the Red Army Base outside of Moscow, or on a reasonably well-manicured field in Nettuno, Italy, the game was the game.

The dimensions are sacrosanct. Whether measured by the locals in the English System or Metric System, we found the bases 90 feet apart and the mound 60 feet, six inches from the rear point of home plate. Red Smith, the noted sports columnist said, "90 feet between home plate and first base may be the closest man has ever come to perfection."

The rules are consistent and for the most part simple. No matter where you play, you get three strikes, four balls, and three outs. A foul line is always in fair territory (OK, so that is not obvious from the name, but it is always true).

During his career as a baseball executive, Bill Veeck was the owner of the Indians, Browns, and White Sox. He was a genius when it came to promoting his teams and bringing fans to the ballpark. He was, as described on the Hall of Fame web site, "an inveterate hustler and energetic maverick." Veeck sent a midget (Eddie Gaedel) to the plate, introduced fireworks at ballgames, installed an exploding scoreboard, started the practice of adding players' names to the backs of jerseys, signed the first black player (Larry Doby) in the American League, and signed the oldest rookie ever, 43-year-old Satchel Paige, in 1948. But while Veeck tinkered with the promotion of the game, he fully respected the traditions and structure of the game itself. He once said, "Baseball is almost the only orderly thing in a very unorderly world. If you get three strikes, even the best lawyer in the world can't get you off."

When we step onto a baseball field, the outcome of the game is in doubt and how we will do as individuals is uncertain. But the structure of the game and the field provide a safe haven. The rules are known, the dimensions are familiar, the rhythm of play is comfortable. Just as Linus Van Pelt in the "Peanuts" cartoons had his security blanket, so do we—the game and field of baseball.

About five years ago, on a whim I went to a class to learn a little about mysticism. The class unexpectedly included learning some meditation techniques. During several of the sessions, the instructor put on some very soothing music, dimmed the lights, and had us lay on our backs with our eyes closed. To start, he asked us to think about a place that makes us feel happy and secure. It was from this place in our minds that we would explore mysticism and to where we should mentally return if our mystic journey became too uncomfortable. It took me only a few seconds to picture my happy, secure place. I found myself lying on my back with my eyes closed on lush green outfield grass just behind second base. Whether through meditation or in an awake reality, I would surmise that many, if not most, baseball players would identify a space somewhere between the lines as their happy, secure place. The structure of the game is comforting.

The Baseball Community

Perhaps the most compelling reason for our love of baseball, especially as players, is that it affords us the opportunity to meet the inherent human need of belonging. Here is what some senior baseball players have to say about how this concept relates to them.

Bob Pinault, 52, a pitcher from Laguna Beach, California, says, "I love the baseball community—'we are family.'"

Phil Reichle, 59, a pitcher and high school baseball coach in Cincinnati, says, "At our age, we play for the love of the game. Those we meet on other teams share this, and we all seem to become one large extended family."

Anthony Ranieri, 42 a pitcher and shortstop from Massapequa, New York, says that baseball is meaningful to him because of the "camaraderie" and that "the friendships I have made are above and beyond anything I could have expected."

Ed Berkich, 71, a catcher from Cincinnati, says, "My best friends are baseball people!"

Tom Giffen, 57, Roy Hobbs' national organization director says, "Players tell me that they look forward to the tournament every year and so do I. This is my family, and the tournament is like a family reunion. We play ball, drink beer, and tell lies."

As I talk with players from around the country, one of the primary themes that affect their love of the game is their connection to their team, league, and the overall baseball community. Regardless of their diverse backgrounds, there is a seemingly instant connection with fellow baseball players. One needs only to experience pre-game greetings, dugout chatter, interaction with the other team during a game, and post-game parking lot, locker room, or bar discussions to feel the camaraderie that permeates the senior baseball sub-culture.

Roger Angell has made a career by writing about baseball. He is an editor and frequent contributor for the *New Yorker* magazine as well as an author, having written *The Summer Game*, *Five Seasons*, *Late Innings*, *Season Ticket*, and *Once More Around the Park*. Angell wrote the following about the baseball family, "It's like joining an enormous family with ancestors and forebears and famous stories. And it's a privilege. It means a lot." He goes on to talk about those who are out of the game, "...they sense what they are missing. I think that they feel there's something that they're not in on which is a terrible loss. And I'm sorry for them."

Being sorry for those outside of baseball may be an overstatement. But Angell's quotation does serve to emphasize the point about the value those of us inside of the game derive from belonging to the baseball community.

"Team – a sense of the soul of baseball"

In her book, *Breaking into Baseball: Women and the National Pastime*, Jean Hastings Ardell uses the chapter "For Love of the Game" to tell two stories that help emphasize how being part of a baseball team can mean so much to an individual. Throughout the book, Ardell highlights Ila Borders, a left-handed pitcher who progressed through a baseball career despite resistance from opposing coaches, players, and parents, and, sometimes, her own coaches. Her baseball career started in Little League at age ten when she told her parents she wanted to switch from softball to baseball and continued, impressively, through a three-year minor league experience, which ended for her at age 25.

Part of Border's baseball life was spent at Whittier Christian Junior High School, where she had two strong years in seventh and eighth grades. In the seventh grade she not only posted a 0.44 earned run average with 36 strikeouts in 16 innings, she also batted .571. In the eighth grade, Borders led her team to a second consecutive unbeaten season and pitched six shutout innings with 12 strikeouts in the championship game. Despite going on to play in high school, college, and beyond, she fondly recalls her Junior High experience. And despite the statistics she amassed in Junior High, she recalls most nostalgically, "It was the time of my life when I felt most like part of a team."

Ardell also tells the story of Jim Glennie, who, in 1992, founded the American Women's Baseball League (AWBL). Even prior to that, Glennie, an assistant attorney general for the state of Michigan, had been a longtime advocate for women in baseball. He seemed to have a sense for the importance of the concept of team to baseball and to those who play it.

As the AWBL was first starting up, Glennie formed two traveling teams. Many of the players had little baseball experience. That meant they had to develop skills, an understanding of the fundamentals, and something that Glennie emphasized when he said, "...because these were first experiences in baseball for many of the women, they had not developed a deep commitment to the team—a sense of the soul of baseball—that some later would have."

While the reality for many of those women was that they had not had the opportunity to learn about the concept of team prior to playing baseball, the experience of the generation of current senior men players was much different. As I noted earlier, I can look at old team pictures and name teammates back to Khoury League days even though I have not seen some of them for 50 years. As early as when I was seven years old, baseball built a sense of belonging to a community that was seemingly created just for me.

This community has stood the test of time. The best example is the infield that played together at University City High School, winning the state baseball championship in our junior year. Marc Golubock at third, Jackie Mercurio at shortstop, Steve Novack at second, and Alan Spector at first. We played those same positions together in elementary school, summer park programs, Khoury League, and Junior High School before moving on to our high school and American Legion years.

Our Junior High School went through ninth grade, so that, as freshmen, we were not located at the high school, but rather a couple miles away. Yet the four of us made the high school sophomore team; we were picked up by taxi for practices and home games. For away games the team bus would pick us up on the way and we changed into our uniforms on the bus.

In the high school state championship game, our infield turned a vital double play in a key game situation. At the banquet to celebrate our state championship the keynote speaker was Bing Devine, the Vice-President and General Manager of the St. Louis Baseball Cardinals. In his speech, Devine said that we were rated as the top high school defensive infield in the country. To this day we do not know if he made that up or if there really were such a rating—but it sure felt good.

Golubock, Mercurio, Novack, Spector—an infield, teammates, family. To this day, although we live in Phoenix, Western Illinois, Chicago, and Cincinnati, we feel close and get in touch whenever we can.

In 1994, my high school class was planning our 30th-year reunion when I received a letter from Steve Novack. The letter was checking on my interest in having a reunion of the high school baseball team during the weekend of the class reunion. Thanks to Steve and the feelings we all had for baseball and each other, on Saturday afternoon of our class reunion weekend, the baseball team reconnected. Not only did our class members on the team show up, but virtually the entire team was there, including the coaches and trainers. Teammates who lived as far away as California flew into St. Louis only for the afternoon event. When we walked in the door of the team reunion, it was as if we had not been apart for 30 years. We belonged to the team and the team belonged to us.

"We are family"

I played for five years with a group of men, supported by their respective families, who represented what is meant by the phrase "senior baseball team." We were the Cincinnati Colts, most of us 50 or older, who played in the Dayton, Ohio, Roy Hobbs league. Like most senior teams, the Colts were a diverse group who, had it been in most other circumstances, would likely never have connected at all, let alone become close friends and family. In two stanzas of a poem that I wrote about the Colts, I highlighted the diversity of the players.

We are teachers, businessmen and PhDs.
We are fan builders, maintenance men and counters of beans.
We are postmen, mechanics, and retirees from Procter.
We are firemen, computer programmers, cartoonists, and doctors.

Yet, we come together in a special way.
We stay together come what may
Because we love the game as well as each other.
While we are teammates, we are more like brothers.

The Colts were not unique in this regard. If you ask players on most senior teams what their occupations are, the answers will be diverse. Yet baseball brings them together. In his book, *Baseball for Real Men: Seven Spiritual Laws for Senior Players*, Nelson W. Wolff describes his reasons for having returned to play baseball some

30 years after playing in his youth. Wolff writes, "...something was missing in my life. I longed for a connection to other males. I wanted it on terms where we were equals, regardless of our station in life."

The Colts played together in two leagues, the one in Dayton and a traveling league in Toledo, Ohio, a three-hour drive. We practiced in the fall, sometimes indoors, then went to Fort Myers together for two weeks of the Roy Hobbs World Series every November. Following the Florida trip, we could not wait to get back together indoors after the new year to get ready for the upcoming league season.

The Colts played hard and partied hard. There is a bar on Fort Myers Beach called Dusseldorf's, which we dubbed "Colts Central." Virtually every evening of the two weeks of the World Series, players and families would gather there to review the day and look forward to tomorrow. There were a few beers consumed along the way. Each week, there would be a "rookie night" at which those who were joining the Colts in Florida for the first time would be generally debased, but all in good humor. And it was not uncommon for the Colts to run a fundraiser at Dusseldorf's to benefit local baseball leagues and deserving local residents.

While many of the aspects of the game of baseball rely on individual actions and achievement, it is still a team game. And it is the attraction of belonging to a team and to the overall baseball community that draws so many of us to continue to participate. I feel fortunate to have the opportunity virtually all year long to be looking forward to and then actually reuniting with baseball friends either in a local league game or in a tournament. Restating what Bob Pinault said, "I love the baseball community—we are family."

"The hard is what makes it great."

The comfortable structure of the game and the sense of belonging to something greater than ourselves are only two reasons we love baseball and continue to play. Another reason is that playing baseball as we get older helps us gain the respect of others as well as respect for ourselves.

Alexander Cartwright said that baseball is played by those who love the game, want to compete, and enjoy the camaraderie. There is more to it than that. There is a level of personal satisfaction that comes from doing something well that relatively few others are doing or can do. In that regard, the movie, *A League of Their Own,* brought us one of the greatest baseball quotations and perhaps one of the best movie lines ever. Coach, former great major leaguer, and drunk, Jimmy Dugan, is trying to convince catcher and team-star Dottie Hinson not to leave the team to return home with her husband.

Jimmy: "...Dottie, if you want to go back to Oregon and make a hundred babies, great, I'm in no position to tell anyone how to live. But sneaking out like this, quitting, you'll regret it for the rest of your life. Baseball is what gets inside you. It's what lights you up, you can't deny that."

Dottie: "It just got too hard."

(Here comes the line that may be the insight of why many of us continue to play the game.)

Jimmy: "It's supposed to be hard. If it wasn't hard, everyone would do it. The hard...is what makes it great."

In 2003, *USA Today* published a series of articles as they sought to determine and describe the hardest thing to do in sports. Their conclusion was that the most difficult sports feat is hitting a baseball squarely. While one might contest their conclusion, there can be no argument that hitting should certainly be among the top picks.

Combine hitting with the other requirements of the game and one could conclude that baseball, in general, is among the more difficult sports to play. There are two quotations by Hall of Famer Ted Williams that apply. Of Williams, Stan Musial said, "Ted was the greatest hitter of our era...loved talking about hitting and was a great student of hitting and pitchers." Given that Williams is considered by Musial and most others as one of the all-time great hitters, his comments mean even more. Williams contended: "Baseball is the only field of endeavor where a man can succeed three times out of ten and be considered a good performer." And he said, "The hardest thing to do...is hit a round baseball with a round bat, squarely."

Baseball is a difficult game to play at any level and at any age. It is increasingly difficult as we get older. We are competing not only with the game and with our opponents, but also with the aging process. There is, therefore, a great deal of esteem associated with still being able to play.

In the second inning, "Who Are These Guys?" I noted a number of lines I have heard from friends and family when they find out that I am still playing baseball. "You mean softball, don't you?" "What about your knees?" "I wish I were doing that. I still love the game." "How do you find the time?" "If I were only in shape…" "I'm proud of you."

These statements indicate that I had earned the respect of others. I do not flaunt it. It just feels good.

One night during my 40th-year high school reunion weekend, my classmate, Les Berger, was speaking to the crowd assembled in the high school gym. There were more than 200 classmates there, many with their significant others. Les was talking and joking about how we had changed since graduating in 1964. He said, among other things, that we were not as physically active as we once were. Then he paused and said, "…except Alan Spector, who is still playing baseball."

We all, albeit to different degrees, need recognition, attention, appreciation, dignity, and status. Playing baseball helps us to meet those needs in the eyes of people outside the game. Baseball allows us to gain recognition from those within the game as well. While baseball is a competitive game, it is also a gentleman's game. It is part of baseball tradition and practiced especially well within the senior amateur community to visibly recognize the achievements of others. How many times have I seen a senior player give a high-five to an opponent who has gotten a solid hit or made a great defensive play?

Moving to field a ground ball in Nettuno

Recall the story of the Chinese team stopping the game to applaud George Goodall to express how much they appreciated who he was and what he was doing. In Nettuno, Italy, I had a particularly good game at third base, one of those games where I was in a zone and nothing got by me left or right. An Italian player came up to me after the game. He told me that his teammates had chosen him because of his reasonable English skills to tell me how much they appreciated watching me play the position and thanked us all for coming to Italy to play baseball with them.

Major leaguers, for all their faults, have served to set an example for recognizing accomplishments, even for opponents. Who can forget the California Angels applauding Cal Ripken, Jr. and giving him high-fives on his recognition lap around Camden Yards on September 6, 1995, when he played in his 2,131st consecutive game, breaking Lou Gehrig's record? Major league fans also recognize accomplishment of opponents. Knowledgeable fans in most cities will applaud a great catch or pitching performance as the player comes off the field.

Shawn Henn plays with me in our Roy Hobbs league. He is in his 30s, owns Encore Plumbing Inc. in Cincinnati, and is the very proud father of three. Shawn was invited to play minor league ball the day before he learned that his wife was pregnant with their first child. He searched his soul and decided that a minor league life, with its small salary and no promises for the future, was no way to raise a family. Without regret, he moved on to his successful plumbing business and his wonderful family.

Shawn is delighted to be back to baseball but still, appropriately, misses games to attend to family priorities. He is a joy to play with and have in the dugout. At one Sunday morning game, Shawn and I were sharing a corner of the dugout. The game had slowed to an easy rhythm, and the other team was making a pitching change. Out of seemingly nowhere, he proceeded to tell me that I was a role model and baseball mentor to him. He wanted to be in and stay in shape, continue to play ball as he gets older, and continue to play at a competitive level, even against younger players. He then informed me that his personal nickname for me is Spectomatic.

Shawn's words were especially heartwarming, not just because I felt appreciated for what I do in baseball, but for the way that I had affected someone else's life. In some small way, I experienced what it must be like to be George Goodall, who has been such an inspiration to so many senior players. It also reminded me that I have a responsibility to others, as do all of us who are continuing to play as we reach our 50s, 60s, and beyond. We can be role models in a way that promotes the game and the positive experience of senior baseball. This responsibility is also part of the basis upon which I felt that I needed to write this book.

No Brag, Just Fact

Gaining the respect of others is important. Gaining self-respect is critical.

I was blessed to have had parents and other close relatives who consistently gave me positive reinforcement. By doing so, they instilled in me a sense of independence and confidence that became the foundation for me to build my life skills. When they introduced me to baseball and spent their time and their patience to help me learn the fundamentals, they set the stage for both my younger and older baseball careers. Significantly, both my mom and dad are among those to whom this book is dedicated.

Baseball has been an integral part of my life and one of the activities that has helped me gain self-respect. I have also been fortunate to play on a long list of good to great teams and have been blessed to be on championship teams at all levels. I was on the Lapp Printers Khoury League team that won the Missouri–Illinois championship in 1958. In 1963, our University City High School team won the Missouri state baseball championship. In my senior year at the University of Missouri at Rolla, we won the 1968 Missouri Intercollegiate Athletic Association league championship. My Cincinnati Colts won the AAA division Roy Hobbs Masters Division World Series championship in 2002. I have also been on teams that have won championships at Baseball International's Spring Training Tournament and Legends of Baseball Cooperstown and Coney Island Tournaments.

This litany is not about me, nor is it really about the teams that won the championships. It is rather about the opportunity over time to get positive feedback from the game of baseball. That feedback comes in many forms. It can be a comment from a teammate after you make an error, "Nice effort." It can be driving home from a game knowing you went two for three with a walk and played an errorless game. It can be playing for a team that won eight games one year after winning only one in its inaugural season the year before. It can even be about winning championships.

While baseball is a team sport, it is also a game of individual achievement. As we continue to play the game, it enables us to gain and increase our self-respect on two levels. One level is to demonstrate to ourselves that we are competent enough to find a place to play, without embarrassing ourselves, somewhere on the senior baseball circuit. The second level is that we are maintaining our adequate level of capability at an age when most have hung up their spikes a long time ago and cannot even envision playing the game.

It feels good to be able to look in the mirror and say to myself, "I am a moral, ethical, and respected person. I am 60 years old and have, with Ann, created a happy, healthy, and self-sufficient family, including having two wonderful grandsons. I am well into a fulfilling retirement after a very successful 33-year career with the Procter & Gamble Company. And, importantly, I just got back from playing a baseball tournament in Cooperstown where I played a doubleheader each day for five days." That is self-respect.

Walter Brennan played the lead role in the 1960s TV western *The Guns of Will Sonnett*. When facing a nasty gunman who was challenging him, Brennan would look the gunman straight in the eye and say, "Some say my son Jim is fast. Well he ain't. I am. No brag, just fact."

A Baseball Player Must Play Baseball

In 1954, Abraham Maslow first published his book, *Motivation and Personality*, which included what has become to be known as the "Hierarchy of Needs." When he did his research for the book, most psychology dealt with the abnormal and the ill. Maslow, however, was fascinated with high- performing individuals and studied them to determine why they were able to be at their best. His resultant "Hierarchy of Needs" postulates that human beings are motivated by unsatisfied needs and that certain lower order needs must be met before higher order needs can be satisfied. Once the lower deficit needs are met, we can then operate at high levels of achievement.

The deficit needs from lowest to highest are physiological needs, safety and security needs, belonging needs, and esteem needs. Once these are substantially addressed, Maslow contends, can we reach our full potential, which he calls "self-actualization."

Maslow described self-actualization, "Even if all these needs are satisfied (referring to the four deficit needs categories), we may still often...expect that a new discontent and restlessness will soon develop, unless the individual is doing what *he*, individually, is fitted for. A musician must make music, an artist must paint, a poet must write, if he is to be ultimately at peace with himself. What a man *can* be, he *must* be. He must be true to his own nature. This need we may call self-actualization."

Talking to senior players, I see a consistent theme. They seem to have been drawn back to the game and feel as though this is where they belong, where they are fulfilled. Maslow could have added that a baseball player must play baseball.

CRACK OF THE BAT

"Tradition, tradition! Tradition!"
Tevya from "Fiddler on the Roof"

*"This game—baseball—is rich with strategy, talent,
challenge, excitement and yes, tradition."*
Mike Schmidt

*JR: "Jack, you really sat on that fast ball. I love the crack of the bat
when it sounds like that."*

Al: "That put us up 4-1."

*Jack: "Am I glad we switched from metal a few years ago. We're
back to playing the game the way it should be played."*

*Ken: "I only hope they change a few of those other rules. I know they
mean well, but some of the rules are just not traditional baseball.
And that's what we should be playing. Jack, you know that Palm
Beach tournament you're considering. There's no stealing or
advancing on passed balls and wild pitches. That takes the catcher
out of the game."*

*Jack: "I'd rather that not be the case, but I'm probably going to go
anyway."*

JR: "Al, how's your thigh feeling? You barely got your glove on that line drive before it hit you."

Al: "I'm just glad we weren't using aluminum. I'm not sure I'd have touched it at all before it got me. Well, we got the out and I can still walk. So, I guess it all turned out OK."

The Pickle Barrel League

Our love of baseball is, in part, sustained by the traditions of the game. The constancy of baseball is comforting—the dimensions, the rules, the history. In his great monologue, James Earl Jones, playing Terence Mann in *Field of Dreams*, talks to Ray Kinsella about why people will "come to Iowa." He says, "The one constant through all the years, Ray, has been baseball. America has rolled by like an army of steamrollers. It has been erased like a blackboard, rebuilt, and erased again. But baseball has marked the time. This field, this game: it's part of our past, Ray. It reminds us of all that once was good and it could be again. Oh... people will come, Ray. People will most definitely come."

Certainly, there have been changes over the years that have enhanced the game. For example, the game was once played without batting helmets. Later, players used hat inserts, then earless batting helmets, and finally helmets with protective ear flaps. In youth baseball in the 1950s, we used red wrap-around one-size-fits-all padded plastic head protection.

Another example of a change in the game is that we now wear gloves to play defense and we carry them into the dugout with us instead of leaving them on the field. And the gloves have dramatically improved. The transition of the use of gloves has not fundamentally changed the game. The physics of getting to and catching a ball are the same regardless of the tool used to do so. Ozzie Smith, among the greatest fielding shortstops of all time, could not afford a glove when he was young. He formed one out of a paper bag. He then used the paper bag with a rubber ball to develop his hand-eye coordination.

My dad told me about an annual ritual of his that began in late winter when he was a young player in the 1930s. He would join his friends at the local deli. Each of them gave the proprietor a nickel and in return would get two things. One was a dill pickle from the barrel. The second was the right to dip their glove hand in the brine of the pickle barrel. The intent was to toughen the skin on their glove hand for the upcoming season to compensate for the poor protection afforded them by the gloves of that era. For hours, they would eat their pickles, talk baseball, and soak their hands. One baseball tradition has been the "hot stove league." For my dad, it was the "pickle barrel league."

Despite these few changes, in large part, baseball has stayed fundamentally constant throughout the modern era. I previously referred to Bowie Kuhn's Rip Van Winkle Theory. "I believe in the Rip Van Winkle Theory: that a man from 1910 must be able to wake up after being asleep for 70 years, walk into a ballpark and understand baseball perfectly."

I had earlier proposed the Man Without A Country Corollary to Kuhn's Theory. A second corollary is: a 60-year old player, who has not played baseball since his youth, is able to go to a fantasy camp, or sign up for a tournament, or join a league, and play a game he understands perfectly. The constancy of the game and the traditions that support it allow him to feel at home on the field. This is the Senior Baseball Corollary to the Rip Van Winkle Theory. It is scientific; look it up.

Let Catchers be Catchers

Senior baseball does have a number of rules that are different from those of the major leagues and the rules by which we played youth baseball through high school and college. In many cases the changes appropriately accommodate the intent and needs of senior baseball and its players. Others, I believe, are changes that, while well intended, have unnecessarily chipped away at the foundation of baseball and its traditions.

Rules vary from event to event. These are examples of senior baseball rules that serve to maximize participation and ensure player safety.

- unlimited defensive substitution
- the use of substitute runners when warranted without the original runner leaving the game permanently

- removal of a pitcher after he hits some predetermined number of batters per inning or per game
- allowing a batting order of more than nine players
- continuation of the batting order from game to game in a tournament versus starting over every game.

Other rules changes at various tournaments address when a batter can and cannot bunt. Some of these are very restrictive, allowing no bunting at all. My personal preference is for the full bunting rules to be allowed. In the 2006 48-and-over Roy Hobbs World Series, the team I was on squeezed successfully three times. It is an exciting play and forces the strategic thinking so important to making baseball the exciting, yet subtle, game it is. But if bunting must be restricted, the best set of rules I have seen is that in which bunting is allowed in any situation except when a runner is on third base. While this does take the strategic and exciting squeeze play out of the game, it can be rationalized as a reasonable tradeoff—to minimize the risk of an injury caused by an uncontrolled play at the plate.

There are, however, rules changes at some senior baseball events that, in my judgment, have diminished the game. These rules relate to when runners can and cannot advance on the bases. Many tournaments and most, if not all, fantasy camps play what are sometimes referred to as Cooperstown rules. By these rules, a runner is not allowed to steal a base nor advance on passed balls or wild pitches. In addition, the batter is out even if the catcher drops the third strike, regardless of the number of outs and runners on base. While the catcher is still important to the defense and to calling the game for the pitching staff, these rules serve to marginalize the role of the catcher. Doing so is a meaningful loss to the traditional rhythm of a baseball game. Are there those who are catching senior games for whom these rules are helpful? Yes. But the value for these catchers and for the games in which they are playing is more than offset by the loss of an important aspect of a baseball game.

The only exception to my aversion to the Cooperstown rules is the very oldest of the age divisions. These rules may be appropriate for the 60- and 65-plus divisions where teams may find it difficult to recruit two or three catchers (more than one catcher is critical to being a successful tournament team) who can manage the full game rules. That being said, I have played with and against 60-year-old-and-over catchers who can still throw runners out. Remember, the base stealers are older also.

Scott Green's Play at the Plate rules begin to address the issue. Green set up his tournaments to be played using the Cooperstown rules but included a clause that if two teams want to play full rules, they are allowed to make that agreement before the game. Although this has not yet happened in one of his tournaments, Green has said that someday he hopes to have a tournament with full baseball rules.

For a couple of years the Cincinnati Colts, for whom I was playing at the time, joined a league centered in Toledo, Ohio. That league had a rule, which, to this day, I cannot figure out. If there were a passed ball or wild pitch, each runner was allowed to advance one base, unless the catcher chose to chase the ball. In that case, runners could advance as far as they wished at their own risk. This seems to me to be the same as drinking half-decaffeinated coffee.

There is another explanation of why Cooperstown rules are detrimental to the foundations of baseball. I consistently hear from senior players that one of the reasons they have returned to baseball after playing softball for a number of years is the difference in the importance of strategy. While I am not intending to detract from softball (I played and enjoyed it for many years), it lacks a dimension present in baseball. Softball is a "station to station" game, even in fast pitch where stealing is allowed, but seldom attempted. Once one gets on base, the only way to advance is to be forced by a hit ball or a walk.

The strategy of baseball, by contrast, allows for advancing on the bases by stealing, use of the hit and run, and by the sacrifice bunt (which, while allowed in fast pitch softball, is not allowed in slow pitch, the predominate game of softball played). The intricacies of baseball that derive from the ability to lead off, steal, and sacrifice bunt are a compelling feature of the game.

As an example, assume there is a runner on first in a baseball game. Will he attempt to steal second? What has to be considered by the players and coaches to answer this one simple question?

- How many outs are there?
- What is the score?
- Is it early or late in the game?
- What is the count?
- What is the speed and starting quickness of the runner?

- How good is the pickoff move by the pitcher?
- How good is the hitter?
- Is the hitter right or left handed?
- Should the pitcher throw over to first to keep the runner close?
- Should the pitcher slide step to home?
- Should the pitcher hold the ball longer in the stretch to tighten the runner's legs in his stance?
- How strong and accurate is the arm of the catcher?
- How quickly does he get rid of the ball?
- Who should cover second for the throw from the catcher?
- Should the first baseman hold the runner on or play behind him?
- Where should the second baseman play to both cover second on the throw from the catcher yet cut down the hole as the first baseman is holding the runner?
- Should the catcher call for a pitchout?
- Should the catcher call for a more easily handled fast ball even though an off-speed pitch may be warranted?
- Should the batter take the pitch or swing to protect the runner?
- If a runner is also on third, should the catcher throw through? If he does, should the runner on third take off for home? Will the second baseman cut the ball off if the runner on third tries to score?
- How do the fielders position themselves to be prepared for the additional possibility of a bunt or hit and run?
- Has the defensive team stolen the signals?

These questions and others you may think of are asked and answered by coaches and players in those few seconds before every pitch with a man on base in a baseball game that is being played with full rules. Cooperstown rules may have their place, but I would prefer that the full strategy and intricacies of the game be part of the senior baseball experience. Let catchers be catchers; let baseball be baseball.

"Is Nothing Sacred?"

There is another aspect of senior baseball rules that has historically chipped away at the traditional foundation of baseball. Which would you rather use, an aluminum/composite bat or a wooden bat? For many players the answer is changing. After a long-standing trend to aluminum going back to the early years of senior baseball, the tournaments and leagues that I play in have already moved or are quickly moving back to wooden bats.

ESPN's online magazine edition ran a poll of readers asking, "What are the worst sports innovations of all time?" Thankfully, the readers were insightful enough to rank performance enhancing drugs as their first pick. Second was artificial turf with ESPN quoting Dick Allen from 1970, when he said, "If a horse can't eat it, I don't want to play on it." Third was the college football BCS (Bowl Championship Series).

The next ranked item as the worst sports innovation of all time was "aluminum bats." This is what ESPN online magazine had to say to represent what they heard from their readers about metal bats, "Politicians often do the wrong things, and sometimes say the right things. So we'll just quote from a speech given by Illinois representative Richard H. Durbin in 1989: 'Designated hitters, plastic grass, uniforms that look like pajamas, chicken clowns dancing on the baselines, and of course the most heinous sacrilege, lights in Wrigley Field. Are we willing to hear the crack of a bat replaced by the dinky ping? Are we ready to see the Louisville slugger replaced by the aluminum ping dinger? Is nothing sacred?'"

By the way, the ESPN readers also disliked titanium golf clubs, oversized tennis rackets, and indoor football, among other things.

Wood is Poetic

There are two primary reasons for the wood movement; tradition and safety. When I asked Tom Giffen of the Roy Hobb's organization why he has relentlessly transitioned his World Series from metal to wooden bats, he simply said, "It's the way the game is supposed to be played." He then went on to talk about how the safety issues influenced his decision as well.

The value of maintaining tradition is a subjective argument. The facts that the baseball started with wooden bats and the professional leagues continue to use them fall on deaf ears to those who eschew tradition for more batted-ball speed. It is likely, therefore, that those same non-traditionalists will not be moved by the fact that poetry has been written about the wooden bat. By contrast, have you ever seen anything poetic about the metal bat alternatives?

From "*Diamonds are Forever*" by an unknown poet:

> A Louisville Slugger;
> a baseball, that perfect object
> for a man's hand; the smell of
> varnish and leather; and a well-
> worn and well-used, older
> brother's glove.

From "*Seaver and Stargell*" by Glen Clifford:

> Props are few. Wooden bat, not yet cracked,
> An outfielder's glove, almost broken in,
> And the remnant of a hardball wrapped in electrical tape.
> The breeze off the Atlantic, a mile away, blows in.
> The sun spectates, changing position for a better view.
> A neighbor's dog umpires from the shade.

From "*How Life Imitates the World Series*" by Thomas Boswell:

> Ever since the first caveman picked up the first cudgel,
> went to the door and smacked the first nosy saber-
> toothed tiger in the snout, mankind has known the
> atavistic power and pleasure of the bat.
> From Robin Hood's quarterstaff to Paul Bunyan's ax,
> men of myth have loved the taper of the handle,
> the texture of the wood grain, the centrifugal surge
> in the end of the whirling mass.
> Axes and stout staves have dwindled in everyday use.

Now, that ancient inherited desire for thudding force,
for an instrument that will deliver a satisfying blow,
has descended to the baseball bat.

From *"The New Player"* by Lowell Bergeron:

He came in fresh and green
Wearing a suit sparkly clean.
In one hand, he held an old bag,
In the other, a glove like a rag.
His hat at a slant did rest.
Of his confidence, did attest.
He lugged a big wooden bat
And introduced himself as Nat.
They showed him to his stall
For his rookie year of baseball.
At once, he was part of the team.
He had realized his baseball dream.

From an untitled poem by Justinas Marcinkevicius:

I fear for that old song now silent,
and for the bedspread time has tattered,
and for the wooden bat now rotting,
I fear for the old-fashioned flail.

Incidentally, Justinas Marcinkevicius was a Lithuanian, born in 1930, and the poem had nothing to do with baseball. Nevertheless, it applies so perfectly.

Christine and Thomas

Poetry is well suited to help us relate an abstract concept like the value of the wooden-bat tradition. Another way is to visit a place where you can smell, see, hear, and feel the tradition. Take the winding back roads of Cape Cod to the quiet community of

Centerville, Massachusetts. Find 40 Pleasant Pines Avenue but do not expect to see a business sign. Pull down the driveway around back into the trees. You have arrived at wooden bat tradition central, the Barnstable Bat Company.

Christine Bednark's one-woman office, showroom, and laser engraving machine are housed on your left. Thomas Bednark's one-man wooden bat making operation is in front of you in the barn turned workshop. Thomas was exposed to woodworking as an apprentice guitar maker in his teens. He joined the building trades on Cape Cod but was never really happy on the job. As a baseball fan, he had closely followed the historic Cape Cod league that bills itself as "Where the Stars of Tomorrow Shine Tonight." With a vision in mind, Thomas and Christine combined a wood craftsman's background with a love of baseball to establish the Barnstable Bat Company. They have found their place in baseball and life.

Enter the small office/showroom and you are surrounded by finished bats of all lengths, styles, and colors. There are even long thin bats that are specifically made for stickball and wiffleball. To me, they looked like corkball bats but that is probably because I am from St. Louis, the reputed birthplace of that game. The Bednarks make baseball bats of ash, maple, and what they refer to as "imported wood." For now, the type of the imported wood and its country of origin are trade secrets, but I was impressed by how light it was compared to other bats of its size. Thomas says the secret wood makes a durable bat with the flexibility of ash. I am definitely going to give one a try.

Standing in the showroom surrounded by bats, hearing wood against wood as I remove samples from and replace them to their racks, is a sensory experience in itself. When you step into the workshop, it is sensory overload. You are surrounded by the roots of the game. From this workshop, wooden bats have gone to the Cape Cod league, Little League, the major (having been the 13th bat maker to be officially approved by major league baseball) and minor leagues, to vintage baseball, and elsewhere.

Each bat starts as a "billet" of round or square wood about four inches across and about 40 inches long, weighing between six and seven pounds. The skill that Thomas then brings to picking the individual billet for the specific bat design he is making, setting up the lathe, and finishing the wood turns the unformed billet into a thing of beauty with a sweet spot about one-sixth of the length of the bat from its business end.

Stand in the workshop and smell the shavings come off the lathe, hear the sound of wood on wood, see the billets turned into base hits. The Barnstable Bat Company gets you as close to the abstract concept of wooden-bat tradition as you can get, short of playing the game. Go there and shake Christine's and Thomas's hands and thank them for being part of the game. They are isolated on the back roads of Cape Cod yet inextricably linked to all of us who value what they are doing. Whether or not a batter is gripping a Barnstable Bat creation, if he is using wood, he comes to the plate with tradition in his hands.

Bat Cost and Performance

Abstract concepts aside, there are objective reasons for preferring wooden bats. But before discussing the relative safety risks of wooden and metal bats, it is only fair to consider the arguments in favor of aluminum bats. I have heard two of them: lower cost and more offense. There is little doubt that aluminum bats generate higher-scoring games than do wooden bats. Anyone who plays in both environments can tell you that qualitatively. There is quantitative support as well.

The NCAA introduced aluminum bats to college baseball in 1974. In the four years before the switch, the annual cumulative batting average across all Division I players ranged from .262 to .267. Since then the average has not fallen below .270 and, since 1980 has been higher than .288 each year and over .300 for six of those years. These are not the averages of only the top offensive teams in college baseball—they are the averages across all players on all Division I teams.

Run production for the four years prior to 1974 ranged from 4.96 to 5.07 per team per game. Since 1980, the average has not been below 6.07 with two years at 7.00 or higher. One could argue that batting average and run production increases could be the result of poorer pitching or defense. But both strikeouts and defensive fielding percentage have also improved over this timeframe. It is too coincidental that the increase in offensive output correlates with the introduction of the aluminum bat in 1974.

Given that pitching and defense have not deteriorated, the only logical reason for the higher offensive statistics is that the aluminum bat creates a higher batted-ball speed (BBS) and, therefore, higher offensive statistics, more consistently than does the wooden bat.

In 1999, J. J. Crisco, PhD, (Associate Professor of Orthopaedics and Engineering, Brown Medical School) and R. M. Greenwald, PhD, (Executive Director of the National Institute of Sports Science and Safety) reported on their study comparing the performance of metal and wooden bats. Nineteen batters, of whom nine were professional and ten college and high school, used two wooden and five aluminum bats in a commercial batting cage at two different pitching speeds. Bat speed, location of the ball relative to the "sweet spot," and batted-ball speed were measured and recorded. The baseballs were standardized (Wilson A1001). The two wooden bats had a weight (in ounces) minus length (in inches) of -3 (L=34, W=31). The metal bats varied from -3 to -5.

To test the difference among the bats, the researchers used the top ten percent of hits as measured by batted ball speed. The metal bats that were -4 and -5, exhibited significantly higher BBS than the wooden bats, ranging from 4% to 8% faster. The average of the top 10% of hits from the fastest metal bat was over 106 miles per hour, while BBS from the top 10% of wooden bat hits was just under 99 miles per hour.

This means, for example, that a third baseman has 8%, or .05 seconds less to react to a ground ball or line drive. Or for a ball hit up the middle, the pitcher has only .38 seconds to react if the bat is metal. These fractions of a second make the difference between a fielded ball and a base hit. Similarly, the BBS determines whether a ball will get through the outfielders in the gap or be cut off.

For the -3 metal bat, the difference in BBS relative to the wooden bats was reduced to just over 2%. While this is a smaller difference, the performance and, therefore, the offensive advantage of the metal bat still holds. There is little qualitative or quantitative doubt that metal bats generate more offense. The question is whether that is better for baseball or, more specifically, better for senior baseball.

Given the age and capability differences among senior players, where it is not uncommon for 30-year-olds to be playing with 50-year-olds, which bat is right? In my Cincinnati Roy Hobbs league, there are two divisions, an upper one made up of the stronger teams and a lower one. We play each team within our division three times per year and use metal bats. We play each team in the other division once per year and wooden bats are required. The reason for using wood is to level the inter-division games by reducing the offense-multiplying effect of metal. If it is appropriate to do this across divisions, why is it not appropriate, given what I would hope would be a preference for balanced competitive play, to do it for all of our league games? And if that is so, why not use wooden bats in all leagues and tournaments?

Given that wooden bats seem appropriate for senior baseball for reasons of competitive balance, what about the argument that metal is better from a cost perspective? While I am sure you can find a bat costing outside the following range, the cost of a good -3 aluminum bat can run from $180 to $260. The $260 bat is the Rawlings 2006 -3 Liquidmetal Plasma Bat. I am not sure what that is exactly, but they claim their "shell technology has over 5X more Liquidmetal and 35% more barrel flex provides a 30% larger sweet spot versus previous models...translates to 20 feet added distance...frame 8.5% stronger and 13% thinner." Somehow, that does not sound like a traditional baseball statement to me, but, for now, we are talking about cost, not tradition.

By contrast, a good wooden bat (e.g. Louisville Slugger Pro Stock C271) can be purchased for under $40 with a maple version just under $70. While less expensive than metal, wooden bats have one problem: they break.

To create a hypothetical situation, we will have one player, Ken Schug, one of our dugout denizens, purchase a metal bat for $200. He gets a lot of use from the bat and it holds up well. But after using it for four years, he learns of a new technology bat (maybe it is the new Liquidmetal Plasma Bat) and needs to keep up with the offensive output of his teammates and opponents. He goes to his local store or an internet merchant and buys his new bat. So, in Ken's case, he spent $200 and got four years from his metal bat.

Player two, Jack Herbert, also one of our dugout guys, chooses to use wood and wants a C271 model Louisville Slugger Pro Stock bat for $40. But Jack knows that wooden bats break, so he buys five bats for a total of $200. What Jack cannot estimate is how many bats he will break per year. Before making his bat order, he asks me about my personal experience, knowing that I play up to 80 games per year and, over the last five years, about 80% of those have been wooden-bat games. I search my memory and tell him (and this is fact, not hypothetical) I have broken six bats in five years. Actually, I have broken five, while a teammate of mine borrowed a bat without asking and broke it for me. But to be fair to our comparison, the fact is that I had six fewer wooden bats than when I started.

To help us make the comparison even more favorable for metal, I will assume that the six bats I broke happened within four years versus five. So, if Jack has the same experience I had, he will use up his five bats and need to buy another in the four year comparison period. Jack will have spent $240 on bats compared to $200 that Ken spent on his metal bat. So, even with the conservative bat breakage assumption, Jack will have only spent $40 more over four years to use wood versus aluminum. I contend that the benefits (tradition and safety) of using wood are well worth the small incremental cost difference.

Moving from the hypothetical to reality, there is an even stronger argument for all senior baseball converting to wooden bats. The reality for many senior players today is that they need to own both metal and wooden bats. That is because each is used in various tournaments and leagues. So the cost to the senior player, in reality, is $200 for a metal bat and the cost of a wooden bat supply, perhaps two or three. A conversion to all wood precludes the need for a metal bat and its cost. In fact, a player does not have to wait for the league or tournament he plays in to convert to wood. He can make that choice himself. Tournaments and leagues which allow aluminum do not preclude the use of wooden bats.

One could argue, therefore, that neither of the primary reasons typically given for using metal over wood, higher offensive production and lower cost, are compelling for senior play. One could even argue from the analysis that for competitive balance and cost, wood is preferable to aluminum. When we throw in the safety factor, the decision becomes a no-brainer.

BBS-Slower is Safer

Safety may be the most critical factor when assessing the bat we should use as well as deciding other factors concerning the senior baseball experience. Fortunately, baseball is a relatively safe sport. Based on a study by the National Center for Catastrophic Sport Injury Research, the rate of a catastrophic injury in baseball is about half as much as the chance of being hit by lightning. This is not to say that injuries are rare. The U.S. Consumer Product Safety Commission estimates that as many as 8% of adults playing baseball or softball are injured each year. These injuries are primarily abrasions, sprains, strains, and fractures with many of them being ankle or knee related. Thankfully, serious injuries from being hit by a batted ball are rare. They are so rare, in fact, that the statistics cannot discern the difference between the effects of wooden and metal bat usage.

The issue, however, is the risk. Given the speed of a batted ball, if a ball hits a fielder or runner, the results can be very serious if not just painful. It is the potential severity of a batted-ball injury that makes the safety risk comparison for bat types relevant for senior players. While statistics are not available to make the case, we can intuitively conclude that higher batted-ball speed and slower reflexes add up to greater risk. In the previous section, we established that aluminum bats generate higher BBS than wooden bats. How does this fact interact with the changes in reflexes of older players?

It is both intuitive and demonstrated in research that our reaction time gets slower as we age. While this has apparently not been studied specifically related to baseball, there are relevant studies related to other activities (e.g. driving). Reaction time is traditionally broken down into three components: neurological detection, processing, and movement. The consensus is that each of these components is affected by aging, resulting in overall loss of reaction time. Whether the batted-ball risk is associated with defensive players (i.e. pitchers and infielders) or, as Tom Giffen believes, with base runners, slower reaction time is a key element of risk to senior players.

In summary, while there is some argument for metal bats (i.e. more offense and lower cost) wood is clearly better for the senior game. Wood is the traditional choice, has a lower safety risk, helps establish competitive balance across a range of ages and capabilities, and has only a small, if any, cost disadvantage (with an argument that wood is actually cheaper overall). Listen; can you hear the crack of the bat?

Yes, I Can

The clear trend in senior baseball is toward the full use of wooden bats. As examples, Reds Baseball Heaven and other fantasy camps have always used wood and, given they are simulated major league experiences, always will. The Bob Wagner Wooden Bat Classic name speaks for itself. Legends of Baseball's events have always been wooden bat only. When Scott Green recently initiated the Play at the Plate tournaments, he started them as wooden bat only events. As Scott said when I asked him why he made the wooden bat choice, "Why hockey pucks instead of golf balls? Baseball was meant to be played with wooden bats."

The Dayton, Ohio, Roy Hobbs league made the conversion many years ago and is now a wooden bat only league. In 2005, the Cincinnati Roy Hobbs league began playing about 25% of its games with wooden bats and is, according to league president Joe Caligaris, planning to complete the transition. The Roy Hobbs World Series began making the transition by introducing a few wooden bat only games, then wooden bat divisions available in each age group. By 2005, the 48-and-over, 55-and-over, 60-and-over, and 65-and-over age groups were fully wooden bat only. The 38-and-over age group had 57 teams registered, 30 of which had chosen to play in the wooden bat only division. The 28-and-over age group had yet to get enough teams to start a wooden bat division, but Tom Giffen, Roy Hobbs leader, was determined to try again in 2006.

The Baseball International Spring Training Tournament and international trips are wooden bat optional. The Spring Training Tournament precedes the Bob Wagner Wooden Bat Classic each year and some players use the Baseball International event as a warm up by using wood. There is a practical reason to use aluminum on the international trips. Each player is responsible for bringing his own bat(s). Given the logistical difficulty of taking all of the baseball equipment needed on the trip, it is much simpler to carry one aluminum bat than two or three wooden bats, needed in case one or two are broken on the trip.

I suspect that in the next few years it will be difficult to find metal bat leagues or tournaments. So, can I hear the crack of the bat? In deference to Sammy Davis, Jr., "Yes, I can."

37 Years Later

There are other traditions woven into the fabric of senior baseball, thereby helping to enrich the experience. The playing ritual starts when we pack our equipment bag in preparation for a game or for traveling to a tournament. Depending on the game's location and the event, we dress for the game at home, in a motel room, or in a locker room. We make our way from the car or locker room to the field and go through our pre-game routine. For seven or nine (or for some reason at the Bob Wagner Wooden Bat Classic, eight) innings, we are really participating in two games—one on the field and one in the dugout. There are post-game activities, which begin with handshakes and end in parking lots, locker rooms, and bars. When we tell someone we are playing a ball game, what we really mean is we are spending an afternoon, evening, whole day, or a full week participating in the rituals that are senior baseball.

What equipment do you have in your baseball bag when you go to a game? Mine has two gloves, a fielder's mitt and a catcher's mitt. There are five to eight baseballs, depending on how many I have lost track of or picked up at the previous game. I carry two bats, assuming I might break one. If I play in an aluminum bat event, I take that bat and put a wooden bat in the bag as I am likely to use it instead of aluminum and just because it belongs there.

Those few items seem like they should be enough to play the game, but they are only the beginning. I always wear a protective cup when I play, and its home is the baseball bag. I had some elbow problems years ago, so my two elbow support sleeves are always with me even though I have not used them since the problem was resolved. Does the "Peanuts" character Linus come to mind? I wear a glove under my fielder's mitt, so I need to have one in my bag. Because I need one, I have seven—go figure. Actually, not all of these gloves reside in the bag. Two or more are attached to the carrying handles. Because I perspire so much, they need to dry out between games, and they do that best outside the bag. I never know what to call these gloves. They are not batting gloves because that is not what I use them for. If I refer to them as fielding gloves, they get confused with the mitt.

You would think with bats, balls, mitts, cup, elbow sleeves, and the gloves I wear under my glove, I would have what I need to play. But there is still more. I carry one or two sweat towels, a pullover warmup jacket, a bottle of water or more, depending on whether water is readily available at the game, and, depending on game time, some snacks. While I do not normally eat during a game, it is comforting to know that I could if I wanted to. I generally go for granola bars. If we are playing a doubleheader and do not have time to go to lunch somewhere, I also carry some fruit—maybe raisins and an apple or banana.

The last thing in my bag is another bag that houses incidentals. These include a basic first-aid kit with band-aids of all sizes, antibiotic cream, Bio-Freeze, antiseptic wipes, gauze, adhesive tape, and scissors. The bag also has a container of Flex-All, a glove repair kit, a couple of Ace bandages (the kind big enough to hold on an ice pack), extra adhesive tape, a glass-cleaning rag (I wear glasses when I play), sunscreen with SPF 45, sunscreen lip balm (SPF 15), a foam pad, and a wrist sweat band.

The fully loaded equipment bag, including my spikes, which are tied to the carrying handles, must weigh about 25 pounds. Thankfully, I am able to borrow catcher's equipment when I need it, and helmets are provided by teams or tournaments. But many players carry this equipment as well. The upside is that the bag is packed to ensure that anything I might need during a game is available. The downside is that the bag has to be carried from the parking lot or locker room to the field. These treks can be anywhere from 20 yards to a quarter mile. Some bags have built-in wheels and a pulling handle. Some have shoulder straps, which spread the load evenly. Most merely have carrying handles or single shoulder straps. For tournaments where I know the walk is far, I sometimes take a wheeled luggage-carrying cart I can attach my bag to. And expect a baseball equipment bag to feel heavier after a game than before it and even heavier as a tournament week wears on.

Another tradition involves the constant chatter that is an integral part of baseball. We may not always be the best conversationalists from our wives' point of view. I heard a comedian once say that on average a woman uses 5,000 words per day while a man only uses 3,000. That is why at the end of the day, she wants to converse, but he is out of words. When it comes to baseball, however, our word limitations are magically lifted. We talk continuously from arrival at the park until the last goodbyes are said.

As players approach the field with bags in tow, the traditional baseball chatter begins. In November 2000, I was walking from the parking lot at the Fort Myers Lee County Sports Complex to field one for a game in the 48-and-over Roy Hobbs World Series. I was walking next to a player I did not know but noticed that he had a tee shirt on which said "St. Louis University." Being from St. Louis, I asked him if he had attended the school. He answered that he had not, but was from St. Louis also, although he was then living in California.

As I mentioned earlier, the next line when two people find out they are both from St. Louis is, "Where did you go to high school?" We shared that he had gone to Chaminade and I to University City. As soon as I mentioned U City, he asked me if I knew Kenny Holtzman and told me he had played against him in high school. After a few more questions and answers, we established the following. He and I had played against each other in the first game of our eight-game state tournament run in 1963. He had pitched for Chaminade; Holtzman had pitched for us; we had won the game and we went on to win the state championship. I could not recall and could not find records of how I hit against him that day in 1963. But I got the chance again in 2000 as it turned out he was pitching against us that day. I batted against the same pitcher 37 years later. Oh, and I went two for three with a walk.

Long Toss

Ritually, each player has his routine to prepare for the game. Some predictably arrive 45 minutes to an hour before the game while some walk up with barely enough time to get their spikes on before the game starts. Some go through a rigorous running and stretching routine while others immediately grab a glove to start throwing or a bat to take a few loosening swings. Some take advantage of batting cages if they are available while some stand around and kibitz. The common theme is that, in general, whatever a player does, he does it for every game. The tradition is the pre-game warmup. The superstition, whether conscious or subconscious, is the individual player's routine.

My routine is to arrive about 45 minutes early, jog, and stretch both lower and upper body. Then I run some sprints although they are probably not recognizable as such by anyone watching. It is then time to throw to warm up, starting close and moving to long toss. And finally, I take the bat I will be using that day out of the bag and take some swings.

I frequently have the opportunity to play in tournaments with Tedd Schaffer who, until recently when he hurt his shoulder, was our number one pitcher and center fielder. Schaffer is a lefthander who could pitch back-to-back games in a doubleheader and be ready to relieve the following day. While I have a reasonably strong arm, I needed to be careful if Schaffer was my pre-game throwing partner. His arm was so live that he played long toss at distances where I needed either to strain to keep up with him, play with a relay man, or throw it to him on a bounce or two. To protect my arm, I had learned not to pick option one. It is not unlike playing catch over that huge oak tree with Steve Novack in high school. Happily, Schaffer's shoulder is on the mend and his pre-game long toss is getting back to normal.

Did you hear the one about...?

Baseball is a fascinating game on a number of levels. One of its peculiarities is that it is an intense game requiring unparalleled concentration and explosive movements. Yet, at the same time, it is a tranquil game with lull periods that lend themselves to relaxed socialization. It is not uncommon during a game, between pitches, for example, for fielders to have time to visit with each other or with base runners or umpires. A catcher and the plate umpire can carry on a game-long conversation, which frequently engages the batter of the moment. But there is no place more social than the dugout. Whether during a team's defensive half inning when the non-playing team members are isolated or during the offensive half when the dugout is full except for coaches, base runners, and the batter, the chatter can be constant.

"I heard your wife was ill; how is she doing?"

"Are you going to this year's Cooperstown tournament? Should we try to put together a team?"

"The Reds still don't have any pitching."

"I'm really hurting; who has some anti-inflammatories?"

"If you're going to be drinking all night again tonight, you're going to do it alone. I'm too old to do that anymore."

"Hey, nice try on that ground ball last inning. If you'd lose a few pounds, you might have been able to bend down and get to it."

"I still can't believe Yoke's not in the dugout with us anymore."

"If that guy bunts down the first base line again, I'm not going for the ball. I'm just going to run up his back. Or maybe I should just pitch him high and tight to let him know who's boss."

"When did you buy those spikes, in high school? Break down and buy a new pair."

"Did you hear the one about...?"

"I really don't feel sorry for the clowns back in Cincinnati who decided not to come down to Florida with us. We're playing ball in

75 degree sunshine and they're shoveling snow."

"When I was playing high school ball..."

"He's followed every fast ball he's thrown for a strike with a breaking ball. Next time up, I'm going to take a strike and sit on the curve."

"OK, so I was sitting on the curve and still couldn't hit it; what's your point?"

I have kept these examples clean and not as aggressive as the chatter sometimes gets. The best teams I have played on are the ones where it is not only tolerated, but expected, that players get on each other in a kidding, yet serious way to keep everyone on their toes. Whether for purely social purposes or for baseball reasons, socialization on the field and in the dugout is a tradition of the game. Why is it that so many senior baseball players become friends over the years of playing with and against each other? There are many reasons, but one of them is the personal connection that is made as we talk the talk of baseball and of life during those times in between the intensity and explosiveness.

Who do we appreciate?

When a senior baseball game is over, another set of rituals kicks in. The first of these is shaking hands with the other team. The post-game handshake is a part of baseball and many other sports at all levels. I believe, however, for senior baseball players it is not merely procedural but, rather, a true show of appreciation for the competition.

I remember in Khoury League when we were as young as seven, we would gather around our coach after a game and cheer for the other team, "Two, four, six, eight, who do we appreciate? The Rockets." The cheer was expected of each team, and I am pretty sure we did it because it was expected versus really feeling the intent of the cheer.

Every game played as a senior is precious and we treat it as such. Certainly there are rivalries in leagues and tournaments. But, without exception, in my experience, those rivalries and all other games are friendly. The post-game handshake is sincere. This is especially true when playing in tournaments against friends that you have played with and against in the past. The handshake is for the game and for the joy of reuniting in a special way; playing a baseball game.

Once greetings are complete, the verbal dissection of the game begins. It starts during the collection of equipment in the dugout, continues as groups form to walk back to the parking lot or locker room, and is sometimes completed in one of those two places. But many times the real review of the game or games played that day begins in earnest later, in the local bar, a tournament-favorite restaurant, or the lodging's hot tub.

After local league games or practices, some portion of the team heads to a local establishment. We buy pitchers, order wings, and begin the diagnosis of the game.

"If we had made that one play in the second inning, the game was ours."

"How many bad hops did you see today; that was the worst shape I've ever seen that field."

"I think that home run I gave up in the fifth is still going."

"We finally started hitting the ball today."

"Should we have hit and run in the seventh with one out?"

"The relay we made from left center in the fourth was exactly like we'd practiced it."

"Hey, did you hear the one about...?"

At tournaments each team tends to have a favorite watering hole where players and fans get together in the evening.

"Who do we play tomorrow, and what do we know about them?"

"Who's pitching for us?"

"We need to be stealing more."

"How are we going to make up for three of our guys being hurt?"

"Hey, did you hear the one about...?"

Senior baseball players are far from single minded. They are a diverse group with far ranging interests. While baseball is at the center of the conversation, I have been in discussions ranging from microbiology laboratory functions to the issues facing over-the-road truckers, from the procedures for fighting a skyscraper fire to the pluses and minuses of selling the family business, from whether we believe in current government policies to what was it really like to be in Viet Nam. But at tournaments, despite the depth or breadth of the subject matter being discussed that evening, the last thing virtually every player says before leaving the bar or restaurant is something like, "Just to confirm, our first game tomorrow is at 10:00 on field 2 at Lee County, right? Hey, let's win two."

The traditions of baseball are comforting. Sharing them with our fellow players and fans is uplifting. Continuing to be a part of the traditions is heartwarming. Passing them on to future players is priceless. Whether hearing the crack of a wooden bat or loading up the equipment bag or warming up before a game or talking to a base runner on second while playing shortstop or chatting in the dugout or rehashing a game at the local watering hole, we are part of the traditions of baseball and, importantly, of the rituals of senior baseball.

ATHLETIC
SUPPORTERS

"Love is the most important thing in the world.
But baseball's pretty good too."

Greg, age 8

"There's three things in my life that I really love:
God, my family, and baseball. The only problem—
once the season starts, I change the order around a bit."

Al Gallagher

Ken: *"Walks to leadoff hitters are always trouble. That was the beginning of their three-run inning."*

Al: *"I'm really struggling to get my curve ball over, assuming that off-speed pitch I'm throwing is really a curve ball."*

JR: *"Well, let's just suck it up and win this inning."*

Ken: *"Jack, you were talking about playing in Palm Beach and in China. Have you come into some inheritance you haven't told us about? Between league fees, the costs of this tournament, and the other two you're talking about, it really adds up. To say nothing of the time that all takes—where are you coming up with all of the vacation time?"*

Jack: *"Sheryl and I talked about it and decided it is worth it to make the investment in time and money. It'll be a stretch, but we're both looking forward to it."*

JR: "We're all pretty lucky. Pat, Kim, Ann, and Sheryl all are really supportive, and I know they enjoy coming to the tournaments."

Al: "Well, I know I'm fortunate for the support Ann gives me. I'd be even more fortunate if you guys could support me and get me some runs."

Standing Room Only-Sort Of

In November 2003, I was playing for the Cincinnati Colts in the wooden bat division of the Roy Hobbs 48-and-over World Series. It was another great day in baseball paradise. We were playing on field five at the Lee County Stadium Complex, the spring training home of the Minnesota Twins and the minor league home of the Class A Fort Myers Miracles. In the fourth inning, I walked over to the bleachers, which were behind the screen between the plate and our dugout and where Ann and the other Colts' faithful were sitting. I was not going to bat for awhile in the inning and had the time to check with Ann to see how she was doing.

She told me that a couple of innings before, a player from the other team had come over to the Colts' supporters and said he was impressed that we had over 20 fans. His team, from the Cleveland area, had none. He asked, with tongue in cheek, "How much would it cost to get half of you Colts' fans to move over to our bleachers and root for us?"

Most of our supporters, which included spouses, children, and friends, had traveled more than 1,000 miles from Cincinnati, some flying and some driving. They had all committed time, energy, and family resources, which, for most, were not trivial commitments. Vacation time was precious. There were many other activities and responsibilities vying for their energies. And family finances could be strained by the costs of the week or two playing and watching baseball in Florida. Yet, to a person, every player and supporting fan was totally committed to their choice. The joy of family mixed with the joy of baseball was an intoxicating combination. Of course, spending a week in Florida away from the emerging winter in Cincinnati also influenced the decision-making process.

One of the many things baseball has going for it is that it is, with the occasional exception, played in warm weather. Senior baseball tournaments can be good reasons to move from cold weather to warm, if only for a week or two. As an example, in 2004-2005, Ann and I were in warm weather locations four of the five cold Cincinnati months. We drove to Fort Myers for the Roy Hobbs World Series in November, to Port Charlotte for Baseball International's Spring Training Tournament and Fort Myers for Bob Wagner's Wooden Bat Classic (back-to-back tournaments) in January, and Play at the Plate's Palm Beach Classic in April. I am also counting the Baseball International Caribbean Baseball Cruise in February. When that trip was cancelled for a lack of players, Ann and I went on the cruise anyway.

In the 2003 Roy Hobbs World Series, each of the Cincinnati Colts felt great as individuals and as a team that many of our families had joined us. Our supporters had created an environment of combination fraternity party and family reunion. In retrospect, however, the team from Cleveland was not without support. Nor were those Colts and the many other players at the tournament who did not have someone with them in Florida. Most had family members back home who had agreed to support their ballplayer spouse, parent, or significant other as he or she took the time and resources to make the trip.

While there are likely some families who are conflicted because players want to go to tournaments against others' wishes, virtually everyone I have talked to indicates that is not the case for them. Support for the senior player is typically strong and unwavering.

$7,500 per Year

So, why would a spouse or significant other be supportive of the baseball experience? Why would a wife give her husband a $4,000 birthday gift for a once-in-a-lifetime experience to go to fantasy camp? Why would another wife support her husband going to five or six tournaments a year? Why would yet another travel the country and the world with her husband to share the baseball experience?

The family commitment during any given senior baseball year can be substantial. One hypothetical player's name is Aaron Jordan (OK, so those are the first names of my two grandsons, but hey, it is my book). Since being reintroduced to senior baseball by attending a fantasy camp three years ago, Jordan has played on a local team that plays two league games per week, one on Sunday and the other on Wednesday. He needs to provide his own equipment and chip in his fair share for the team's uniforms. He also plays in the league's post-season national tournament in Florida, as well as in two other one-week tournaments each year, one in Florida and one in Cooperstown. Last year, Jordan took advantage of the opportunity to go on a Baseball International trip to China. He lives in Cincinnati, is still working (three years from retirement), and is married with two children, one of whom still lives at home.

The costs for a three-year span of Jordan's baseball activities are charted below. They do not include the cost of his wife or children joining him on trips, the cost of gas for local games, miscellaneous expenses on trips, or incidentals like off-season visits to the batting cages or to the local pub after practices and games. For simplicity, the costs are estimated and rounded to the nearest $100.

Jordan flies to the Florida events where he rents a car, but he drives to Cooperstown. He stays in the motel that is recommended by the tournament to get the best rates and, when his family does not join him, he shares a room with a teammate. He tries not to be extravagant for meals, although he tends to join other players for whatever they may be doing for dinner and drinks each night.

Cost Item	League (3 yrs)	Tournaments (9)	Fantasy Camp (1)	China Trip (1)
Equipment/ Uniform	$900			
Fees	$900	$3,300	$4,000	$1,900
Travel		$3,400		$1,000
Lodging		$4,400		
Meals		$2,500	$300	
3-year Total	$1,800	$13,600	$4,300	$2,900
Average/Year	$600	$4,500	$1,400	$1,000

Notes:
- Equipment includes a glove, spikes, a metal bat, three wooden bats, and incidental uniform needs (e.g. socks, jocks, cups, belts).
- The league uniform and the uniform provided at fantasy camp are used for tournaments and in China.

Aaron Jordan and his family committed a total of about $22,600 over the three-year period or about $7,500 per year for him to play senior baseball. Certainly, many play less baseball than this because of economic or time constraints. Perhaps they play only in a league, which still translates to 30 or more games a year. Some may play only in a tournament or two. Some play the same number of games as does Jordan, but do not participate in the more expensive fantasy camp or international baseball events. There are also those who play all of these and more.

In the three-year period from 2003 through 2005, I was fortunate enough to play in my league each year, attend one fantasy camp, play in 15 tournaments, and go on two International Baseball trips. (One was the Caribbean baseball cruise which was cancelled because of a lack of players but on which Ann and I decided to cruise anyway.) While this seems like a lot, there are a number of players that I saw at virtually all of these events and some who were doing other tournaments, fantasy camps, and international trips as well.

Vacationing with the Baseball Family

While of great importance, cost is only one component of the commitment families make to participate in the senior baseball experience. How much time did Aaron Jordan spend on average during each of the last three years? His league schedules games, including playoffs, from May 1 through the end of September—about 20 weeks. Taking into account some weeks with only one game scheduled, rainouts, and personal conflicts, Jordan plays in 30 league and playoff games, half on Sunday (nine-inning games) and half on Wednesday evening (seven-inning games).

The nine-inning games typically last for three hours while the seven-inning games are about two and a half hours long. The pre-game and post-game time at the park adds another hour, and Jordan's round trip drive is 45 minutes. Not counting time to dress before leaving for each game, showering after the game, and any spontaneous team trip to the local bar, a combined Sunday–Wednesday pair of games requires a nine-hour commitment. Given there are 15 Sunday–Wednesday pairs, Jordan and his family commit 135 hours of his time to league baseball—or almost eight and one-half 16 hour days each year (everyone has to sleep sometime) or more than 25 days over the three-year period.

Jordan's family joins him for some or all league games, thus they are participating together. My non-scientific estimate of significant others attending league games typically ranges from zero to 30%. I have seen it as high as 60% to 70% when the conditions were right. We can look at this in two ways. One is that the family is using the baseball game as a time to be together. The other is that more than the player alone is committing significant time to the game. In either case, a significant commitment is being made.

Jordan plays in more than his league games. Over the three-year span, he participated in nine tournaments and a fantasy camp and he joined the China baseball trip. Each of these required a one-week commitment or 11 weeks over the three years. Thus the cumulative time for baseball over the three-year period was 102 days or an average of 34 days per year, almost 10% of all available time.

Recall that Jordan, who is 52, is still working. He is three years from retirement and has amassed four weeks of vacation per year. His baseball commitment has now tied up 11 of those 12 weeks over the three years. As a result, in Jordan's case, the family has chosen to use baseball trips as family vacations. Jordan's wife joined him in China, in Cooperstown two of the three years, and in Florida for four of the six tournaments there. Their child who is still at home also joined one of the Cooperstown and three of the Florida trips.

On the minus side, family participation has added to the cost of baseball trips. On the plus side, the Jordan family is spending on baseball what they may have already intended to spend on other vacations. The question they need to answer is whether the whole family accepts committing virtually all of their vacation time to baseball tournaments.

Family vacations spent at baseball events have both advantages and disadvantages. On the downside, the flexibility for the family for the week is constrained by the tournament schedule. Most tournaments play one or two games each day, without a day off. This schedule forces the family to make choices about how many games, if any, the non-players spend at the fields. My experience is that if a family comes to the event location, they come to most games. The exception is the Baseball International trips where spouses tend to spend more time sightseeing versus attending games.

When a family chooses to come to the games, non-baseball vacation time is limited to evenings, half-days before or after games if only one is being played, and days toward the end of the tournament if the player's team has been eliminated. Time at the beach, at museums, seeing the local culture, or other normal vacation pursuits are, therefore, constrained.

For families that want to use their vacations to visit different places, there is another disadvantage. It is common that once a player finds a tournament that he likes, his tendency is to return each year. As an example, between the Roy Hobbs World Series in November and the Bob Wagner Wooden Bat Tournament in January, Ann and I have spent several weeks each year in Fort Myers, Florida. For us, it is not an issue because we are retired and take advantage of the opportunity to travel to many other places during the year. But if we were using precious vacation time, it would limit the diversity of our travel.

There are positives as well. Baseball is a warm-weather sport and tournaments are typically played in beautiful locations. Whether attending tournaments in Florida or Arizona or another warm weather spot, the family escapes from the cold weather at home. In many locations, there are beaches and swimming pools galore. Another advantage is that the tournament areas are typically in tourist locations and many are a short distance from fresh seafood—the dining experience at senior baseball tournaments can be a great part of the vacation.

There is a more subtle advantage, at least for Ann and me. When we were young, most of our vacations, whether we were living in Pennsylvania just after we were married or in Cincinnati with young children, were to St. Louis to see family. We still frequently travel to St. Louis or the northeast to visit family.

But we have found that we are now part of a new family. We have established many new and deep friendships within the senior-baseball community. We see more of some of these non-Cincinnati friends than we see some members of our real family. Remember Aaron Jordan spent almost four weeks each year with his baseball family. During those weeks, he (and sometimes his wife) ate, drank, played, and schmoozed with friends they had gotten to know so well. Vacations can be about the locations we visit but also, and perhaps mostly, about the people we are with.

Value Equation

Having spent my career working for Procter & Gamble, I learned to understand the value equation—benefits received by a consumer divided by the price the consumer pays. The value equation is not only useful in a purchase decision between two competitive consumer-goods brands. Families also use the value equation to help decide how to spend their finite resources. Should they buy a new family car or new furniture? Should they replace their worn-out carpeting or the refrigerator that is about to die? Should they upgrade their insurance, take a vacation, or increase the monthly college-fund deposit?

The choices are endless, but the final decisions come down to the value equation. Of all the options, each one competes with all of the others based on relative benefits and costs. Given these many choices, and given, for most families, finite resources, the decision to invest in senior baseball is far from simple. The costs in money and time can be significant. But up to 125,000 families are making the choice. We can draw one of two conclusions: (1) senior baseball is played only by those who have so much discretionary income that the expenditures are relatively meaningless, or (2) the benefits to the family are worth the cost.

While some players can easily afford the cost of senior baseball, many more struggle to do so. While the population of senior players may have, on average, a higher economic profile than the general population, most players and families must make tough decisions, especially if they stretch the experience beyond league play to include tournaments, fantasy camps, or international trips.

I know players who take on second jobs to pay for specific tournaments. I also know of a player, who is a day laborer, who quit his job to play in a tournament, then looked for work again when the tournament was over. (He was single at the time.) For most families, choosing to play senior baseball means choosing not to do or buy something else. I can only conclude, therefore, that the benefits of participating in the senior baseball experience justify the costs. If that is so, what are those benefits as perceived by the players and by their families?

A Hole in the Lineup

Chris Yocum embodies the supportive senior baseball fan. She has steadfastly continued that support despite having had to deal with the unimaginable.

On August 18, 2005, there was a tragic motorcycle accident on East Miami River Road in Miami Township just outside of Cincinnati, Ohio.

Senior baseball lost one of its most beloved players, organizers, and advocates. I lost a dear friend. And Chris Yocum lost her husband. Roy Yocum was on his way to a ballgame when he crossed the center line on his bike and hit the side of an oncoming car.

The loss of anyone we love is cause for grief. When that person is only 53 and more full of life than anyone you know, the grief is magnified. When that person is as widely loved as Yoke was, the grief is unbearable.

Yoke wore many hats in his life. He was a proud retired firefighter, having risen to the position of District Chief. Roy and Chris were competitive and exhibition dancers. Yoke loved music and it showed, as he was a popular local party disc jockey. He was a very good ballplayer, loved the game, and was always working to organize teams for leagues and tournaments.

Roy was a genuine extrovert—one might even say an exhibitionist. Perhaps the best way to reflect Yoke's makeup is through a story that Ann tells. We were in Fort Myers for a tournament. One evening after a game, a number of teammates and spouses were settled in at The Cottage, a local hangout overlooking the Gulf of Mexico on Fort Myers Beach, having an adult beverage or two, listening to the surf, and smelling the mixture of the restaurant grill and the beach. Ann was sitting next to Ray "Radar" Nease and across the table from Chris and Yoke.

Yoke was being Yoke; singing and dancing in his seat as the conversation jokingly turned to exotic male dancers. Ann told Radar that, years earlier, she had been to a friend's 40th birthday party for her only experience seeing a male stripper. She recalled the tear-away clothes, that the guy was pretty sweaty, his name was Max, and that he ended up wearing nothing but an elephant head. We all got the picture. To Ann's amazement, Radar quietly pointed across the table at Yoke and told her, at that very moment, she was sitting across from Max, our baseball friend, the male stripper.

Some things about Roy were not as evident. We only found out after his death that it was not uncommon for him to stop by a local school where he grew up and spend time reading to the children. And he had quietly supported firefighters and their families when the need arose.

When Yoke died, almost immediately, a local park where he grew up was named for him as was the Play at the Plate spring baseball tournament. It would not have been a surprise if a firehouse, dance floor, schoolroom, baseball field, party room, or bar were also named for Roy Yocum. All would have been appropriate and well deserved.

Within hours of the accident, the word went out nationwide. Firefighters and ballplayers traveled from all over the country to join locals at the funeral, which was the most impressive one any of us had ever experienced. Roy was recognized with full military honors including a 21-gun salute to commemorate his military service. There were hundreds of tearful firefighters standing in attention in their formal uniforms. The firefighter honor guard, with bagpipes playing according to the 150-year Scottish Rites tradition, led the procession to the grave site. The service ended when the local aircare helicopter honored Yoke with a fly-over.

Some estimates were that more than 2,000 came to pay their respects. Firehouses from all over the community sent available firefighters. Yoke's motorcycle friends showed up on their bikes in full leather. His baseball friends, many who came in their team uniforms, showed up in force. Some players and firefighters also came from out of town, flying in from as far away as New York and Florida and driving from Michigan and the nearby cities of Columbus and Dayton, Ohio.

It was heartwarming to see how many wives of Yoke's fellow ballplayers came with their husbands, reflective of the family aspect of the senior baseball community. Most of the wives had traveled with Roy and Chris to tournaments and sat for long hours watching local games. They came to honor Yoke and to help support Chris.

When the funeral was over, there was a long caravan to The Meadows, where Yoke had DJ'd so many parties, including great New Year's Eve blowouts. Along the route, which was through areas of the community in which Roy had lived and played, people had put up signs honoring him. When we arrived at The Meadows, we found that Jason, Chris and Roy's son, had set up Yoke's sound equipment to DJ a celebration party for his father and given by The Meadows. It was a special day for a very special man.

Chris, while clearly and understandably in deep mourning, was strong throughout the ordeal. Both the firefighter and baseball communities quickly acted to support her as she had supported them for so many years. When the two days of viewing, services, and partying were over, we were ready to leave The Meadows. Chris came over to the baseball teammates and wives. She went around and hugged each one of us and said, "I'll still be coming to your games and tournaments. You all are family." We cried again for Yoke and said we would not have it any other way.

Within days of the funeral, Jason decided that he wanted to play with us in our next tournament, which was scheduled for about six weeks later in New Orleans. Scott Green initiated the tournament the previous year and already renamed it the "Roy Yocum Memorial Cajun Classic." Green was one of those who had traveled to the funeral, having flown from his home in Hampton Bays, New York, to pay his personal respects to his baseball friend. Jason had not played baseball since his teens but felt he needed to replace his dad in the baseball family and we were proud to have him. Chris also, as promised, came to several league games and to that first tournament as did most of the wives. We all needed to be close together.

On August 29, 2005, hurricane Katrina changed all of our plans when she hit the gulf coast and put New Orleans under water. Green acted quickly and moved the tournament to Palm Beach, Florida, where he runs an annual tournament each April. Overcoming the late change in plans, the team, including Jason, and the supporting wives, including Chris, made the trip to Palm Beach to be together with the people we care about and play the game we all love. Green also did a great job of organizing a baseball memorabilia silent auction in Yoke's name, proceeds going to Chris' favorite charities.

Chris and Jason Yocum at the October 2005,
Play at the Plate Palm Beach Classic, played in Roy Yocum's memory

Prior to the tournament, on the Sunday morning after Yoke's services, we played our first Cincinnati C-Hawks game without Roy. Our catcher, Glenn "Roomie" Fiebig, brought a can of red spray paint and wrote "#14 RY" at deep shortstop. Jeff "Butch" Butcher knelt in prayer before he led off for us in the first inning. And virtually all of the C-Hawk wives and children were at the game, some who had not been to any other games that year. Roomie's wife, Alma, who is also our official team photographer and scorekeeper, brought an elegant red or white carnation for each of the wives to remember Roy. Geno Rueckert had arranged for many of us to be wearing game jerseys with "Yoke" and number 14 on the back. Players from the other team gave us meaningful hugs both before and after the game. The baseball family was together and supporting each other the way we always have.

> There's a hole in the lineup
> That can never be filled.
> There's a hole in our hearts
> Since the night Yoke was killed.
>
> He loved baseball and life
> And played both of them hard.
> He loved us, his teammates
> His friendship we'll guard.
>
> There's an empty seat in the fire chief's car
> And Yoke's white bean chili's gone cold.
> Firefighters nationwide grieve
> As he is remembered and stories are told.
>
> There's a gap on the dance floor
> Now that he's gone.
> Yoke danced to his own music.
> His life was a song.
>
> There's a wound in the family
> That very slowly will heal.
> Yet Chris's strength upholds us
> As for Jason and her we so deeply feel.

There's an ache in our hearts
For the loss of a friend.
Yoke made each of us feel special
He was loyal to the end.

There's a hole in the lineup
That can never be filled.
There's a hole in our hearts
Since the night Yoke was killed.

Roy Yocum

"You've got to keep movin' to keep movin'"

While growing up, Chris frequently visited her grandmother, who had been born in Italy, lived for a while in Brooklyn, and eventually followed family to Columbus, Ohio. Chris recalls that every time she visited, her grandmother would have the Reds game on TV. Chris did not learn the game from her grandmother but established a feeling about it that vividly came back to her years later.

She met Roy in college at auditions for a play at the University of

Cincinnati. He was trying out for a part while she was involved in the play's set design. They began dating, and it was not long before Yoke invited Chris to come to his Sunday morning baseball games. The feelings for baseball she had developed at her grandmother's home came back to her, and she quickly learned the game, although she does admit to some early lack of knowledge. After the first game, she asked Roy why there were two second basemen. It took him awhile to figure out that she was asking that if there were obviously only one first baseman and only one third baseman, why not have one second baseman, instead of a second baseman and, what he taught her, was the shortstop.

Baseball became a centerpiece of their relationship. But their mutual interests were many. Roy was teaching ballroom dancing for the Cincinnati Recreation Commission, and Chris was taking the class. It was the disco era and dance competitions were cropping up everywhere to emulate the movie, *Saturday Night Fever*. The couple decided to give it a try and became hooked. Competitive dance morphed into dance exhibitions and they joined a number of groups. Chris believes that one similarity between the baseball and dance communities is that many participants continue to pursue the activity as they age. As she puts it, relative to the older dancers, "You've got to keep movin' to keep movin'."

Maybe she summed it up for senior baseball as well: "You've got to keep playin' to keep playin'."

Among their many activities, baseball came first. This was not only Roy's decision. Chris loved the game and drew benefits from it that made the financial and time commitments well worthwhile. Some of these benefits accrued directly to her and some indirectly through Roy. She knew that playing ball made Roy happy and kept him busy. He loved the game, the competition, the people, and the roles he filled as player, organizer, motivator, friend, and court jester. His perpetual excitement about playing ball rubbed off on Chris and their marriage. Baseball was one of the building blocks to their mutual happiness.

But enjoying baseball through Roy paled to the benefits she felt directly. She supported Roy's deep involvement in the game in large part because she loved it as well. Chris is a student of the game and enjoys its strategic aspects. While she clearly loves the action of a baseball game, she enjoys even more the time between pitches as she considers what each player should be thinking in preparation for the next pitch. The leisurely aspect of baseball with its spurts of action is attractive to her. In fact, that is why she liked it much better when Roy was playing baseball versus softball—it is a much more strategic game.

The length of a baseball game is also something Chris relishes as it gives her the time to build relationships with the other fans and players. She relates that when there are no other spouses at a game, she works her way into the dugout to visit with the players and get closer to the game. If a couple of other spouses show up, but she does not know them well, she visits with them and keeps score to stay in the game. When a large group of spouses are at the game or when some are close friends, she admits that every few innings she needs to remind herself there is a game going on.

Chris had joined Roy on the Italy Baseball International trip, and we were playing in Nettuno. Almost every player had a spouse on the trip and for one game they all came to watch instead of going sightseeing. It was after this game that first baseman Ronnie Weiss and his wife, Patricia, were to renew their wedding vows on the field. During the game, we would look up into the stands behind home plate where the "crowd" was assembled. We noticed that some time in the early innings, they had found a local store and returned with gallons of local wine and plastic glasses. They really did not care if there was a baseball game going on—they had started the vow-renewal celebration early.

Chris' involvement in the game did not stop when it was over. She and Roy debriefed every game on their way home. Chris was not only able to comment on the overall flow of the game, but prided herself for her specific contribution to Roy's game. As Chris puts it, "He needed a coach. I needed to be there." If she wanted to let him know about a coaching point during a game instead of critiquing it afterwards, she had "the look" which Roy could read. Without speaking, she communicated to him what he needed to know about his game.

Chris has stayed involved with her baseball family, not as an obligation, but, as she says, "It's for me." She says that throughout Roy's baseball career and now after it, she feels like the senior baseball community is her family and enjoys the support that she both gives to and gets from it.

Angie Butcher, Chris Yocum, Alma Fiebig, Karen Caligaris, and Ann Spector at the 2005
Play at the Plate "Roy Yocum Memorial Fall Classic" in Palm Beach, Florida

Chris concluded that the benefits were well worth the commitment of costs and time. There are tens of thousands of stories of senior baseball supporters. While Chris is only one of these stories, in many ways she represents them all, whether they show their support by attending games or not. Thank you, Chris and Alma and Karen and Angie and Ann and every family member and friend who helps make senior baseball possible through your support.

"I look forward to it"

One day after Ann and I were engaged, my mother sat us down to have what she said was to be a serious discussion. That sounded to me like we were going to talk about something like family or financial planning. As we settled in, Mom looked Ann in the eye and asked her if she knew what she was getting into. I gasped inside. What was my mom doing?

She went on to explain to Ann that there was something she thought my bride-to-be had not yet considered. "Mom, stop now," I thought, but did not say.

Mom then got to her subject. She told Ann that I did not smoke, drink, run around with other girls, gamble, or have any other vice she could think of. What I did do was play sports—I played them a lot. Mom said that she knew from experience that even after I was married, I was going to continue to play a lot of ball. My dad had done so, and I was even a more active player than he had been. She asked Ann if she were prepared to either join me at games or be all right when I went to play when she could not make it.

To Ann's credit and my delight and relief, she responded as though she had already thought it through, "Absolutely," she said, "I look forward to it." And, she has now acted on that statement for 38 years, probably attending well close to 2,000 games.

Ann grew up in a home that was anything but baseball-centric. But she remembers going to her brother, Jerry's, youth baseball games. And her high school friend, Lisa Middleman, was an usherette at Busch Stadium and niece of the St. Louis Cardinals' team physician. Lisa would occasionally get tickets, and Ann would join her at the ballpark.

Ann does not recall other specifics of the relationship she might have had with baseball when growing up, but she finds herself very comfortable with the game. Upon reflection, she believes the game was all around her. St. Louis was, and still is, a baseball town, and the culture of the game and the team ran deep in the city. Conversations about baseball and the Cardinals were everywhere. Baseball news was on the front page of the *Post Dispatch* and *Globe Democrat*—she did not even need to open the sports page to know how the Cardinals did. Players were visible in the community and visited schools to speak to and meet the children.

And, like so many St. Louisians growing up in our era, Ann was familiar with the rhythm of Harry Carey, Jack Buck, and Joe Garagiola announcing the games on KMOX. Just as Chris Yocum became comfortable with baseball because her grandmother always had the Reds game on TV, so did Ann become comfortable with the game that surrounded her.

She is also comfortable the senior baseball partnership we have today. Ann is an integral part of my teams. While I attended my first Reds Baseball Heaven and first two Roy Hobbs World Series without her, she has joined me for every other tournament trip since then. These have included trips to China, Russia, and Italy, two Cooperstown tournaments, two in northern Ohio, two in Coney Island, and about 20 in Florida. Add to that nearly 200 league games to get a sense for Ann's personal commitment to the senior baseball experience and for the support she gives me.

The Wives' Team

Ann genuinely enjoys baseball for a number of reasons. "I understand it," she says, "the goal is simple." The environment at a game is enticing to her. It is outdoors and normally in good weather. And everyone, players and fans alike, whether at a major league or a senior game, is excited about being there.

These advantages help her overcome the times when a game is moving at a snail's pace or is being played sloppily, or when the seating is not comfortable.

Senior baseball has specific attraction for Ann. She is a consummate people person and revels in the camaraderie of the team, including what she calls "the wives' team...both a separate entity and part of the whole."

She enjoys being "one of the guys" as well, occasionally sitting in the dugout and keeping score. Our Bob Wagner Wooden Bat Classic coach, Dave Lupert, calls her "the Ron Roth of Wooden Bat." Roth is the official scorer of the Cincinnati Reds.

Ann says that she likes watching me play because I am doing something I like so much. And traveling to local games and tournaments gives us time together that is sometimes difficult to find. This was especially true when we were both working, but remains so as we are retired but still busy.

Ann especially enjoys senior baseball tournaments—they are played in nice locations, on nice fields, and in weather typically nicer than at home. And there are many things to do in addition to watching games. We have approached every tournament as an opportunity to find interesting places nearby or on the way to or from the event. The tournament, therefore, is only the basic reason to create a multi-dimensional vacation experience.

All is not always rosy. Field sites for local games are often fan-unfriendly. Seating areas are sometimes dirty, and bugs can be a constant annoyance. Bathroom facilities for women are either nonexistent or generally inadequate. And at times, Ann finds she is the only fan, sitting by herself for a whole game.

Taken on balance, however, Ann is a baseball fan in general and a senior baseball partner. She is among the most supportive and participative wives in the community. We are both part of the baseball team. Ann is a member of the wives' team. And she and I are a team in baseball and life. I am very blessed.

Charley, Katrina, and Wilma

Families are not the only support that senior players need and get to help them continue to play the game. Because of some very special people, we have the luxury of just checking the schedule, donning the right uniform, and showing up. To afford us this ultimate convenience, the behind-the-scene efforts are extraordinary. There are tournament directors, league administrators, groundskeepers, umpires, ex-professional players at fantasy camps, and many more.

The work of a tournament director is a labor of love of the game as well as a business. Making a tournament work is a process that lasts all year as arrangements are made for fields, umpires, recommended lodging, welcome and farewell parties and myriad other details. The work also involves promoting the event, recruiting players and teams, getting everyone registered, and generating schedules. All this needs to be done in a way that caters to the players while making the level of play more competitive and evenly balanced each year.

The list of things to organize is long, and no item on the list is trivial. One might think, for example, that making sure umpires are available would be a simple phone call. For smaller tournaments, local umpires are typically available, but even then, arrangements need to be made, confirmed, and reconfirmed. For the larger tournaments, like the national organizations' World Series events, local umpiring staffing is not adequate. Umpires must be found, recruited to travel to the event site, lodged, and then coordinated. This effort is a project in itself, yet is only one of the many details that are critical to a successful, well-run tournament.

The yearlong work only sets the stage for all of the possible problems that can arise just before and during the event. The organizer and his staff must respond on a moment's notice to make adjustments. Roy Hobb's Tom Giffen says, "The success of a tournament is determined by how the crises that arise are managed before and throughout the event."

Scott Green learned this early in his startup of the Play at the Plate organization. He found when he showed up in Palm Beach for his inaugural tournament that the caterer that was to supply the lunches had decided to renege. Green scrambled and was fortunate to find a nearby bar that would deliver lunches to the tournament each day. He says that he now knows to have backup plans for all of the critical event components.

Other adjustments are necessary because the attendees for these events are senior baseball players coming from all over the country and, sometimes, the world. They have jobs, families, disrupted travel plans, and conflicting priorities. Players and teams can drop out with little time for organizers to modify rosters and schedules. Tom Giffen was confronted with this issue at the 2005 Roy Hobbs World Series in Fort Myers. The 28-and-over age group was to have started games on Sunday, October 23. While early the week before, she was heading northwest toward Cancun, Mexico, Hurricane Wilma was predicted to intensify, shift to the northeast, and hit Florida, including the Fort Myers area, over the weekend. What surprised the forecasters and made tournament management even more difficult was that Wilma slowed down over the Gulf of Mexico before getting to Florida.

Giffen, who owns investment properties in Fort Myers, makes the city his home base at tournament time. His tournament staff had joined him, as they do every year, a week before the tournament to set up the event. Because of Wilma, they spent much of the setup week monitoring weather websites and talking on the phone and e-mailing with team managers from all over the country. As Wilma took her time, schedules were done and redone. Equipment, concession stands, banners, and signs, which are normally in place during that week, were all staged on pallets in the bowels of Lee County Stadium—to both protect them from the storm and ensure the items were ready to be deployed as soon as possible.

Eventually, Wilma hit the area on Monday, October 24. While the Fort Myers area was affected, it did not take a direct hit. Giffen, with help from the local grounds crews, predicted and communicated to teams that the fields would be playable on Wednesday—and they were. The tournament was played in full with teams playing two to three games per day. But several teams and a number of individual players did not arrive, causing schedules to be affected by both lost days and lost teams. Giffen, reflecting on his Wilma experience, exemplifies the attitude of tournament directors when he said, "the whole idea is providing a place to play."

The 2004 and 2005 hurricane seasons were record-setters. The effects were devastating throughout Florida and on the Gulf Coast. While immeasurably less critical than the damage they did to people's lives, the storms also had an effect on baseball plans. During this time, Ann and I traveled to play in three tournaments at which the organizers needed to make "major" hurricane-related adjustments.

Baseball International's Spring Training tournament was to be played in January in Port Charlotte, Florida, at the facilities of the Texas Rangers. On August 12, 2004, Hurricane Charley hit the west coast of Florida, severely damaging the Port Charlotte-Punta Gorda area. The time between the hurricane and the tournament was several months and the baseball complex was unaffected, except for light stanchions at the stadium being damaged.

But the motels that were recommended by tournament organizer, John Gilmore, were sufficiently damaged such that they were still not available at tournament time. In fact, while we were in the area for the event, we drove by the first recommended motel and learned why it was not available—its second floor was in its first floor. Gilmore was able to confirm all of the plans for the tournament, identify a backup motel, and keep the players informed that the tournament was still on.

While the effect of Hurricane Charley caused Gilmore significantly more than the normal level of planning adjustments for his January event, it pales against the stories later that year for the Play at the Plate Cajun Classic and the Roy Hobbs World Series. Hurricane Katrina walloped the Gulf Coast on August 29, 2005. Levees in New Orleans failed, dumping the waters of Lake Pontchartrain and the Mississippi River into the city. Five weeks later, we were scheduled to play at the home field of the minor league team, the New Orleans Zephyrs.

In only a couple of days following Katrina, Scott Green hustled to make arrangements to move the tournament from New Orleans to the Cardinals–Marlins spring training facilities in Jupiter, Florida. Despite the uncertainty that all of us felt and our need to make alternate travel arrangements, Green's speedy action allowed almost every player to change plans and come to the tournament in Florida.

I already mentioned how Tom Giffen had responded to the impact of Hurricane Wilma on the Roy Hobbs World Series. These three hurricanes—Wilma, Charley, and Katrina—were the fifth, third, and first costliest of all time, costing an estimated $14.4 billion, $15.4 billion, and $75 billion, respectively. The devastation of these storms taught us what baseball tournament organizers mean to all of us— they provide us with the opportunity to play the game regardless of what it takes, even in the face of natural disasters. Thank you John, Scott, and Tom. And thank you to all the tournament organizers who, while they do not have to deal with a hurricane for every event, work hard to make baseball conveniently available to us.

The Tournament Must Go On

In late 2005, I hurt my back and spent some months managing the pain and rehabilitation. As a result, I needed to cancel plans to play in the January 2006 Baseball International Spring Training and Bob Wagner Wooden Bat Classic tournaments. I e-mailed John Gilmore, for whose tournament I had already registered, to let him know I would not be coming. I got a surprising e-mail in return. John explained that he had also hurt his back, playing racquetball, and had been in bed for three days.

Over the next month, John had surgery to repair a cracked vertebrae, spent ten days in the hospital because the operation was more complicated than expected, returned home with continual numbness in his leg, was getting around only with the aid of a walker, began to try to get ready for his tournament, experienced blood clots in the bad leg, returned to the hospital for three days, came back home still unable to use his leg, and finally decided he could not go to the tournament he had nurtured from its infancy and was responsible for running.

With help from his friend, former work colleague, fellow Ann Arbor, Michigan resident, and senior baseball compadre Dick Kruger, and from John's wife, Olga, they packed up all of the tournament equipment, give-away shirts, packets of schedules, and miscellaneous other items and shipped them to Sarasota. John then wrote out the script for Dick so he could be on-site tournament director. John coordinated the tournament remotely with Dick's leadership and the support of the seven team managers who had previously agreed to run their teams. The tournament must go on, and it did.

Drizzled Out

One of the joys of playing senior baseball tournaments is that they are predominantly played on pristine fields. Most are at major league spring training complexes and stadiums. Those that are not are still played on fields that yield few bad hops and are in beautiful settings. These fields are designed to drain well and maintain their carpet-like grass and smooth infields. Despite the design, however, the fields would not be in the shape they are in were it not for the local groundskeepers.

When Hurricane Wilma hit Fort Myers, dumping torrential rains and strewing debris everywhere, it was less than 48 hours later that the Roy Hobbs World Series was being played. The local groundskeepers got the Lee County Baseball Complex, Terry Park, City of Palms Park, and 5-Plex all ready to go. These fields did not only need to be made ready to play after the hurricane—they had to be able to withstand three to four games played on them each day that week. And every field needed to be in shape to accommodate the next three weeks of heavy usage by the older age divisions.

The groundskeepers not only know their fields; they also know the local weather. We were scheduled to play at Doubleday Field in Cooperstown in August 2004. We got to the park under an overcast sky and forecast of 50% chance of rain. As we began to put on our spikes, the head groundskeeper, Joe Harris, came over and asked if we would help him put the tarps on the plate area, mound, and infield. We asked him why he was going to cover the field when it had yet to even start drizzling. Harris responded that it was going to rain and soon. He also told us that once the field was covered, the games were cancelled for the rest of the day.

We wanted to play and began to give him some grief, but Harris just calmly said that he was going to cover the field with our help or not. By this time, a very light drizzle had begun. We decided to help and had the field covered in about five minutes. Fifteen minutes later the skies opened up and drenched Cooperstown. Once we had helped him, Harris came over and explained that Doubleday Field gets a lot of use each season with almost 400 games being played. He needed to protect the field as much as possible to make sure it was available and in optimal condition for all of those who want to experience the thrill of playing on the historic field. He was right, of course. He knew his field, knew the local weather patterns, and cared about presenting Doubleday in the best way he could. We ended up agreeing with him and appreciating that we were able to finish the tournament because he protected the field. We also recognized it was the first time any of us had been involved in a game that had been "drizzled out."

On February 2, 2006, the Legends of Baseball web site posted a report that Joe Harris had just had successful quintuple bypass surgery but was doing well in recovery. We hope to see Joe at Doubleday soon.

Wet fields are managed in different ways. I recall a game I played when I was about ten. I do not remember the importance of the game, who we played, or the result. But I vividly remember that the field was too wet to play when we got there and what happened next. A number of fathers left and came back with cans full of gasoline. We were told to step back as they poured the gas on and lit the field. I will never forget that sight or the intense heat we felt as we watched the field drying in flames. We played the game.

Missing a senior baseball tournament game due to rain is a rarity. I have lost only two games despite playing three to five tournaments per year for seven years. There have been more frequent postponements, but groundskeepers and tournament directors combine to ensure most rain-postponed games are rescheduled and played. Sometimes this means playing a tripleheader or two but such is the life at a senior baseball tournament. Field design, highly capable groundskeepers, and sometimes a healthy dose of field drying agents combine to keep rainouts at bay.

Fields of Dreams?

Groundskeepers for the tournaments at major and minor league facilities do a great job each day to keep the fields in prime playing shape. They are on the fields after each game, getting them ready for the next one. Sometimes fields host three or four games a day, yet the keepers maintain virtually bad-hop-free surfaces.

Despite their hard work throughout the tournament, much of the reason for their success is hidden from us. The ability of a field to drain and to keep a consistent playing surface is largely determined by its design. This is especially true of the skinned surfaces, those that makeup the infield "dirt," mound, and plate areas. In an article entitled "The Art of Infields" in *Grounds Maintenance* on-line magazine, Tom Burns, director of grounds for the Texas Rangers, explained the critical elements of designing and maintaining an optimum skin field area. Some additional information was gleaned from an on-line article entitled "The 'dirt' on Infield Skins" in *Landscape Management*, written by Paul Zwaska, former head groundskeeper for the Baltimore Orioles.

Think about the quality of the fields you play on in your local leagues. If they are anything like mine, you will marvel at the contrast. The composition of good infield soil is typically in the range of 60% sand, 15% silt, and 20% clay. (OK, so that does not add up to a 100%, but I did not want to misrepresent what Burns said.) These percentages can then be adjusted to account for local climate conditions. The sand/silt/clay combination should be four to six inches deep and tightly packed.

Managing water runoff is also a field-design objective. A good infield is graded 0.5% from front to back to help most effectively move excess water into the outfield grass. Two other things then become important. One is making sure that the base soil is not packed too tightly so that water can be drained down through the surface. Secondly, it is important to make sure the "lip" at the interface between the infield and outfield is not so high that water cannot transition from the skinned surface to the grass. If you are interested in more detail, the articles describe techniques to properly maintain the surface grade and lip height.

The groundskeepers then use various types of topdressings for moisture management, improved texture, and appearance. The right topdressing also provides a barrier between the player's cleats and the base soil to help prevent moist soil from building up on the cleats. Topdressings are typically applied in the range of a quarter- to a half-inch thick. Materials of choice are various types of clay and crushed aggregate (e.g. stone dust, brick dust), which is used in some parts of the country. The clays are also used as a drying agent on wet fields.

With these design elements in place, the next steps are timely and effective spiking to fluff the soil and provide loose material to fill divots and low spots, dragging for leveling, and watering to maintain the right level of soil compaction. The objective of all of this design and maintenance is to provide a skinned field surface that has the right level of traction, playability, and resiliency during normal playing conditions and to ensure optimum moisture management.

If you have been thinking about your local fields, you may, as I do, know that they are not necessarily designed nor maintained as described above. The range of conditions of local fields I have played on in recent years is huge. Haubner Field in White Oak, Ohio, is a delightful neighborhood facility but has no grass on its infield so it can accommodate base dimensions from youth to adult baseball. The infield is kept at a good level of compactness to keep the speed of a ground ball reasonable. Even so, it is more like playing at artificial-surface speeds.

By contrast, the town of New Carlisle, Ohio, built a community ballpark, fielded a senior team in the Dayton Roy Hobbs league, and has been drawing local fans to watch games. They have been persistently improving the field every year. About five years ago, they installed new grass in the infield. For the first couple years, while the grass looked great, any ground ball, no matter how hard it was hit, would barely make it to the infielder, who was already playing in. As the grass wore in, the problem abated.

Ross Avenue Field in Cincinnati has been used for baseball and softball, including a short-lived professional slow pitch league, for all ages for many years. The infield grass only extends a short way from home plate to accommodate youth leagues and softball games. Therefore, most of the infield for senior baseball is dirt. The surface is one to two inches of soft dirt–dust over hardpan. This causes ground ball hops to be very inconsistent. Sometimes an infielder gets the quick high hop, which is primarily affected by the hardpan. Other times the ball stays down as it is grabbed by the dirt–dust. The mound is made up of the same dirt–dust, so that after only a few pitches, the hole in front of the rubber is so deep it is dangerous. You may be able to tell this is not my favorite field.

On June 24, 1970, the last game was played at Cincinnati's Crosley Field before the Reds moved into their newly constructed Riverfront Stadium. You may recall Crosley's distinctive scoreboard and the inclined outfield terrace. The city of Blue Ash, Ohio, in which I live, built a sports complex in 1988. Amid the ten baseball fields and six soccer fields stands a replica of Crosley Field, including the 58 by 65 foot scoreboard, complete with its signature clock and the scores and lineups as they were for its last major league game. The outfield terrace has been replicated, and 400 original Crosley Field seats have been installed. The infield and outfield are very well maintained, and the playing surface is relatively true. It is a thrill to play at this historic replica. However, we once had a rainout because there was a hard ten-minute rain that not only soaked the field, but created puddles on the infield and base paths. On the major league's spring training fields in Florida I have played on, the game would have continued after about 20 minutes of raking. But we were rained out because the design of the field, composition, incline, and lip, was not sufficient.

Among the better fields we play on are those at the local high schools. If you can look past the strange and typically short outfield dimensions, chosen to allow the field to fit on the school's land area allotted to baseball, the fields are good to play on and relatively consistent. Groundskeepers for high school and local recreational fields—where we play our league games—are not as fortunate in the design of the fields they are responsible for. To get an idea of what it takes to care for such a field, I talked to Phil Reichle. He is a strong 59-year-old senior baseball pitcher, who can spot the ball, throw a variety of pitches, change speeds well, and muscle up on his fastball when he needs to. He has also coached baseball at Cincinnati LaSalle High School and Cincinnati St. Xavier High School.

During his tenure at LaSalle, he took it upon himself to take care of their field. Reichle told me that at most of the high school fields he is familiar with, the official responsibility for tending to the baseball field is assigned to the person in the school's maintenance department who also has responsibility for other outside work. If the maintenance person cares about and understands baseball, that works well. If not, which is normally the case, the field can be hurt even though the maintenance person is paying attention.

Reichle has found that despite discussing proper field maintenance with school groundskeepers, grass is mowed in the wrong pattern and with a dull blade, resulting in the grass becoming frayed and brown at the ends. He has even seen a pitching rubber being cut off the mound.

Reichle has also seen fields dragged improperly making them more susceptible to puddling after a rain. Because of these and other problems, it is common for the high school coach to either closely supervise the field maintenance or do it himself, which was Reichle's choice.

The basic composition of LaSalle's field is sandy loam, which, by definition, is less than 52% sand, 28–50% silt, and 8–28% clay. Reichle added Turface MVP, a ceramic soil conditioner that absorbs moisture to help drainage, working the conditioner into about the top two inches of sandy loam. Note the level of sand is less and the level of silt in the base layer is much higher than in the optimum field composition noted earlier. So, while LaSalle's field is in relatively good shape and despite Reichle's best efforts, the field does not have the optimum rain handling capability.

Another difference versus the ideal field, which is evident at LaSalle and the other high schools at which I have played, is the quality of the pitching mound and batting areas. It is common at high schools and other local fields for there to be a deep hole just in front of the rubber and a depression in the landing area. In the batter's boxes, depressions are typical in the areas for both front and back feet. Reichle tried to solve this problem by purchasing bricks of clay and embedding them in the critical areas. He noted, however, that pitchers and hitters felt compelled to "dig in" and in only a few games, the clay had worn away. He gave up because he could not keep up.

One of the issues for local fields, including high schools, is the availability of adequate maintenance budgets. An example that Reichle shares is that all of the advice he was given was to have the field grass aerated four times per year. His budget only supported having it done twice.

So, while most of the groundskeepers of local fields are as dedicated as those on the major league facilities where we play our tournaments, they are confronted by problems that are difficult to overcome (e.g. infield composition, time, budget). Despite all of these issues, the fields are typically in as good shape as possible, and we have groundskeepers to thank for the opportunity to play.

Fields of Screams?

You may think that the range of field quality runs from the major league facilities at the top, to the college and high school fields in the middle, to recreational park fields at the bottom. But I have also played on fields which make our local park fields look pristine. In 2002 and 2003, Ann and I joined Baseball International trips to China and Russia, respectively. We played on a reasonable field in Beijing. It had been built to help attract the summer Olympics, which the Chinese were successful in doing. In fact, they named it Olympic Field well before they were chosen to host the 2008 games. In the interim, the field was being used for China's "major leagues." After playing on this field with its soft all-dirt infield and less than smooth outfield grass, it was all downhill from there.

For example, we played a game against the Tsinghua University team on their campus. Their baseball field was a no-grass, bad-hop laden, dusty, converted soccer field. The field dimensions were determined by those of the soccer field, which is supposed to be 60 yards wide. But their soccer field was not even that wide, so that the right field baseball fence was no more than 150 feet from home plate. We needed to play a ground-rule double for any ball hit over the fence in right. Perhaps we should have played it as a ground-rule out. In addition, there was no pitching mound. Why ruin a "good" soccer field by building a hill on it?

The fields in Russia were no better. In the entire city of Moscow, there was one baseball field. It also doubled as the local cricket grounds. The field was covered with very old, faded green, indoor–outdoor carpeting. Playing there was like playing on a concrete floor. Groundballs shot through the infield and typically through the outfield as well. The one good thing I remember about the field is its setting of historical significance. It sat under the majestic main building of Moscow State University. The building is the tallest of what is known as Stalin's Seven Sisters, which the communist leader ordered built in 1947 as a symbol of Soviet power at the beginning of the Cold War. When it was completed in 1953, the building was the seventh tallest in the world and the tallest outside of New York City.

Robert Siciliano on the field under Moscow State University, one of Stalin's "seven sisters"

We later played at the Red Army Base field about an hour outside of Moscow. While the field itself was about the quality of a lower-level US recreational park, it was burdened by a shallow drainage ditch that ran just outside the third-base line, making it dangerous to round third or chase a foul ball in that direction. It was also difficult to play there over the shouts of what appeared to be drunken soldiers who had settled into the concrete stands to watch. These were the same concrete stands that served as our outdoor locker room before the game.

The Russia baseball adventure then moved to St. Petersburg, which is an eight-hour train ride north of Moscow. In St. Petersburg the baseball season is very short, baseball is not a local priority, and the field quality reflects that. There was only one baseball diamond in the city. It had a dusty and rocky all-dirt infield and clumpy grass outfield. About 20 feet from the third-base line was the dugout, a single bench up against the wall of a decaying brick building.

Catching in St. Petersburg, Russia with "dugout" and brick wall in background

Even though some of the fields we play on at home are less than ideal, they are far better than those we played on in China and Russia. I have played at the Great American Ballpark and Riverfront Stadium, the major league stadiums in Cincinnati, at many of the major league spring training facilities, and at LaSalle and other high school fields. Regardless of the design of the field and the budget available to keep it maintained, my hat goes off to the groundskeepers who take what they have and work hard to keep the field in the best playable shape for us.

Just Show Up

Before attending my first fantasy camp, Cincinnati Reds Baseball Heaven, I called Andy Miller, the director of the organization running the camp. I had a long list of questions, and Andy answered virtually every one the same way. He said, "We will take care of that. We are going to treat you the way the professionals are treated."

But I did not fully appreciate what that meant until I got to camp and had everything fall into place. I am sure Andy would not mind if I pointed out before going on that while he is the official head of Baseball Heaven, the person who really runs the logistics of the camp is Kathy Bender, Miller's assistant. Because of leadership attention from Andy, Kathy, and Doug Flynn, the camp ran like clockwork.

Flynn, a Gold Glove winner, spent 11 years with Cincinnati, (including two as a role player on the 1975 and 1976 "Big Red Machine"), New York (Mets), Texas, Montreal, and Detroit. He is also known both in Cincinnati and New York for being traded, along with Steve Henderson, Dan Norman, and Pat Zachry, for Tom Seaver. While Andy and Kathy managed most of the behind-the-scenes logistics and planning, Flynn ran the daily camp operations.

When 100 campers arrived for the fantasy camp, all we had to do was show up and walk into the locker room the first morning. Airline arrangements were made, airport pickups were available, and room reservations were assured. Our uniforms were hung in our locker and laundered every evening by the professional clubhouse staff. The training room staff, the same who care for the professionals, were readily attendant to our needs. The fields were conditioned and maintained that way, the wooden bats were provided, morning warmups were led, lunch showed up each day between doubleheaders, the umpires were there for each game, and the activity schedule was shared and followed. When there were questions or concerns, they were promptly addressed.

Of course, when you are paying $4,000 for anything, it should definitely be well planned and executed. The leadership and staff of the camp understood this and did everything they could to be sure the experience justified the cost. On balance, I believe they accomplished what they set out to do. The best evidence is that the camp is filled every year with a significant percentage of returning campers.

A critical element of the fantasy camp experience is the presence of the ex-professionals. Over the four years I attended Reds Baseball Heaven, my coaches were Jack Billingham, Pat Zachry, Will McEnaney, Chris Welsh, and Herm Winningham, the first three being members of the Big Red Machine pitching staff. Other ex-professionals took on the role of hitting instructor for the whole camp. Mickey Brantley and Joel Youngblood were the most memorable. Regardless of the skill level of the campers coming into the camp, the professionals had helpful coaching tips.

I have a very open batting stance and have since high school. During a several-game span in my sophomore year, I was not hitting the ball well. Our assistant coach, Dick Greenblatt, thought I was over-striding. At practice one day, he advised me, for batting practice only, to open my stance to be directly facing the pitcher and hit without striding. The idea was that I would get a feel for hitting by only shifting my weight, then go back to my normal closed stance with a reduced stride. I had an extremely successful batting practice, only closed my stance a little, and have hit that way for over 40 years.

When I walked into the camp batting cage in 2000 to have my swing analyzed by Brantley, who was the Mets hitting instructor, he looked at my open stance and his first comment was, "Well, OK, if that's what you do, that's what you do." He proceeded to check the balance of my stance and then had me hit some balls. He liked my swing but indicated I could get even more power were I to close my shoulder a little more even while I maintain my foot position. I tried it and immediately felt more pop on the ball. I have been hitting with my shoulder in that position ever since.

I recently had an opportunity to talk to Joe Nuxhall, who was one of the ex-professionals at each of the camps I attended. Although Nuxie has been struggling with his health lately, at 78 he still looks forward to attending camp every year. I asked him what the attraction of the camp was for the ex-professionals and was surprised by the answer.

I expected him to say that the professionals come back every year because they get a chance to spend time with their former playing friends. While that is a factor, Nuxie said that the biggest reason is that they enjoy the camaraderie with the campers. The professionals are energized by the campers' passion for the game and appreciate being able to talk baseball with people who love it so much. Nuxie was unable to think of one ex-professional who has ever chosen not to return to fantasy camp because they did not have a great time during the week.

Fantasy camps are great, albeit expensive, experiences in themselves. They provide an intense baseball experience for over-30 players of all skill levels. And the camps serve to reintroduce many to the game so that they go on to play senior baseball in other venues. The leadership and staff, including the ex-professionals, provide an environment where players can enjoy every aspect of the game and be treated like major leaguers. And all we have to do is show up.

Thanks, Mom and Dad!

Senior players are blessed with the support of our families. Our spouses, significant others, and family members help us make the commitment of money and time to play the game we love. We are similarly blessed with those who make the game available to us: the league and tournament directors, groundskeepers, umpires, fantasy camp administrators and ex-professionals, and others. Despite receiving all of this backing today, I would argue that the most important support structure we have is the foundation that was built for us when we were playing the game in our youth. That foundation, for many of us, was built by our parents.

Recall the concept I shared earlier that we should be doing when we get older what we were passionate about when we were ten years old. It was our parents and other adults who gave us the instruction, the urging, and the latitude to become passionate about the game. They gave us the financial support, committed their time, got us to our games, coached teams, ran leagues, and shared our joy for the adventure.

So, I deeply thank Ann for supporting me and joining me in my senior baseball experience. I thank John Gilmore, Thom Lach, Joe Caligaris, Scott Green, Greg Wagner, Tom Giffen, Andy Miller, and the many more who, joined by umpires, groundskeepers and others to make the game available to me still today.

Personally, I also thank my sisters, Carol and Marti, who were dragged to all of my games. And, after all these years, I can forgive Carol for the one time I was made to miss a game of mine to attend her dance recital. It was only fair.

But, most of all I thank my parents for giving me the right start on my life and baseball journey. This is the basis for dedicating this book, in part, to them. These are the dedications you may have missed earlier in the book.

To my mother, Jeanette Friedman Spector, who provided me a balance of freedom and support to be the best that I could be, regardless of what I chose to do. I only hope that her wisdom lives well beyond her all too brief 54 years.

To my father, Herman Spector, who established fair play, team play, and baseball as cornerstones of my life. "Oh you're Herm Spector's boy. Wow, can your dad ever hit the ball!"

SIXTH INNING

PLAYING CATCH
WITH DAD

"Baseball is fathers and sons playing catch, the long arc of years between."
Donald Hall

"Hey, Dad? You wanna have a catch?"
Ray Kinsella, *Field of Dreams*

JR: "OK, we're back up 6-5; great ball game. If we can just shut down their four and five hitters, we win this; those guys are killing us.

Al: "I'm going to keep the ball outside on both of them even if I'm off the plate. We'll make the other guys beat us."

Jack: "Al, maybe we need to fly in your son to relieve you next inning. I understand he can play the game."

Al: "Yeah, I'm proud of him. After we played together at fantasy camp, he's back in baseball, playing in a senior league near Boston. I'll tell you, there is nothing I enjoyed more than when he was pitching and I was catching. After playing catch with him when he could barely walk, we were playing catch again almost 30 years later."

Jack: "My daughter could have played the game. She had all of the skills and strength, but there just wasn't a place for her to play. She ended up playing and enjoying fast-pitch softball."

Ken: "Tomorrow we have some time off to watch Alma, Roomie's wife, who's playing in the women's division. There are eight teams this year and some of the players are from the Team USA women's softball team."

Al: "Let's do it. By the way, could you guys get me a few more runs? I need all the help I can get."

Playing Catch with Grandsons Too

In his essay, "Fathers Playing Catch with Sons," from his book by the same title, Donald Hall writes, "My father and I played catch as I grew up. Like so much else between fathers and sons, playing catch was tender and tense at the same time. He wanted to play with me. He wanted me to be good. He seemed to demand that I be good. I threw the ball straight. Then I tried to put something on it; it flew twenty feet over his head. Or it banged into the sidewalk in front of him, breaking stitches and ricocheting off of a pebble into the gutter of Greenway Street. Or it went wide to his right and lost itself in Mrs. Davis's bushes. Or it went wide to his left and rolled across the street while drivers swerved their cars."

Many of us had our own equivalent of Greenway Street or Mrs. Davis's bushes. My street was Clemens Avenue in St. Louis. My son's street was Crosier Lane in Cincinnati. If Kevin threw wide to his right, we ran the risk of the ball being lost in the creek area at one end of our front yard. For my grandsons, Jordan and Aaron, it is Blackberry Avenue in University City, Missouri. So far, they have not been strong enough to throw the ball over the backyard fence onto busy Hanley Avenue, but that time is rapidly approaching.

It was not surprising, when I surveyed a number of senior players, to learn their fathers introduced them to baseball at a very young age. Picture Phil Reichle, playing catch with his dad 50 years ago in Cincinnati. Picture Bob Pinault, in his 50s and living in California, playing catch with his dad in Chelsea, Massachusetts. Picture Anthony Ranieri, in his early 40s and running an MSBL tournament in his spare time, playing catch with his dad in Massapequa, New York, when Anthony was four. Picture Ron Russo, 68 and playing 100 games a year, playing catch with his dad in Johnston, Rhode

Island, at age six.

Recall George Goodall's baseball shrine room in his home in Belleville, Illinois. On a wall, George had a framed picture of his father's Western Brewery Company semi-pro team from 1901. His father, Arthur, introduced George to baseball although George claims that he was born and "came out onto the floor rolling a baseball." Picture George playing catch with his father in Belleville over 90 years ago.

George Goodall's father's 1901 semi-pro team—Arthur Goodall—middle row, far right

My father introduced me to the game before I could walk. I remember playing catch with him draped in his ever-present towel, which he wore around his neck to help manage the relentless heat and humidity of the St. Louis summer and his over-active sweat glands, which I inherited. I also remember playing catch with my grandmother, not because she knew how or wanted to, but because I wanted to. What does a little old Jewish grandmother from Brusilov, Ukraine, know about baseball? She knew her grandson wanted to play catch. So, also picture me playing catch with my father (and grandmother) in St. Louis almost 60 years ago.

Has a movie ever made you cry? There is one that makes me cry every time I see it. I know the scene is coming—I know I am going to cry—I still cannot help myself. In fact, I am a little teary eyed as I am writing this just thinking about it. You guessed it. When Kevin Costner, playing Ray Kinsella, is introduced to his father, John, played by Dwier Brown, near the end of *Field of Dreams*, the tears start to well up in my eyes. After the following dialogue, I lose it.

John: "Well, good night, Ray."

Ray: "Good night, John."

(They shake hands and John begins to walk away.)

Ray: "Hey...Dad?"

(John turns.)

Ray: (choked up) "You wanna have a catch?"

John: "I'd like that."

That scene is not only about baseball. It is about father-son relationships, both the good parts and the bad. It is about memories and regrets. But it is about baseball and how it bonds not only fathers and sons but families, generations, and communities.

The late Luther Vandross featured a song entitled, "Dance with My Father." The lyrics include:

"If I could get another chance, another walk, another dance with him

I'd play a song that would never, ever end

How I'd love, love, love

To dance with my father again."

Wouldn't you like to play catch with your dad right now? I would.

Many of us are bound to the game and to the memory of playing catch with our fathers. Many of us have also experienced the joy of sharing the tradition with our own sons. And some of us have even had the opportunity and joy to play catch with our grandsons.

Get to Everything

Playing catch is at the foundation of the game of baseball. It creates a feel for the ball and an ability to anticipate its flight. It is the most fundamental way to begin to build a respect for teamwork. Playing catch builds an understanding of the importance of defense.

Playing catch taught me never to anticipate that a ball thrown to you is going to be perfectly thrown. If you assume you will have to move for the ball, you will more likely get to and catch an errant throw. And the balls that are thrown right to you can be looked at as a bonus. This approach also pays dividends for batted balls. The ones right at you are great, but assuming you will not be so lucky gives you a head start when needing to move to a ball to the right or left or in front or in back of you. While playing defense, before every pitch, I say three words to myself, "Get to everything." This concept and the words are also not a bad philosophy of life to help you prepare for the "balls" that are not hit perfectly to you.

Playing catch not only builds skills, it creates bonds. Whether playing catch with your father or warming up a teammate, the chatter is constant. There is talk of baseball and families and politics. In high school (OK, maybe as we get older also), there is talk about girls. Playing catch builds fundamentals and it builds relationships.

Signed Mashed Potatoes

In the first inning, I mentioned that Joe Garagiola was one of the three Hall of Fame announcers, along with Jack Buck and Harry Carey, that I grew up with—listening to Cardinals' games on KMOX in St. Louis. I have had the opportunity to meet Garagiola on three separate occasions. The first time was at the Chase Park Plaza Hotel in St. Louis. My father took me to a professional wrestling card called "Wrestling at the Chase," mostly to see Lou Thesz, the foremost wrestler of that era and a St. Louis native. He held the world title for 13 straight years and won 936 consecutive matches. Oh, sure, it was fixed then too, but he was also a legitimately good wrestler and athlete. The broadcaster for "Wrestling at the Chase," which was covered on local television, was Joe Garagiola. After the matches were over, my dad took me over an introduced me to him. What a treat!

The second time I met Garagiola, he was the speaker at a father-son Cub Scout banquet in St. Louis when I was ten years old. My dad and I were sitting near the head table, close enough to hear some of the conversation during dinner. My best friend growing up was Marc Golubock, who eventually played third base on our Missouri State

High School championship baseball team when we were juniors. Marc had such small hands that even in high school he needed to hold the top of the ball with his three middle fingers to get a good throwing grip. He was the consummate fielder and led the team with a .368 batting average in our championship season.

Marc and his dad were sitting at the head table next to Garagiola. Marc whispered to his dad that he would like to ask Mr. Garagiola for his autograph. Before Mr. Golubock could answer, Garagiola, who had heard the request despite the whisper, said, "Push your plate over here." He then proceeded to sign his name with his finger in Marc's mashed potatoes. After the laughter died down, he gave Marc a real autograph.

Joe Garagiola, Marc Golubock, and Ralph Golubock at 1954 Cub Scout banquet

Fifteen years later, I was working for Procter & Gamble and doing a lot of traveling. One trip I made frequently to a raw material supplier near Niagra Falls was on a small plane of 20 or so seats out of Scranton, Pennsylvania. I had made the trip so often, I was in that traveling zone in which you do not really pay attention to what is going on around you. I checked in at the gate (this was before highjackers and airport security), boarded the plane, and found my seat. After settling in with something to read, I looked up and across the aisle from me was Joe Garagiola. I introduced myself as being from St. Louis and honestly was able to tell him how much I enjoyed listening to him do the Cardinals' games. Then I related the mashed potatoes story to him. I am not sure if he was just being nice, but he said he remembered the incident. I reveled in the next 60 minutes as I had a chance to talk baseball with Joe Garagiola. He was a real gentleman.

So, what does Joe Garagiola have to do with how baseball is passed down from generation to generation? In Garagiola's case, he is the exception to the rule—he definitely did not pick up his love for baseball from his dad.

In *Baseball is a Funny Game*, Garagiola's marvelous 1960 book about the inside and insight of professional baseball, he describes how Yogi Berra and he grew up playing baseball in a section of St. Louis called "The Hill." He describes his father's relationship to the game as follows. "There was no Little League in Italy, so it was hard for Papa Garagiola or Papa Berra to understand why you had to catch a ball, let alone have a glove to catch it with, and why you needed special shoes to run in...Papa saw the paper, but he never read the sports pages. He didn't know third base from the coach's box; in fact, he didn't know there was a third base or a coach's box."

Notwithstanding his father's disconnection with baseball, Joe quickly grew to love the game. Clearly, while the generational rite of passage is part of why the game of baseball means so much to many of us, the game can carry itself without parental support. But parental support is helpful, even when the parents do not agree. Garagiola reports in his book, It's *Anybody's Ballgame*, that when Harmon Killebrew was elected to the Hall of Fame in 1984, he said, "My father taught me and my brother to play ball in the front yard. One day my mother came out and told him we were ruining the lawn. My father told her, 'We're raising kids, not raising grass.'"

Despite stories like that of Joe Garagiola and his father, one of the things that draws many, if not most, of us to baseball is that it reminds us, whether consciously or subconsciously, of our relationships with our fathers and sons. Our baseball memories are frequently linked to those intergenerational relationships.

"What if he is a girl?"

"Wait a minute! Could it be? What the hell! What if he is a girl?"

As Billy Bigelow, in the musical Carousel, sings his "Soliloquy (My Boy Bill)," he contemplates the possibility of having a son and all of the things that they would do together. He then pauses, thinks, and realizes that he could be having a daughter instead. While Billy could not quite relate to a future relationship with a daughter in the way he could with a son, he knew instinctively that he had the same responsibility regardless of his child's gender.

Relative to baseball, a father's relationship with his daughter can be the basis of her lifelong love of the game, regardless of whether she ever plays it. Many women are as avid baseball fans as men and, like men, can tie their love of baseball to their relationship with their father or other family members.

The movie, *A League of Their Own*, introduced us to a part of the history of women's relationship to baseball. In July 2005, I met Pat Scott, who had an impressive pitching career in the All-American Girls Professional Baseball League (AAGPBL). Pat pitched briefly with the Springfield Sallies in 1948 before returning home because of a family illness. Max Carey, Pittsburgh Pirates Hall of Famer, was managing in the AAGPBL. He contacted Pat and asked her to return to the league, which she did, pitching for the Fort Wayne Daisies in 1951-1953. She ended her career with a 2.46 earned run average and recalls pitching an 11-inning shutout against Battle Creek in 1951. She was also the pitcher of record in her team's 5-1 championship victory that same year against the Rockford Peaches.

Pat's love of baseball started when she was very young. She remembers playing catch when she was two, and traveling to Cincinnati to see big league games at the old Crosley Field. Pat had three sisters with whom she played ball, but she also spent a lot of time at the nearby school lot, where the boys were playing. She spent every spare minute either at the schoolyard or throwing at an old basket nailed to the side of the barn on the family farm. The skills she developed allowed her to take advantage of the semipro team that played on the baseball field on her family's farm. She would shag flies, pick up equipment, and occasionally play in a practice or game. Her skill and confidence grew—she knew she could compete with the guys, but she had no outlet to play regularly. That was until her father saw in the paper that a girls' baseball league was holding tryouts in Chicago. The family supported her in making the trip, and her professional career was born.

Pat, now 76, is still competitive and participates in multiple events in the Senior Olympics. While there is not an outlet for her to continue to play baseball, she works out three times per week. In an interview in the Cincinnati Enquirer she said, "I...think I could still throw harder than most of the girls playing ball today."

Pat Scott and me at the Cincinnati Reds Hall of Fame in July 2005

While my mom, Jeanette, never played baseball, I am sure she would have been a good player. She had great hand-eye coordination and timing, and she was quick, as evidenced by her table tennis game. She played the game right up against the table and, regardless of how hard the ball was hit at her, she returned everything, forehand or backhand. I was well into high school before I was able to beat her in table tennis or H-O-R-S-E on our small basketball court in the backyard. Mom was one of the family members I was able to drag outside to have a game of catch. She threw well and was clearly strong enough to have played the game. I regret never having talked to her about whether she wanted to. Also regrettably, if she had wanted to play, there would have been no playing opportunity.

Pat Scott's playing opportunity in the AAGPBL was unusual, while my mom's and other athletic women's baseball playing options were and are few. Until 1972, female athletic opportunities were limited regardless of a woman's sport of interest. In that year, Congress passed the Education Amendments to the Civil Rights Act of 1964. Title IX of the act's amendments reads, "No person in the United States shall, on basis of sex, be excluded from participation in, or denied the benefits of, or be subjected to discrimination under any educational program or activity receiving federal assistance."

Women's sports programs began to flourish in colleges and trickled down to high school and youth leagues. While colleges and high schools do not have girls' baseball teams, fast-pitch softball teams are prevalent. It has been a prominent Olympic sport and is among the most exciting sporting events to watch on television. High school and youth girls' fast-pitch has grown exponentially in participation and support. It is not uncommon, for example, during the winter, for us to compete for time in batting and pitching cages with girls practicing softball.

In 2003, when my son, Kevin, joined me at Reds Baseball Heaven, he had not played baseball for a number of years. Having played only slow-pitch softball, he was concerned about facing the speed of a baseball pitch. Prior to camp, we were both in St. Louis for a family event and decided to head for the batting cages. As at most batting cage facilities, the speeds were posted. This facility's cages threw from 55 to 85 miles per hour.

We decided to start at 70 and work our way up. I had been playing for some time and was typically facing these kinds of speeds. It took Kevin awhile to regain his baseball swing, but he did so in short order. As we were talking about moving to a higher speed cage, a young lady walked up to the cage area, put on her batting helmet and stepped into the fastest cage. From pitch one she was hitting line drives. We watched for a while and then asked to share the cage. As we rotated through our turns and as Kevin and I tried to keep up with her hitting, we had a chance to talk to her. She was rehabbing after a knee injury, evidenced by the brace she was wearing, trying to get back to her small college fast-pitch softball team. The only way she could get to see speeds anywhere near what she saw in her games was to practice at the fastest of baseball cages. There was little doubt in our minds that she could be playing baseball if she wanted to and the opportunities were available.

Fast-pitch softball is not the only outlet for women. The Roy

Hobbs World Series has a Women's Division that in 2004 drew eight teams. That year, we went to watch one of the women's games because Alma, the wife of our catcher, Glenn "Roomie" Fiebig, was playing. Some of the players in a game on an adjacent field were from Team USA fast-pitch softball.

There are also women's baseball organizations sprinkled throughout the United States and Canada. Perhaps the most prominent is the American Women's Baseball Federation that runs tournaments and a World Series. These events are relatively small, however. Some are four-team tournaments, and the World Series, which in 2005 was held at the Disney's Wide World of Sports Complex, drew only nine teams. These are all open age group events and primarily populated by younger players. During the World Series, the AWBF also ran a 13-and-under tournament but drew only two teams.

Interestingly, in both the open and the 13-and-under divisions, there were teams from Australia, which now has about 60 active women's baseball teams. The Australian approach has been to organize as sister teams to already organized men's adult baseball teams. There are women's baseball activities in other countries as well, including Japan, which has about 200 teams. For now, most Japanese teams play with a "soft" baseball, although that is starting to change as they compete internationally. It is appropriate to point out that the women's baseball sanctioned by the AWBF, including the international tournaments, is played with 80 feet between bases and 56 feet as the pitching distance.

In 1948, when Pat Scott first played in the AAGPBL, the field dimensions were 72 feet between bases and a 50 feet pitching distance. They were also using a ball that was over ten inches in diameter. Over time, the dimensions lengthened, and the ball size was reduced and made livelier. By the time the league closed in 1954, the base paths were 85 feet, and the pitching distance was 60 feet. In the middle of that season, the AAGPBL converted to a regulation baseball. One can conclude that given time and demonstrated performance, current women's baseball would be played at full-field dimensions everywhere.

But women's connection to baseball is not just measured by their participation. Women can love the game with equal or greater passion than even the men who play it and, like men, many were introduced to the game by their fathers, thereby having feelings for the game that are inextricably linked to those relationships. Consider Jean Ardell and her father, Bill, Danielle Gennaro and her father, Vince, Arleen White Bly and her father, Sam, Doris Kearns Goodwin and her father, Michael, and Ila Borders and her father, Phil.

Jean Hastings Ardell wrote the book, *Breaking into Baseball: Women and the National Pastime*. She loves, lives, studies, and writes about baseball. She reports that one of her earliest memories involves joining her father on the elevated train as they traveled from Queens to the Polo Grounds to see their beloved New York Giants play. She viewed herself as her father's "baseball companion" and reveled in his stories about the glory days of John J. McGraw's teams of the 1920s.

Ardell later developed dreams of replacing Billy Martin at second base for the Yankees, her favorite team. Unfortunately, she discovered a gap between her dream and her talent. Nevertheless, she was hooked on the game. As she writes, "Thanks to my father, I had been imprinted with baseball at an early age..."

While still in high school, Ardell developed the idea that her future was in writing about baseball and, over time and with much effort, that is what it became. Her baseball life also went beyond writing. She married Dan Ardell, "...who had his cup of coffee with the Angels during their inaugural year in 1961..." And she energetically nurtured her two boys' youth baseball experiences. But she ties her life and her future to her past when she writes, "The game connects my husband and sons with my father, who died before they were born."

In his book, *Field of Dreamers*, Vince Gennaro, writes, "Baseball isn't just my past; it's also a central part of my future. It has become an important part of my relationship with my daughter. Not because I overtly encourage it, but because she sees its virtues. I will teach Danielle many of life's lessons... perseverance, the will to win, fairness, losing graciously ...through baseball. Danielle genuinely enjoys going to a ballgame, learning the rules, playing catch in the backyard, or even searching for statistics in the Baseball Encyclopedia. For Danielle and me, one of the tablets on which we have our dialogue is baseball."

I'm sure that in the future, when Danielle Gennaro is grown and goes to a baseball game with her children or perhaps is playing the game herself, she will be reminded vividly and fondly of her relationship with her father.

At least every ten years, I reunite with my high school class. Among those I see is my first really special girlfriend, Arleen White. Over the past several years, Ann and I have had a chance to see even more of Arleen and her husband, Howard. Despite knowing her pretty well, until recently I thought the only connection she had to baseball was through Howard.

Howard is the ultimate memorabilia collector. Their basement in St. Louis is full, wall to wall and floor to ceiling, of primarily Cardinal, a lot of Yankee, and general baseball nostalgia. Literally the entire basement is dedicated to what must be a multi-million dollar collection. Just as a few representative examples, Howard has the Hall of Fame Induction Bats for every 500-home run inductee and every living inducted pitcher with more than 300 wins. He has over 400 autographed items from Stan Musial, including 30 bats, and more than 150 autographed items each from Bob Gibson, Lou Brock, and Ozzie Smith. Howard also has rookie baseball cards for every Hall of Famer from 1955 to date and autographed items for every Hall of Famer from 1950 to date. And these represent just a minute fraction of the collection, which is featured in Rich Wolfe's book, *For Cardinal Fans Only*. As Arleen jokingly (I think) says, "Don't you think that he should sell it all, and we should retire to Tahiti?"

As it turns out, however, Arleen's connection to baseball is much more personal, connected to her childhood, and very deeply felt. She and Howard recently visited Cooperstown and we shared e-mails throughout their trip. In her final message, Arleen wrote the following about their visit.

Howard "was in 7th heaven. It was wonderful. I wondered if I was the only one (presumptuous of me) who was holding back tears through the tour. I felt so nostalgic, remembering how my Dad (who died in 2000) loved baseball, especially the old Hall of Famers. I remember that baseball played a large part in my life growing up, as we went to many games, had games playing on TV, and had many discussions, heated and otherwise, about which teams had the best players and why. My dad was so knowledgeable and loved debating about the teams. We also had the greatest comedy routine running continually...'Who's on First' with Abbott and Costello. I watched it over and over, remembering how my Dad loved Abbott and Costello, and especially that routine. I could hear the sound of his laughter. Anyway, that experience was sad and sweet at the same time."

Arleen's Cooperstown experience brought back so many powerful feelings and memories for her. Baseball was clearly an integral part of her relationship with her father, Sam. The intergenerational father-daughter theme is also foundational to the personal story that Doris Kearns Goodwin narrates in her book, *Wait Till Next Year, A Memoir.*

Goodwin is a Pulitzer Prize winning historian and an avid baseball fan. She was a prominent storyteller in Ken Burn's Public Broadcasting System documentary, Baseball. In her book Goodwin wrote, "...baseball was an indistinguishable part of my childhood..." and "...thinking about the Dodgers summoned recollections of my family, my neighborhood, my village, and the evolution of my own sensibilities."

Goodwin then, on the very first page of her book, captures the essence of many women's, and men's, connection with baseball. The book begins, "When I was six, my father gave me a bright-red scorebook that opened my heart to the game of baseball." She ends page one with, "By the time I mastered the art of scorekeeping, a lasting bond had been forged among my father, baseball, and me."

Goodwin hits the nail on the head for George Goodall, Phil Reichle, Bob Pinault, Anthony Ranieri, Ron Russo, Danielle Gennaro, Arleen Bly, and so many others as she relates her experience of going to her first baseball game with her dad. She writes, "...what I remember most is sitting at Ebbetts Field for the first time, with my red scorebook in my lap and my father at my side."

At least one women-in-baseball story, however, is one of participation. Jean Ardell features Ila Borders in Breaking into Baseball. The book details Borders's career as a left-handed pitcher, which ended in her fourth minor league season. Like so many men and women, including those noted above, Borders was introduced to baseball by her father, who had played some professional ball. Her mother even got into the act by fielding balls during Borders's batting practice. Borders said, "I really learned to appreciate the game from my dad. When I was younger, we were always watching games on TV, going to the ballpark, or playing catch."

Phil Borders remained closely involved throughout Ila's baseball career. He helped her deal with the barrage of reporters interested in her story, thereby allowing her to keep her grade-point average in the 3.3 range while balancing studying with her baseball practice. And when she was invited to the training camp of the St. Paul Saints, an independent league team, her dad made it clear why she was called when he said, "This is not a gimmick. She is not going there for anything but the right reasons: to be a legitimate left-handed pitcher based on her abilities."

I also had a father-daughter sports-based relationship with my daughter, Dana. While she never played baseball, she was a gritty soccer and softball player. She loved the games for their competition and reveled in adversity. Bruises, sprains, or scrapes never kept her from being in the middle of things.

Dana, with her competitive sports mindset, and her brother, Kevin, are at the center of one of my favorite stories. They had both gone off to college at Washington University in St. Louis. Dana was studying and eventually got her Masters degree in Occupational Therapy. Kevin received his degree in Economics. Within a single week, Ann and I got the following phone calls.

From Dana: "Hi, guess what I did yesterday. You know that co-ed flag-football team I've been playing on? Well, it was late in the game, and we needed a score, and they threw me a pass for a touchdown. Did you hear that? I scored a touchdown!"

From Kevin: "Hi, guess what I did yesterday. I got an ear pierced."

Dana and her husband, Vince, have built a wonderful family and are rearing two boys who both have an affinity for games with bats and balls. I played catch with Dana on the front lawn as she was growing up and am now playing catch with her sons 30 years later.

Whether it was at the stadium, in front of the radio, across the dinner table, at our youth ballgames, at batting practice, or during a game of catch, we, as both daughters and sons, were using baseball to help forge our relationships with our fathers, our mothers, and our communities. And as fathers we have done and are doing the same with our sons, daughters, and grandchildren.

Playing Catch with His Daughter—Again

A very special father-daughter story unfolded at the 2003 Reds Baseball Heaven camp. Among approximately 100 campers that year were Jim Mannix and his daughter, Lisa. At the time of the camp, Jim was 71 years old and Lisa was 38.

She came to Sarasota as a well-conditioned athlete, whose primary sport was soccer, which she played in college. She still plays three to four games per week in both women's and co-ed leagues against younger players. Her soccer team is made up primarily of players over 40. In one league, which has a 25 age limit, Lisa's team's name is "Old Enough to Be Your Parents." Her exceptional conditioning paid off for the Mannix's Baseball Heaven team because, by the end of the week, Lisa was pinch running for nearly everyone on the team as they were suffering from sore knees, sprained ankles, tight hamstrings, and general fatigue.

Jim came to camp in a very different physical condition. As noted, he was over 70. He had not played any sports since his 30s when he was a left-handed slow-pitch softball pitcher in a Cincinnati industrial league. Jim also has a physical disability. During birth, the doctor misused forceps and damaged some of the nerves in Jim's neck. This left him with less than full use of the right side of his body. Fortunately, after Jim finished high school, he found a doctor who performed complex corrective surgery so that Jim gained somewhat more use of the arm and hand.

Once the Baseball Heaven organizers realized Lisa would need her own locker room and worked with her to compensate for the fact that men's baseball pants are not designed for a woman's body, Lisa and Jim settled into the camp routine along with the rest of us. Their team, coached by then third-base coach for the Reds, Tim Foli, and Reds legend and radio broadcaster, Joe Nuxhall, lost their first three games by a run each, but caught fire and went on to win the championship. I remember their championship win vividly because I was the starting pitcher against them that day.

But the Mannix baseball story is not really about fantasy camps or championship games. It is about their life relationship from when Lisa was a child to now that she is a widely published and respected physician who specializes in headache management.

Jim, like most boys, became interested in baseball because his dad was an avid fan. While Jim tried to play baseball when he was young, his physical limitations made it impossible. But he did not give up. He "made" his younger brother play with him, and Jim found, when he was 12, that he could play slow pitch softball. He played in elementary school, church leagues, and went on to pitch in an industrial league.

When Lisa was old enough, Jim had her out in the back yard playing catch and taking batting practice. Lisa has two memories of those times. One is that she was already highly competitive by nature and was, therefore, frustrated that she could not hit the ball consistently. The other memory is that one time when she did hit the ball, she shattered the bedroom window. Lisa went on to play softball recreationally through high school, but it was never even a thought that she should play baseball. In that era, the option just did not exist.

While they both played softball, Jim and Lisa were avid baseball fans. They would listen to the Reds games together on the radio on WLW in Cincinnati. And they found ways to go to as many games as they could even though resources were limited. Every year, the Reds would give away tickets to students who got straight As, which Lisa consistently did. And her mom collected coffee can lids because, as a promotion, Maxwell House lids could be traded in for baseball tickets. As Jim says, "We drank a lot of coffee."

Jim and Lisa continued to be baseball fans, although Lisa's loyalty shifted to the Indians when she worked in Cleveland for awhile. Then, in 2002, Lisa saw an advertisement for Reds Baseball Heaven and knew immediately what she was going to do. She and Jim went to dinner and she asked him that if she went with him, would he want to go to baseball fantasy camp? She wanted to give the week to him as a gift. Despite not having played any ball game for 40 years, never having played baseball, being 70-plus, and having the physical limitations, Jim did not hesitate to say yes.

From Jim learning to love the game from his father in the 1930s, to playing catch with Lisa in the back yard when she was seven, to their mutual love of the game and the Reds as Lisa was growing up, to their continued common enjoyment of baseball, and finally to the 2003 Red's Baseball Heaven experience, Jim and Lisa Mannix have traveled the road together. They played catch in the early 1970s and they played catch again in 2003.

A Man

I can relate to how Jim Mannix felt as he joined Lisa at the 2003 Reds fantasy camp because I have had the same experience. My son, Kevin, was born in 1973, and, as you may have guessed, we had a ball in his hands shortly thereafter. We moved to Cincinnati in 1976, and began playing catch on our new front lawn. Twenty-seven years later, at the same fantasy camp where Jim and Lisa Mannix played, Kevin and I also played together. We not only played catch on the green carpet-like grass of the Reds' Sarasota complex, but there were a couple of games that week in which we were a battery with Kevin pitching and me catching. What a thrill!

Ann and Kevin with me at 2003 Reds Baseball Heaven

Following the fantasy camp, Kevin and I played in a couple of other tournaments together. But that was not enough baseball for him. After a 15-year hiatus, he returned to playing regularly the game he was passionate about as he was growing up. Kevin recalls his early youth baseball experience in ways with which every baseball player can relate.

"Our weekend game might have been at 2:00, but I was dressed by 10:00 and ready to go."

"Somehow I remember that it was a sunny day whenever we played."

"When you're seven or eight, baseball is summer."

"There was nothing I didn't like about baseball."

When Kevin was about 12, he ran into a small problem. Actually, the problem was that he was small. While all of the other players his age were growing, albeit at different speeds, Kevin was not. For perspective, he wrestled in high school in the 119 and under weight division as a junior. When he went to get his driver's license at age 16, he was 5'1". The woman making out his license asked him how tall he was, and he said 5'6". He looked her in the eye and said, "That is what I will be." So she wrote it down. It turned out Kevin underestimated his potential growth. He went off to college and grew to be 5'11" and now weighs a muscular 180.

But in Junior High School, while he had the baseball skills, the speed and strength of the game, as he puts it, passed him by. The size issue kept him from playing high school and, perhaps, college ball. After his college growth spurt, he again began playing ball, but this time it was softball, and that is where he stayed until that fantasy camp. And the passion is still there. As a youth, he dressed by 10:00 for a 2:00 game. Now, he gets up at 7:30 on Sunday morning to make his baseball game on time. Kevin, not a morning person, says, "What else other than baseball would I get up so early for on a Sunday morning?"

I would like to believe that Kevin's passion for the game, in part, reflects our relationship as it existed when he was growing up—and as it is now. He recalls long baseball talks with me and with my father. They had a special relationship and every time Kevin visited, he and Grandpa would go, by themselves, out on the back porch to talk. No one ever imposed on their time and space together nor asked what they talked about. Recently, Kevin told me that baseball was in the mix of those conversations; stories of Musial and others. Only now do I know that among other skip-generation wisdom, my father was passing on the traditions, intricacies, language, and love of the game to my son. Whether it was talking the game with Grandpa on the back porch or playing catch with Dad on the front lawn, Kevin ended up with it in his blood. As he is now married and openly talks of his future children, Kevin fully expects that he will pass the baseball torch to them. I asked him what baseball means to him, and, among other things, he summed it all up, "It's who I am."

That was not the only answer Kevin gave me to the question of what baseball means to him. He paused for a long time and shared his thoughts. He told me that baseball is "tradition," not explaining further as if that one word says it all. Kevin told me that baseball is "summertime" with all that implies. He said baseball is "a day at the ballpark." By explanation, he supported my belief that baseball is not about the major leagues, but rather about the game itself. Kevin and his wife, Lisa, had flown to Colorado for a wedding. While there, he had some spare time while driving around one afternoon, and came upon a Little League game. Drawn to the game, Kevin parked the car and began to watch. As he said, "It was a beautiful day to watch, even if it was being played badly. It was baseball. The kids loved it, and so did I. I stayed quite awhile."

Kevin then used two other words to describe what baseball means to him, "lifestyle" and "culture." We were sitting in Kevin and Lisa's apartment, and even though they have many interests, Kevin made his lifestyle point when he said, "Just look around. This apartment has baseball pictures and books and videos. There are trophies and baseballs and bats leaning against walls. Baseball is everywhere around me." He went on to explain that baseball is so ingrained in our culture that he has found he can talk baseball to a stranger anywhere. That is no trivial statement as Kevin is a frequent traveler, is personable, and enjoys conversation, so he has the opportunity to meet a lot of strangers.

While it is Kevin who described what baseball means to him by using the words, "tradition," "summertime," "lifestyle," and "culture," and the phrase, "It's who I am," he captured, in many ways, what baseball means to me as well. I am confident that it means that much and more to so many, especially senior players. My thrill is that these mature, thoughtful, profound insights were coming from the little guy who held a ball as soon as he could grip anything and with whom I played catch on the front lawn. My now-not-so-little guy is a senior baseball player and a man.

CHARACTERS

"It's a mere moment in a man's life
between the All-Star Game
and an old timer's game."
Vin Scully

"He is the man. He is the man."
(referring to Cal Ripken, Jr.)
Sammy Sosa

Ken: *"That squeeze play surprised the hell out of me. Game's tied."*

JR: *"This is definitely the kind of game that Yoke loved; a close one. I think about him all of the time."*

Jack: *"He was definitely a character. Never a dull moment when Yoke was around. No one could keep a dugout loose like he could."*

Ken: *"I think he'd have been trying to convince us that he had the squeeze smelled out."*

JR: *"Well, I know the only thing Yoke liked more than a competitive game was winning it. He'd be all over us to get in gear."*

April Fools

When someone mentions baseball characters, what comes to mind? Characters in major league baseball are typically identified as such because of their off-center personalities and antics. And there are characters in baseball fiction. Many of these are also a bit off center, making them all the more interesting. When hearing stories about baseball characters, it is sometimes difficult to separate fiction from non-fiction because the major league characters and the fictional characters have similar traits.

"The Bird" was the American League rookie of the year in 1976, winning 19 games with an earned run average of 2.34. In the remainder of his five-year career Mark Fidrych won only ten more games. The *ESPN Classic* web site gives us some indication of what "The Bird" brought to the game, "...along came Fidrych—wiggling and jiggling on the mound, talking to the ball, discarding balls with which opposing batters had managed a hit, chasing away groundskeepers so he could landscape and groom the mound himself, shaking hands with teammates after outstanding plays." He played the game with joy. As Red Sox pitcher, Bill "Spaceman" Lee said of Fidrych, "He's like the little boy that's thrown into a pile of horse manure and he's bobbin' up and down and they say how can you be so happy and he says there has to be a pony in here somewhere. His glass is always half full."

Is Fidrych really any different from Ebby Calvin "Nuke" LaLoosh in the movie, *Bull Durham*? LaLoosh talked to himself on the mound, had less than routine mannerisms, and was convinced by girlfriend, Annie Savoy, to wear a woman's garter belt for good luck. He was not very bright. When Annie was trying to introduce him to poetry, LaLoosh said, "Ooh, I've heard of stuff like this."

Annie followed with, "Yeah? Have you heard of Walt Whitman?"

LaLoosh responded, "No. Who's he play for?"

Characters abound both in professional baseball and in fictional settings. Jimmy Piersall was a classic. During his 17-year major league career he was renowned for his stunts. He ran the bases backwards for his 100th home run—in the right order, but backwards. He would act like an ape while on the base. And once he was called out on a close play, pulled a water gun out of his pocket, and squirted the umpire.

Al "The Mad Hungarian" Hrabosky, sporting a Fu Manchu

mustache and long hair, was a reliever, mostly for the Cardinals. His routine, when he came in from the bullpen, was to finish his warmups, turn his back to the plate, put a scowl on his face, slam the ball into his glove, and turn to glare menacingly at the hitter. Hrabosky once said, "I want the hitter to wonder if maybe I am a little crazy."

Bill Lee may be the prototypical non-fiction baseball character. "Spaceman" spent most of his 14-year career with Boston, went on to play in the short-lived professional senior league, and still plays amateur senior baseball. He is well known for his counter-cultural baseball behavior and his pointed quotations. The *Baseball Reliquary* reports that he "...talked to animals, championed environmental causes, practiced yoga, ate health foods, sprinkled marijuana on his buckwheat pancakes (an indiscretion for which he was fined $250 by Commissioner Bowie Kuhn), pondered Einstein and Vonnegut, quoted from Mao, and studied Eastern philosophers and mystics." This is not your typical major leaguer—or person in general, for that matter.

Lee's quotations are legend. Here are three prime examples.

"I think about the cosmic snowball theory. A few million years from now the sun will burn out and lose its gravitational pull. The earth will turn into a giant snowball and be hurled through space. When that happens, it won't matter if I get this guy out."

"The other day they asked me about mandatory drug testing. I said I believed in drug testing a long time ago. All through the 60s I tested everything."

"You have two hemispheres in your brain—a left and a right side. The left side controls the right side of your body and right controls the left half. It's a fact. Therefore, left-handers are the only people in their right minds."

Lee, Piersall, Hrabosky, and Fidrych are not alone on the roster of major league baseball characters. Among others are Yogi Berra, Brad "The Animal" Lesley, Bill Veeck, Ron Luciano, the San Diego Chicken, and Casey "Old Professor" Stengel, who, not to be upstaged by Yogi, is known for his Stengelese.

"Being with a woman all night never hurt no professional baseball player. It's staying up all night looking for a woman that does him in."

"Good pitching will always stop good hitting and vice-versa."

"All right everyone, line up alphabetically according to your height."

"There comes a time in every man's life, and I've had plenty of them."

Fictional characters also abound. Hayden Siddhartha "Sidd" Finch was introduced in the April 1, 1985, edition of *Sports Illustrated* in an article by George Plimpton. It took many readers a couple of weeks to figure out that the article was really an April Fools hoax. Finch was reported to be at spring training with the Mets. With no known baseball experience, he had emerged from spending years in Tibet where he learned the teachings of "the great poet-saint Lama Milaraspa" and mastered "siddhi, namely the yogic mastery of mind-body." Through this study, Finch had apparently "learned the art of the pitch."

This purportedly allowed him to pitch at speeds of up to 168 miles per hour with pinpoint accuracy. His catcher said that when pitching, Finch looked "like a pretzel gone loony." The righthander frequently wore a hiking boot on his right foot with his left foot bare. At the time of the article, Finch had not decided whether to sign with the Mets or pursue a career as a French horn player.

LaLoosh and Finch are joined in the realm of fictional characters of baseball ranks by, among many others, voodoo outfielder Pedro Cerrano, team owner Rhubarb the cat, Rick "Wild Thing" Vaughn, and even Charlie Brown. They all have their idiosyncrasies and look at the world and at baseball somewhat differently than most of us.

Senior baseball is no exception when it comes to having its characters. There are those who are degrees off center and keep things loose in the dugout and on the field. Every team seems to have one or two and, occasionally, a team is predominately made up of such characters. But, within the senior baseball community, the characters worthy of note are not necessarily those players who are several degrees off kilter. Rather, they are the seniors who represent the experience, are an integral part of what makes it great, and have contributed more than their fair share to the game's vitality.

There are thousands of players to choose from. The following four well represent the senior baseball community. Not only are they players. They are also organizers and leaders. Bob Hawkins organized the Cincinnati Colts and is their heart and soul. Scott Green developed Play at the Plate and continues to nurture it. Joe Caligaris is a Roy Hobbs league president and team sponsor. And

John Gilmore initiated and leads Baseball International. As we asked in the second inning, "Who are these guys?"

Hawk

Bob Hawkins, in many ways, had the most to do with reintroducing me to baseball and getting me involved in the senior game. He is a tall left-handed pitcher and first baseman, who can hit the ball a long way. He hit the only walk-off home run that I ever recall being associated with. Hawkins sports long hair, straggly when it gets sweat soaked during a game, and a large mustache, both which he allows to grow as the season progresses, and only cuts back after each November's Roy Hobbs World Series.

I am convinced "Hawk" has an ancestor who played major league ball although he claims there is no family lineage. In August 2002, Ann and I visited the Baseball Hall of Fame during the week of the Legends of Baseball Cooperstown tournament. We were in the Hall looking at plaques and came across Charlie "Old Hoss" Radbourne, who had been inducted in 1939. Radbourne's plaque reads, "PROVIDENCE, BOSTON, AND CINCINNATI NATIONAL LEAGUE 1881 TO 1891. GREATEST PITCHER OF ALL 19TH CENTURY PITCHERS. WINNING 1884 PENNANT FOR PROVIDENCE, RADBOURNE PITCHED LAST 27 GAMES OF SEASON, WON 26. WON 3 STRAIGHT WORLD SERIES GAMES."

Although Old Hoss was right handed and considerably shorter (5' 9") than is Hawk (6' 4"), the image on the plaque could have been either of them.

Bob "Hawk" Hawkins and Charlie "Old Hoss" Radbourne

With only about a five-year interruption, when he broke his left arm in a swimming pool accident and needed a plate inserted in the late 1980s, Hawk has been playing baseball all of his 51 years. His father, Ralph, introduced him to the game in their small town of Fremont, Indiana (population less than 1,000). Ralph Hawkins was a local legend. He pitched for the Fremont town baseball team for eight dollars per game or twelve for a doubleheader on Sundays and did bare knuckle boxing on Saturday nights.

Some of Hawk's fondest memories are of his baseball relationship with his dad. His father helped any way he could with Hawk's Little League team. And he threw batting practice to the neighborhood boys almost every day. Ralph would come home from work, take off his tie, and throw for hours in their big back yard. It did not matter that the baseballs were sometimes held together with black electrical tape or that the bats were taped and screwed together when cracked. What mattered is that they were playing baseball, father and son, together.

"Baseball was always part of the family." Bob says. His mother never missed coming to his games and, even into her mid-80s, would travel to see Hawk play senior ball.

He recalls being a hard throwing 12-year-old in Little League and, says jokingly, that he even had some control back then. When Hawk entered high school, he was only five feet tall and weighed 98 pounds. When he graduated, he had grown to his current 6' 4" and went on to play college basketball.

But baseball was his real and lasting love. All through high school, college, and until he experienced that broken arm, he played summer baseball and fast pitch softball on a traveling team sponsored by a local realtor. He played for $100 per week for 12 weeks every summer. Once he was married, he thought about this money as Christmas funds, that extra cash that allowed the family to buy nice presents for each other.

After the five-year hiatus following the broken arm, Hawk's career in the trucking industry led to a transfer to Cincinnati in 1990. He was told of an MSBL league, went to watch a game at the rebuilt Crosley Field, and talked to a manager about getting back into the game. Hawk was given a tryout and became a relief pitcher for the rest of that season. He was back in the game.

Over the next couple of years Hawk was introduced to the Roy

Hobbs organization when he was asked to play on a 40-and-over team at the World Series. Shortly thereafter, he and several of the older players started up a team of their own. Bob's relationship with these players centered on their mutual love of the game, and he recalls that the friendships he made were, at the time, the closest he had ever experienced in his life.

Then misfortune struck. Hawk was in a very serious car accident that threatened his life, and almost led to him losing a leg. He was in the hospital for a month and off of work for a year. During his first few days in the hospital, his doctor told him he thought he could save his leg, but Hawk would likely not be able to use it much and would only be able to walk with crutches.

His teammates came to the hospital nearly every day, as did representatives from the Houston Astros. Years before, Bob had met a Houston scout who introduced him to the head of scouting. A conversation and some training later, Hawk contracted with the Astros to become an "associate scout" with a focus on the Cincinnati area. Bob recalls the constant attention from the Astros and his teammates had a lot to do with his improvement in the hospital.

But when he returned home, he was still disabled by most people's standards, and very discouraged. He then got a call from teammate Pete Coleman, who told Hawk that he intended to pick Bob up and get him to every game the team was playing. The love shown him by Pete and his ability to be with his team led Bob to say later, "That alone gave me the inspiration to get better."

Hawk worked hard on rehab and started coaching the team. His sister Julie, who, like Hawk, loves horses, sent him her horse, Dakota, for Bob to ride. The riding helped him to build his leg muscles needed to maintain his balance on the horse. The leg was getting better beyond what the doctors had predicted.

A team made up of players from his league decided to go to Florida for the November tournament and Hawk went with them to coach. Late in the week, the team was down by a bunch of runs, and asked Hawk if he would like to pitch an inning or two. He decided it was worth a try and, while shaky, did pretty well. Hawk was back.

The core of the Florida team decided that "playing with children their own age" was preferable and, with Hawk's leadership, started what was to become and still is the Cincinnati Colt 45's. The naming of the team was easy. Bob was scouting for the Astros, who had started as the Houston Colt 45's. And the average age of the players who originally talked about putting the team together was 45.

The Colts won their first game that first year and not another for the rest of the season. As Hawk puts it, "Pitching was a problem. We used to say 'If a pitcher couldn't throw 200 pitches in a game, he couldn't be a Colt.'" But the team improved every year, did some recruiting, practiced together in the offseason, and in 2002, won the Roy Hobbs AAA division of the 48-and-over age group. That celebration lasted for a long time.

Bob's love of baseball came full circle in a couple of ways. Hawk was able to see his son, Gordon Tyson "Ty" Hawkins, play catch with his grandfather, Ralph. And Bob has been able to play in baseball games with Ty. The first time that happened, Ty's team in the Cincinnati Recreation Commission 18-and-over league needed pitching. Ty asked Bob if he would like to pitch and Hawk told his son, "Only if you'll catch me."

As they were walking up to the first game, a friend of Ty's, who played for the other team, asked Ty if the older guy that he was walking with was his coach. Ty proudly answered, "That's not our coach; that's our pitcher." Hawk, who was 42 at the time, was feeling pretty good about his son's answer until the other boy asked, "Does he have insurance in case we hurt him?"

Bob Hawkins represents all that is good about baseball. He loves it and plays it with heart. He gives back to the game even more than he gets from it. He is tied to the game by the intergenerational relationships formed with his father and his son. And he plays it with the vigor of his youth. As he says, "I get so excited before games and tournaments that I can't sleep at night just hoping it won't rain so we can play."

What does baseball mean to Hawk? "If you accept the life lessons this game gives you, it will guide you through life. I know no one who has played the game as they've gotten older who's not better off for it."

Hawk is 55 now, and when asked how long he'll play, he answered, "They'll bury me with my baseball glove."

Greenie

At 50, Scott Green is working to change careers. Over 26 years, he has built a very successful landscaping business that specializes in masonry work. Yet he is getting ready to move on. Toward what new career area is he moving? Baseball.

"Greenie" developed his passion for baseball on the streets of Queens in New York City and at Yankee Stadium. His father introduced him to the game and he remembers, as a five year old, playing catch and taking batting practice with his dad using their garage as a backstop.

While space to play baseball was limited, the boys in the streets of Queens had two things going for them. One was access to plenty of players. Every boy in the densely populated neighborhood knew when and where to be to get a game started. The other thing was stickball.

As noted on *Streetplay.com*, "With only a broom handle, a rubber ball, a bunch of guys, and a street, you can engage in a full scale, bona fide, serious, respectable game similar in feel to classic baseball. And talk about a field. Who can beat manhole covers for bases, cars and walls for foul lines, roofs for bleachers, and the fire escapes—the mezzanine?"

How many New Yorkers began to learn their baseball fundamentals playing stickball? One was Scott Green.

His father was a "tremendous baseball enthusiast" and an avid Cardinal fan, having kept scrapbooks from the Redbird teams of the 1940s. His father got tickets to Yankee Stadium as frequently as he could and took Scott to games. They shared the thrill of seeing Roger Maris hit number 61. And they saw game four of the 1964 World Series, in which Kenny Boyer hit a fifth-inning grand slam with his Cardinal team down two games to one in the series and three runs to none in the game.

The Cardinals and their ace, Bob Gibson, went on to win the seven-game series. From the time of that series, Greenie chose to follow in his father's footsteps, and has been an avid Cardinal fan ever since. This was not an easy thing to do for a youngster from Queens, a cornerstone of New York baseball team fanaticism.

At age 13, Scott moved to Florida with his mom after his parents divorced. While in Florida, his mom remarried, and he was fortunate to have a step father, Manny, who loved Scott and baseball. And Manny had a son, Adam, who instantly became more than Scott's brother—he became his life partner. The brothers are bonded by family and baseball—playing together to this day.

After high school he continued to be a fan of baseball but moved away from playing it. He enjoyed his tennis playing and went on to become a teaching pro. And he began playing softball, primarily fast and modified-fast pitch. It was two softball friends, Butch Cavuto and Paul Vargo, who told Greenie, then in his mid-40s, about the Legends of Baseball Cooperstown tournaments. He decided to give it a try, fell back in love with playing the game, and has not been away from it since.

He quickly recognized that he was learning a lot, just by observing, about what it would take to run a successful tournament. The decision was simple. Greenie chose to immerse himself in the game by starting Play at the Plate while still continuing to play. Since then he has been running tournaments, and is also developing the capability to conduct fantasy camps. And he envisions playing competitively until he is at least 60.

As Green reflects on his return to baseball and why he loves the game so much, he attributes it to a number of things. Not surprisingly, his reasons are the same as they are for many of us. He views it as a wholesome escape from the every day world. This was important to him when he was young and remains so today. He revels in the camaraderie. The stickball games with the neighborhood boys run together with the games with his senior baseball friends.

Greenie takes personal satisfaction in working at something that is difficult and being rewarded with noticeable and continual improvement. This has been true of his baseball playing and now his baseball business. And perhaps his most meaningful reason to love baseball is the combination of the memories of his baseball relationships with his father and stepfather, and the baseball relationship he has with his son, Ian, who plays in the Play at the Plate tournaments.

As baseball has become increasingly more a part of his life, it has made Greenie very happy. Why not? As he says, "I live for baseball."

Cal

Dr. Joe Caligaris is a 50-year-old, mustachioed, big bear of a man—as gentle as they come. In his spare time between playing, coaching, and watching baseball games, going to coaches' meetings, making calls to line up umpires and fields, and rounding up teams to go to a tournament, "Cal" is husband, father, civil war buff, baseball memorabilia collector, and an OB/GYN in solo practice—on call 24/7. Despite being so busy, Cal always has time for a smooth drink, a fine cigar, a great meal, and, most of all, his friends.

Cal grew up with baseball in Massachusetts, having been introduced to the game by his father, who loved and played it. By age five, Joe, his friend, John Shanahan, and his brother, Dave, had set up a field in their cul-de-sac and were playing for hours on end. They moved on to Little League with a Caligaris battery, Dave the pitcher and Joe the catcher. They had a great team, falling one win short of going to the regional tournament one year when they lost in the state finals.

But Little League was not enough baseball for Cal and his friends. There was a large field in the neighborhood, but the grass was high. One day, they took lawn mowers and cut down the foot-high grass, set up bases, and began to play. From then on, only his mom ringing a bell would disrupt the game and bring Cal home for dinner. The lot was not finely groomed and there was no corn serving as an outfield fence, but it was his field of dreams.

In high school, Cal and his brother chose different sports. He concentrated on football and baseball, while brother Dave focused on tennis and basketball. Dave went on to play basketball at Northeastern University in Boston, where he set scoring records, and was known as "the greatest pure shooter in the history" of the school. He was drafted by the Detroit Pistons in the fifth round, but, not making the roster, followed his family heritage and moved on to play professionally in Greece for several years.

Cal went on to play both football and baseball at Amherst University, and did so through his junior year, when he was seriously injured in a football game. He sustained a fracture in the C1-C2 vertebrae, commonly known as the "hangman's injury." Cal was lucky, however, in that no paralysis resulted—this is the same injury that paralyzed Christopher Reeve.

With sports behind him for the time being, he focused on his undergraduate degree, medical school, internships, and his residency. Not until he was working in Cincinnati in 1992 was Cal reintroduced to baseball. A friend and fellow physician, Dr. Mike Leadbetter, called Cal's wife, Karen, saying he was putting a baseball tournament team together and had heard Cal had played some ball. He asked Karen to talk Cal into playing—she did.

It was Clearwater that year and the Roy Hobbs World Series in Fort Myers the next. Cal was hooked. By 1994, Cal joined Leadbetter in forming the Cincinnati Astros, a team that for more than a decade has been highly competitive in both leagues and tournaments. The team was the focus of Mike Shannon's book, *Coming Back to Baseball: the Cincinnati Astros and the Joys of Over-30 Play.*

As the Astros were forming, Leadbetter and Cal attended the local MSBL coaches' meetings. The league was struggling financially and looking for new direction. Behind the scenes and unbeknownst to Cal, Leadbetter lobbied for Cal to take over league leadership. At one meeting, nominations were opened for league president. Before Cal knew it, he was nominated, seconded, and unanimously elected.

Gladly taking on the challenge, Cal has been running the league ever since. Over the years, the league moved from MSBL to Roy Hobbs to be more consistent with the number of players who were attending the Hobbs World Series each year.

Under his leadership, the league has flourished. Cal is a master at building relationships. As a result, local field managers made more and better fields available. And the teams worked together to put the league back on sound financial footing.

Cal dedicates more than his time to baseball. He is financially invested as well. Cal manages and financially supports two teams. One is an 18-and-over team that plays in the Cincinnati Recreation Commission league. The other is a 28-and-over Roy Hobbs team. While he asks the players to pay a nominal fee, Cal covers a significant portion of the overall cost.

In addition, he has now invested in Scott Green's Play at the Plate organization and looks forward to being part of seeing Greenie's business plan play out. Cal is also looking for other senior baseball investments. His plan is to make baseball a focus of his eventual retirement from his medical practice.

Why does Joe Caligaris spend his money and scarce time dedicating himself to playing, leading, coaching, sponsoring, and investing in senior baseball? Cal says that he fundamentally loves the game and wants to be near it now just as he was in the cul-de-sac, on the Little League field, and in the hay-mowed field behind the house. He loves the guys with whom he plays and cherishes the relationships he has built with them.

And Cal views baseball as a stress reliever. His medical practice keeps him constantly on the go. The few hours he is on the ball diamond are stress free. His trips to tournaments are the best of vacations. He and Karen use baseball as a recreation—a reason to be with close friends. It has become a way of life. "It just feels good."

Cal's plan is to play as long as he can. This was challenged recently when he severely dislocated his elbow. But, despite pain and a loss of range of motion, he was back playing as quickly as possible. Cal needs senior baseball and senior baseball needs him.

Man of Good Cheer

John Gilmore's baseball experience may be the most diverse of any in senior baseball. His playing career through college was extensive, but consistent with that of many players. He grew up in Hazlet, New Jersey. His father was a baseball fan, listening to games on the radio. His mother played first base for the Con Edison women's softball team and was an avid Brooklyn Dodger fan.

Gilmore, his two brothers, and neighborhood friends played ball in the street. Home plate was right in front of the Gilmore house and sewers were perfectly located to simulate bases. Because cars and houses were in close proximity to their "field," they played with a rubber baseball purchased at Sears. The experience with the rubber ball would, years later, make him comfortable playing against Japanese teams that use a rubberized ball.

Organized ball took him through Little League, high school at Christian Brothers Academy, and a short stint at Georgia Tech. At the time, Georgia Tech was not yet in the Atlantic Coast Conference, nor did they have a well-developed baseball program—the baseball team had only one scholarship that was being split between two players. Despite loving the game, Gilmore chose to focus on his education and dropped out of baseball for the time being.

In his early-30s and working in Atlanta, Gilmore heard about an MSBL tryout. He attended and has been involved with senior baseball ever since. He played in his MSBL league games and got involved in the early years of the Legends of Baseball Cooperstown events. One of those years, Gilmore was among a number of men who contributed to a fund that bought tarps for Doubleday field. They are recognized on a plaque at the field, being referred to as "Men of Good Cheer."

Shortly thereafter, Gilmore's senior baseball career became more diverse. In 1990, he saw an advertisement in *The Sporting News* asking for men who had played some college baseball to sign up for a trip to Russia to play against local teams. He joined the trip on which they played 17 games over 21 days in Moscow against teams in the Russian Baseball Federation.

Within the next couple of years, Gilmore was traveling to Russia on business, met players against whom he had played, recognized the need they had for equipment, and began bringing some with him on every trip. In 1994, he was asked by one of the teams, the Moscow Red Devils, to bring a team over to play. The Russian league oscillated between having only eight and ten teams each year, and they were looking for some variety in their competition.

Gilmore put the word out and recruited two teams, each of which would be in Moscow 11 days. Gilmore stayed through the entire time and played 18 games in 22 days. The trip was a success—Gilmore recruited teams for the following year with some players returning. To make the trip more attractive to returning players, he added baseball games in St. Petersburg. The third year, the teams stopped in Amsterdam and added games in Ukraine.

These early trips were the basis upon which John Gilmore's Baseball International was founded. Since then, he has been organizing and leading baseball, sightseeing, and equipment-donation trips all over the world. He is the consummate international baseball ambassador.

As part of his Baseball International calendar, Gilmore runs his annual January tournament. The original intent was to bring international players to play in the United States. The concept was beginning to take hold when 9/11 happened, making it very difficult for foreign players to get the necessary paperwork to make the trip.

Most recently, Gilmore's diverse baseball career added another international component. He became the Cincinnati Reds scout for Asia. Over the years, not only has Gilmore led baseball trips to Asia, but he has traveled there extensively on business. As he has, he has become deeply interested in the baseball programs in many countries, starting with Japan. Because he had developed the expertise and many contacts, he was approached by the Reds to take on the scouting position.

From his years as a skinny shortstop on the streets of Hazlet, New Jersey, John Gilmore has played around the world. For much of the international baseball community, he is the face of American baseball and we should be proud to have him represent us.

John is currently hampered by the remnants of a back problem. While that has gotten in the way of continuing to play, it has not kept him out of the game he loves nor deterred him from his mission to improve baseball programs around the world.

A Hole in the Lineup

These four characters well represent the senior baseball players around the country. Their personal histories and what they give to the game help tell the story of senior baseball.

It would be remiss, however, to pay tribute to senior baseball's characters, without recognizing those who have passed away. One of the giants of senior men's baseball was Bob Wagner, who, in 1997, founded the Wooden Bat Classic, and now for whom it is named. Bob died in 2001 but his senior baseball legacy lives on. When you hear Bob Wagner's name mentioned near anyone who knew and played with him, a smile is not far behind.

I had the privilege of meeting and playing against Sandy Scharf. He and his brother, Marty, were on the Baseball International trip to Beijing in May 2002. Sandy Scharf idolized Sandy Koufax. He wore Koufax's number 32 on his Dodger-replica uniform. Scharf, like Koufax, was both a left-handed pitcher and Jewish. While Scharf was a little short of Koufax's speed, maybe 30 to 40 miles per hour slower, he was not short of Koufax in heart, and that is saying something. Sandy and Marty were two of only three people (Rob Bohn was the other) on the China trip that traversed, while running most of the way, the Great Wall segment that we visited, overcoming the incredibly steep and uneven steps for about three miles. What is most amazing is that Sandy came on the trip, played ball, ran the great wall, played in a subsequent Cooperstown tournament, and kept an outwardly impressive attitude on life, even while he was in the middle of a battle with cancer. In September 2005, Sandy Scharf lost the battle and was buried in his #32 Dodgers uniform.

You already know about Roy Yocum. And sadly, among tens of thousands of senior players, there are losses like this every year across the country.

The losses are not limited to American players. A future senior player in Russia, Vladimir Muratov, was tragically killed in Moscow in 2004. Vladimir's father, Sasha, is well known in parts of the American senior baseball community, having played in the Bob Wagner Wooden Bat Classic, Baseball International's Spring Training Tournament, and Legend of Baseball's Cooperstown Tournament. Some of us played and partied with Sasha and both of his sons, Vladimir and Andrei, on Baseball International trips to Russia. Upon learning of Vladimir's death, Ted Simendinger's No Bats Baseball Club provided the funds to erect a memorial to Vladimir in Cal Ripken, Sr.'s yard in Aberdeen, Maryland. The senior baseball family extends well beyond our country's borders.

I am convinced that baseball made Bob Wagner's, Sandy Scharf's, Roy Yocum's, and Vladimir Muratov's lives more fulfilling. But each of them and the other senior players whom we have lost, leave a hole in the lineup that can never be filled.

LOSING A STEP

> *"Put the right pitching mechanics together with good health,
> and there's nothing surprising about lasting a long time."*
> Nolan Ryan

> *"It is not strange that desire should
> so many years outlive performance."*
> William Shakespeare

Al: "I think I've about had it. JR's coming in for me to finish it up. I'm pretty sore."

JR: "I'll go warm up. I'm glad my knee rehabbed pretty well. I'm ready to go."

Jack: "I'm not sure there are any of us senior citizens who doesn't have something that's hurting. But we do a pretty good job of living with it."

Ken: "I'm not sore; I'm numb."

Jack: "Tough it out. We're up two and if we win this, we have a good shot at a high seed going into the weekend."

Al: "Remember when we used to come down to the tournament with 12 guys until we realized the week was a war of attrition. Now that we're bringing 15 or more, we have a better chance of fielding a *reasonably healthy team by the end of the week."*

Ken: *"Yeah, growing old sucks, but growing old playing baseball is heaven."*

The Walking Wounded

As I am beginning to write this inning, it is November 5, 2005, and I am fortunate to be sitting under palm trees at the swimming pool just outside of the condominium Ann and I are renting in Fort Myers. It is a classically beautiful southwest Florida day, about 80°, 10 mph breezes rattling the palm fronds, and an SPF 45 sun. Having lost a great baseball game two to nothing, we are eliminated from the 38-and-over AAAA wooden bat division of the Roy Hobbs World Series. Tomorrow, I will join a different team to start the 48-and-over division tournament.

While disappointed to be out of the tournament, we are taking full advantage of the baseball day off. I am relaxing and taking frequent dips in the hot tub, generally working on reducing the soreness that results from the combination of playing two doubleheaders in the last two days, being nearly 60 years old, and experiencing the very early stages of osteoarthritis in both hips.

It is also a day of reflection. I am so fortunate to be enjoying my retirement life with Ann, and to be still playing the game I love with her full participation and support. It is also time to reflect on my concern that the arthritis will, at some point, limit my capabilities and the number of my baseball-playing years. Any senior player, who allows himself to be introspective, will at some time be thinking about the physical aspects of playing and getting older at the same time.

This past week, I was fortunate to play on a very good team, the Cincinnati C-Hawks, which had 15 players on the roster. We had strong pitching with nearly flawless defense and hit the ball pretty consistently. When we lost, it was to a better team on that day. Our team, however, likely typical of most senior baseball teams, was dealing with a number of current and recent injuries and rehabilitation issues.

Andy Poli is a bailiff in the Hamilton County, Ohio, court system and the baseball coach at Summit Country Day School in Cincinnati. In his first at bat in the tournament, he was running to beat out a ground ball, caught his spikes, and tumbled over the first base bag, landing on his right (throwing) shoulder. The shoulder was separated and needed to be treated in the local trauma center. Andy showed up to the next day's game in a sling and, remarkably, by game three, with the help of strong painkillers, was able to bat. Fighting through pain and using virtually only his left arm, he hit well and with power for the rest of the tournament.

John "JR" Reed is a landscaper, who lives in Loxahatchee, Florida. He is recovering from reconstructive knee surgery that repaired an injury incurred in a tournament last year. While JR joined us in a Palm Beach tournament in October, he chose to sit out this week to help his knee recover. The decision was made simpler when Hurricane Wilma blew through his area, knocked out his electricity, tore shingles off his roof, and devastated his extensive foliage. He was spending the week in cleanup and finally got the power back to the house on Thursday, 11 days after the storm.

You met Joe "Doc" Caligaris, one of the characters of senior baseball. Doc dislocated his left elbow in the October Play at the Plate tournament and was unable to play this past week. However, because he loves the camaraderie of the tournaments, he came to Fort Myers to be our full-time manager for the week. And we helped him celebrate his 50th birthday at "Deuseldorf's on the Beach."

Rob Lambert is an emergency room physician at Clermont Mercy Hospital in Batavia, Ohio. He came to the tournament having a torn anterior cruciate ligament (ACL), a partially torn posterior cruciate ligament (PCL), and other strains in his knee. He played the tournament in a rugged brace, doing a great job at the plate, on the mound, and in the field. He is trying to find the right time to have the corrective surgery done to minimize his time away from the game.

Gene "Geno" Rueckert is a building and remodeling contractor in Cincinnati. He has a chronic shoulder problem. His shoulder has been operated on in the past and is again causing him pain. It is limiting his throwing strength although he continues to hit well and play some first and second base. He believes, based on past experience, that the problem is a tear in the labrum and, like Rob, is trying to find the right time for the surgery to minimize his loss of playing time to recover from the operation and allow for rehabilitation.

Tedd Schaffer is a Firefighter–Paramedic with the Cincinnati Fire Department as well as a small-business owner. For the first time since breaking his foot while running the bases in the Bob Wagner Wooden Bat Classic ten months earlier, he is ready to play regularly. The injury was an acute fracture to his metatarsal #5 of the left foot caused by a pre-existing, but unknown, stress fracture. While Schaffer is healthy enough to play, he is still less than 100% as the injury prevented him from working out at his normal frequency and intensity prior to the tournament.

Basically, 6 of 15 players on the roster, were either playing with, prevented from playing because of, or just returning to full form from a serious injury. This may be an unusual percentage of players with injuries, but perhaps not. During the tournament, Ann and I had dinner with six players from the team with which I previously played, the Cincinnati Colts. Among the six was Greg Bauman, who had pulled a quadriceps muscle and split a finger while playing this week. He was planning to sit out the first few days of next week's tournament, hoping to be able to play later in the week. Roy Wimmers had just completed a year of rehabilitation after shoulder surgery in which both a rotator cuff and labrum tear were repaired. Unfortunately, Roy was also nursing an undiagnosed knee problem, which he believes will need arthroscopic surgery after the tournament. And Gary Hester was playing this week after having just had arthroscopic surgery on his knee only three weeks before. Not long after the tournament, Gary chose to retire from senior baseball, not wanting to risk further injury and longer-term knee disability.

One would hope that the high percentage of injured players in these two groups is unusual. Regardless of the percentage, it clearly is not uncommon for injuries, like the ones with which these players were dealing, to occur. Add to these more serious injuries a long list of minor issues from muscle soreness to blisters, from sunburn to sprains, from bruises to joint soreness, and there is an emerging profile of the life of the senior player. My intent here is not to cause undue concern about playing senior baseball. Rather, it is to help acknowledge our reality and propose that each of us can understand what we can do to help prevent injuries and to recover from them as quickly and safely as possible.

You may be among the younger senior players who have never had an injury. If you really love the game and you probably do, you have the opportunity to play it for a long time. In doing so, there are two things to consider as you continue reading this inning. First, injuries are not restricted to the older of senior players. Second, while it may be hard for you to relate to now, you will, at some point, be facing the reality of the physiological changes that come with aging. You are in the best position to take steps to mitigate their effects because you can start taking action now to help prevent injuries as you grow older.

Be Careful Ironing

Injuries are certainly not confined only to the field of play. Gene Coleman, the strength and conditioning coach for the Houston Astros, in his book, *52-Week Baseball Training*, refers to the high cost in major league team performance and dollars of lost playing time resulting from injuries—especially as it relates to shoulder inflammation, tendonitis, or strain. Teams are developing programs to help reduce these and other types of costly injuries. He notes, however, that with all of the managers, coaches, team physicians, trainers, and conditioning coaches, there are some injuries that could not be prevented by the team. Here is Coleman's top ten list of weird injuries.

1. John Smoltz burned his chest while ironing a shirt he was wearing.
2. Wade Boggs hurt his back when he lost his balance while trying to put on cowboy boots.
3. Odiebe McDowell cut his finger buttering a roll at the Texas Rangers' welcome home luncheon.
4. Ricky Bones hurt his lower back getting out of a chair while watching TV in the clubhouse.
5. Kevin Mitchell strained a muscle while vomiting.
6. George Brett hit his foot on a chair and broke his toe while running from the kitchen to the TV to see Bill Buckner hit.
7. Rick Honeycutt injured his wrist while flicking sunflower seeds in the dugout.
8. Chris Brown injured his eye sleeping on his eye wrong.

9. Phil Niekro injured his hand shaking hands too hard.
10. Nolan Ryan was bitten by a coyote.

Playing with Children My Own Age

A reality of senior baseball is that, despite our passion for the game and our desire to play forever, we are getting older. With that comes a range of issues we need to work to prevent, resolve, compensate for, or ignore. Just as one example, according to Dr. Carl Nissen, Orthopedic Surgeon with a Sports Medicine specialty at the University of Connecticut, approximately one-third of people, by age 60, have some disability that affects walking ability. In my case, my lower body range of motion has been decreased by the minor arthritis in my hips and, depending on a number of factors, it sometimes affects my walking gait. But once I warm up and get into a game, the soreness that I sometimes experience just walking on a daily basis is not as pronounced. I am sure that, combined with the normal aging process, the reduced range of motion has caused me to lose a step or two or more on the bases and range in the field.

To be clear, however, I never was the fastest runner around. My dad had two phrases he frequently used to describe my speed or lack thereof. He would say that I led the league in stretching triples into doubles and doubles into singles. He also would tell me, "You run like a water fountain—a whole lot but all in one place." My speed could perhaps best be compared to that of Mike Scioscia, the long-time Dodger catcher and now manager of the Los Angeles Angels. Scioscia's former manager, Tom Lasorda, said of his speed, "If he raced his pregnant wife, he'd finish third."

Relative to speed, there is an interesting phenomenon that occurs as we progress through senior baseball's age divisions. Perhaps it can be called most appropriately the "Slow Down Together" syndrome. As we age, we lose speed from base to base, we lose quickness in the field, we lose arm strength, and we lose bat speed. The 85–90 mph fastball we faced in high school and college is now 70–75 mph with only an occasional pitcher still in the range of 80. The throw from the catcher to second base is neither released as quickly nor rocketed on as sharp a line. The outfielders do not cover the gap as adroitly nor make the solid one-bounce throw to the base.

Both the bad news and the good news is that this is happening, to varying degrees, to all of us together. Because of the "Slow Down

Together" syndrome, it feels when we are in the middle of the game, we are playing at the speed we did when we were younger.

Earlier I shared Red Smith's quotation, "Ninety feet between home plate and first base may be the closest man has ever come to perfection." We no longer get down the line in four and a half to five seconds—if we ever did. But our arms in the infield are no longer as strong either. The plays are still, therefore, cleanly made and are close at first. When we hit a ball in the gap, it does not go as far, and our time from home to second is longer. But the outfielders are slower to the ball, and their arms are not as strong as they once were. So, we can still get our double or be thrown out on a close play at second.

Those watching senior baseball see a game that is still competitive and in which the timing of plays is still exciting. But they also, especially if watching it for the first time after seeing games of younger players, can clearly notice the difference. My St. Louis high school friends, Ron and Elaine Unell, were in the Cooperstown area in August 2004, on their way to visit their daughter, when I was playing in a Legends of Baseball tournament. They planned to stop by to watch a game and have dinner with us. After the game, Ron noted that the speed of the game was slow, but that he was really impressed with the quality of play and the balance of speed and strength that kept the game exciting. He had independently verified the existence of the "Slow Down Together" syndrome.

So it seems our speed, flexibility, reflexes, strength, and quickness change in relation to each other. That is the beauty of senior baseball and age-group divisions. While I am proud to still be capable to compete in 30-and-older leagues and tournaments, there is a certain degree of comfort when I am playing with children my own age.

"Your body...says stop."

In his book, *Extra Innings—A Season in the Senior League*, David Whitford describes the first and only full season (1989) of a professional league comprised of ex-major leaguers, some in their late 30s, most in their 40s. By most amateur senior player standards, these men were in shape and relatively young. Yet even they had to deal with the realities of aging. Here is a telling excerpt from Whitford's book.

The season was less than one week old and already the sentimental veneer was beginning to wear thin. Injuries were piling up, mainly pulled hamstrings, 'the official injury of the senior league.' In the locker room before and after the games, the constant traffic in and out of the whirlpool was a daily reminder of age and limits. "Our mind says yes," said Bill Madlock, "but your body snaps you in the ass, says stop."

Many of us continuing to play baseball at older ages are in better shape than our non-playing counterparts. But it is not uncommon to see bellies hanging over belts. It is prevalent at fantasy camps and some tournaments to have pinch runners for older players, those with infirmities, and those who have been injured earlier in the week. And all of us at some point, despite wanting to play the game forever, will decide we just cannot play any longer because of a chronic condition of some sort.

George Goodall tells a great fantasy-camp-running story that occurred at Busch Stadium in St. Louis. He was 80 at the time and had begun to need a pinch runner, even from home plate. It is typically allowed, for those who need it, to have someone run for them from home plate when the ball is struck. George hit a ball down the left field line and his pinch runner circled the bases for an inside-the-park home run. Everyone congratulated George on his hit. His response was, "Anyone can get a hit, but did you see my speed on the bases?" Despite George's well intentioned humor, the reality was that his body had said, "Stop." He was no longer able to run the bases.

But George did not let that keep him from continuing to play. At that same camp, in his game against the ex-professionals, George batted against John Tudor, the left-hander who pitched most of his career with the Red Sox and Cardinals in the 1980s. After the first two men in the lineup made outs, George came up and lined a hit over the shortstop's head. Tudor later told everyone that it must be time for him to hang it up if he's giving up line drives to 80-year-olds.

Losing a step does not mean losing the ability to play. Evidence George Goodall, who, at 94 was still taking the field. Evidence Ed Berkich, who, in his 70s still catches every inning of every game of a tournament. Evidence Bill Smith, who, in his mid-60s, is playing an average of almost a tournament per month. Evidence William "Doc"

Pollak who, into his 70s still pitches effectively in the 38-and-over division and, in 2004, got what he believes to have been his 1,000th baseball career win. The list goes on and is getting longer.

This inning will address what these gentlemen and thousands like them are dealing with currently or can expect to deal with as they experience playing baseball and growing older at the same time. The intent is not to provide a definitive reference book on the subject. Many of those have been wonderfully written and are readily available. Rather, my intent is to provide a framework for thinking about and acting upon the range of physical issues senior baseball players might need to address.

I am not a physician, sports medicine expert, nor a trainer. So the information in this inning was developed from many sources, interviews with medical and fitness professionals, credible and publicly available studies, my personal experience, and that of other senior players. You can find some of the references I have used embedded in the inning and others listed at the end of the inning. Those professionals who were kind enough to lend their expertise are noted on the Acknowledgements page.

While I hope this inning is a helpful framework, the best thing for each of us is to consider our individual circumstances, learn more about what we can and should be doing to prevent or address any issues, and, when necessary, consult with a professional. In this way, we should be able to best achieve what most senior players have as objectives: continue to play the game we love, play it as well as we can, and continue to enjoy it—as long as we can. If we approach our health and fitness properly, despite losing a step, we will never be too old to play the game.

We are Getting Older

Why is it that we lose speed, strength, flexibility, quickness, endurance, and overall performance on the field? The easy answer is we are getting older. The more detailed physiological answers are relatively well known and somewhat intuitive. A number of things happen to us as we age, most which begin when we are young. By various amounts and rates, we lose muscle mass, cardiovascular function, aerobic capacity, flexibility, and visual acuity. While we cannot fully offset the effects of aging, we can, by taking the appropriate actions, help mitigate those effects to lengthen our playing years and make them of higher quality. And these steps will positively affect our general quality of life as well.

Many of the studies used to establish the science of aging effects are conducted on elite athletes. As proud as seniors are to still be playing, it is clear from participating or watching us that we are not, and likely never were, elite athletes. But the elite athlete studies can give us insights about our own physiology and performance, as well as what we can do to offset aging losses.

What are the relevant effects of aging were we not to take steps to offset them?

We will lose 40% of our muscle mass after age 20. Muscle strength affects every part of our game, from speed on the bases to bat speed, from speed to the ball defensively to throwing velocity.

We will lose about 10% of our aerobic capacity per decade after age 25. While baseball is not generally thought of as an endurance sport requiring great cardiovascular function and aerobic capacity, each of these factors affects the senior player both on and off the field. As aerobic capacity decreases, senior players will tend to move more slowly during games and will likely exercise less between games. As we age, it takes an increasing percentage of our aerobic capacity just to do common things like climb stairs or do chores. It will also become increasingly difficult to maintain the ability to run the bases or move defensively to a batted ball as we once did. The effect is then magnified when playing in multi-game tournaments.

Our maximum heart rate will decrease on average by one beat per year after age ten. The decrease of cardiovascular function, specifically maximal cardiac output, is a primary contributor to the reduction of aerobic capacity.

Other aging factors may affect senior players.

- Range of motion and flexibility of joints will decrease with aging.
- Joints stiffness will increase, thereby acting as less effective shock absorbers.
- Aging will have an adverse effect on the cartilage that covers the ends of bones and enables them to move smoothly over one another. Therefore, joint disease or osteoarthritis can occur more frequently.

- By the age of 50, most of us will experience a change in vision, which will negatively affect sharpness and focusing power. These changes may cause a decreased ability to differentiate colors and contrasts, a difficulty judging distances, and an increased sensitivity to glare.
- The incident rate of rotator cuff and Achilles tendon injuries increases after age 40 and 30, respectively.
- Previously existing conditions that may not have been causing problems may manifest themselves as other changes occur in the body.

Bummer. As a reminder, the intent of this information is not to send us all into a deep depression, jump off a bridge without, or even with, a bungee cord, or cause us to stop playing baseball. It is rather to recognize reality so that we can deal with it as best we can. In that regard, we will take a more detailed look into these aging effects with a focus on how to best help mitigate them.

Managing Strength Losses

It is a given that we will progressively lose muscle mass and, therefore, strength. There are three options we have to deal with this inevitability. We can choose to ignore the reality, do nothing, and attempt to keep playing the way we always have. We can be aware of our changing bodies and make adjustments in our game to compensate for the strength differences. Or, finally, we can elect to engage in strength training to help mitigate the losses. There is certainly nothing wrong with any of these choices as it is an individual matter depending on a wide range of factors. My choice has been to be very aware of the changes and do two things: adjust my game to compensate and engage in strength training.

Many may choose not to do strength training because they have neither the time nor the inclination. The result of that choice will be about a 10% muscle mass loss by age 50 and another 30% at an increasing rate by age 80. As this occurs, we should expect to lose arm strength, bat speed, and running speed. Depending on our age and the quality of the league and tournaments we play in, these losses may not, at least initially, substantially affect our competitiveness or the enjoyment we derive from the game. In that case, a choice not to strength train may be right for you.

We can also choose to not engage in strength training but, at the same time, find ways to compensate for reduced muscle mass. Here are some examples of what I mean by compensating for the loss.

- Do not play as deep at shortstop or third base. This may prevent you from getting to as many ground balls, but you will be more likely to make a good, sharp throw to first base.
- Become a first baseman, where range and arm strength are less critical.
- Stop playing catcher where arm and leg strength are required to throw out base- stealers and just to make it through games and tournaments.
- Play in age group tournaments so the "Slow Down Together" syndrome can apply.
- Recognize that you have lost some foot speed and choose to steal bases or take extra bases in more restricted situations.
- Realize that the fastball that you used to throw by batters is no longer your out pitch. Work on throwing strikes, spotting the ball, and changing speeds. While these are important principles to pitching in general, they are even more critical to the senior pitcher. Pitching speed is perhaps the most evident difference I have seen in senior baseball. While there are still a few pitchers in their 30s or even early 40s who can dominate a game with speed, they are rare. The good senior pitchers walk very few batters and maximize easy ground balls and popups by keeping batters off balance.

Aging Gracefully

The remaining choice we have requires a commitment beyond the baseball field. It is a choice that should be considered whether we intend to begin or continue to play baseball or any other sport. The choice is strength training. As a reminder, I am not advocating nor even discussing bodybuilding. My intent is not to become the next Mr. Universe. It is to advocate for and discuss weight training to mitigate the aging related losses of muscle mass and to improve the overall quality of life and the longevity and quality of the baseball career.

In an interview posted on the *Men's Health Magazine* online site in March 2005, Albert Pujols, All-Star first baseman for the St. Louis Cardinals, talked about how he approaches the game. While certainly Pujols is blessed with a special combination of physique, reflexes, and temperament, he also works very hard at his craft and his fitness. In that interview, Pujols said, "I'd love to play this game for twenty years, and the only way I can do that is to take care of my body. That means lifting, lifting, lifting. I hit each part of my body twice a week and do at least two days of cardio a week. But I don't want to get too big, where I feel like my body's too tight. The only way you're going to perform is if your body is loose and flexible. I stretch for at least ten minutes before and after a workout..."

Extensive research about weightlifting is available. My objective is merely to provide rationale for the importance of strength training and some simple guidelines. The most straightforward summary of the benefits of strength training I have found comes from The Longfellow Clubs, a fitness and recreation organization that addresses the balance of mind, body, and spirit. Their benefits list captures the effects on life in general, but can be applied readily to the needs of senior baseball players. Not every possible benefit that can be derived from strength training is listed, but the list is compelling in itself.

1. Increased metabolic rate causing the body to burn more calories throughout the day
2. Increased and restored bone density to help prevent osteoporosis—yes, men get osteoporosis as we lose bone density as do women, but we happen to start with a higher level
3. Increased lean muscle mass and, thus strength, power, and endurance
4. Injury prevention
5. Improved balance, flexibility, mobility, and stability
6. Decreased risk of coronary disease by decreased cholesterol and blood pressure and by other affiliated benefits
7. Enhanced injury rehabilitation and recovery by strengthening muscles surrounding an injured area, quickening the healing process
8. Enhanced performance in sports and exercise
9. Aging gracefully by enabling full participation longer

10. Feeling better and looking better, including improved self-esteem and self-confidence

I am sure The Longfellow Clubs will not mind if I add one more benefit that I learned from the book, *Strong Women and Men Beat Arthritis,* written by colleagues at The John Hancock Center for Physical Activity and Nutrition of the Friedman School of Nutrition Science and Policy at Tufts University. The book is a plain-spoken report on the results of a study on managing arthritis. One of the its conclusions is that those who followed a simple at-home strength training program "had a 43 percent reduction in pain, a 44 percent improvement in physical function, and a 71 percent increase in muscle strength." Furthermore, the subjects of the arthritis study "also experienced a reduction in depression and a big boost in self-esteem and self-confidence." Strength training clearly provides a long list of benefits.

Perhaps you are wondering whether weight training can really provide the noted benefits even if you are older and even if you are already exercising a lot, for example, running or swimming or playing baseball. There are a number of studies that have been done across age groups that have definitively answered this question. Strength training will help you build muscle mass regardless of how old you are when you start. And it will do so where aerobic exercising by itself will not.

Assuming the benefits are compelling to you and you have the time and willingness to begin a strength-training regimen, you can find guidelines in the "Fitness Guidelines" section of this book in "Extra Innings."

"...he's wearing my clothes..."

There is a Nike poster which may state the best motivation for an older athlete to keep training: "He's soft and he's fat and he's wearing my clothes and he's getting too old and he was born on my birthday and I'm afraid if I stop running, he'll catch up with me."

Aerobic training for the senior baseball player is not about becoming Lance Armstrong, who has an aerobic capacity 20% higher than even the world's elite endurance athletes. It is not about becoming a marathon runner, although I have played baseball with some who do run marathons. It is not about training to participate in a triathlon, swimming over two miles, biking over 100 miles, and running a marathon. Rather aerobic training for the senior athlete is about improving the overall quality of life as well as improving the ongoing baseball experience.

The benefits for aerobic training, like those of strength training, are many. This list is borrowed from "The Exercise and Physical Fitness Page" of the Georgia State University web site. Aerobic training can help in the following ways.

1. Increase maximum oxygen consumption (VO_{2max})
2. Improve cardiovascular and respiratory function
   a. Increase blood pumped per minute
   b. Increase blood pumped per heart beat
   c. Increase blood flow and ability to carry oxygen
   d. Reduce workload on the heart for any level of exercise intensity
3. Lower blood pressure in people with high blood pressure
4. Increase HDL cholesterol (the good cholesterol)
5. Decrease blood triglycerides
6. Reduce body fat and improve weight control

Even though baseball is not considered an aerobic sport, this list is clearly relevant for senior players. Aerobic training affects general health, which, in turn, affects the quality and longevity of playing careers. But it also directly affects playing capacity. For example, a higher aerobic capacity enables us to maintain body temperature with less sweating, thereby helping offset dehydration risks. Said another way, more aerobically fit players will cope with the heat stress of playing all day in the sun. We will deal with dehydration in more detail later in this inning.

Similar to the effects of strength training on muscle mass, the research is clear about the positive effects of training on aerobic capacity. Both training regimens, while not fully eliminating the results of aging, have shown to reduce the effects. Aerobic training, at any age, can improve aerobic capacity significantly, perhaps as much as 15–25%.

It is a common misconception that aerobic exercise builds muscle strength. There was a cartoon in The New Yorker magazine in March 2006. Two hamsters are in their cage standing in front of the exercise wheel. One of the hamsters says, "I usually do two hours of cardio and then four more of cardio and then two more of cardio." Endurance, yes—strength, no.

While aerobic training might be sufficient for hamsters, it is not for us. Because aerobic exercise is many repetitions with low resistance during each repetition, the principles of what causes strength improvement, muscle micro tearing and recovery, do not apply. Therefore, aerobic training, while important, does not substitute for or provide the benefits of strength training. On the other hand, a continuous strength training session has been shown to provide some aerobic training benefit. It is optimal to incorporate both strength and aerobic training into your fitness program. Then complete the program by adding flexibility training.

Doing aerobic exercise correctly is important to deriving the full benefits for the time invested. General guidelines for a successful aerobic training program are in the "Fitness Guidelines" section of this book in "Extra Innings."

If It Is Good for Cal Ripken, Jr.

Every morning at Reds Baseball Heaven, we spent about 20 minutes warming up. After a slow and relatively short jog, the remaining time was spent stretching. Warming up with light aerobic activity before stretching helps prevent injuries.

On most days, the stretching was led by Mark Mann, Reds Head Athletic Trainer. One morning, we showed up ready for stretching, and found the exercises being led by several waitresses from the local Hooters restaurant. We could have conducted a study of the effects of holding the stomach in while stretching. There was no lack of attention and participation.

The research is mixed on whether stretching is effective at reducing injuries. Intuitively, most of us would believe that stretching should help. But the studies have only limited evidence of that effect. And yet, the definition provided for "flexibility" by the President's Council on Physical Fitness and Sports says, "...the intrinsic property of body tissues which determines the range of motion achievable without injury at a joint or group of joints." In this definition the very essence of flexibility is characterized as the absence of injury.

While the data are mixed, professionals I have asked still counsel the use of ongoing flexibility training. Stretching, as part of your overall fitness program, will improve flexibility. And there are data to support that stretching helps promote muscle strength, improve range of motion, and can improve athletic performance. One need not have a vivid imagination to envision the difference in throwing, batting, or running between a player with a full range of motion versus one with a limited range.

Cal Ripken, Jr., Oriole Hall of Famer, who set the major league record for most consecutive games played at 2632, partnered with the American Academy of Orthopaedic Surgeons to develop tips for injury prevention. The first tip is "Always warm up and stretch properly before and after you participate in any physical activity." Ripken said, "Whether it's Spring Training or during the season, I would never play a game without stretching beforehand." If it is good for Cal Ripken, Jr., I will assume it is also good for me.

A successful stretching program should consider the guidelines that you can find in the "Fitness Guidelines" section of "Extra Innings."

See the Ball—Hit the Ball

There is a longstanding expression in baseball that is intended to simplify the art of hitting when a batter is in a slump and thinking too much about all of the complexities of hitting a round ball with a round bat squarely. The expression is, "See the ball—hit the ball." Intended as a simplification of the art of hitting, the statement also highlights the very real importance of visual acuity to playing baseball.

A study was conducted among almost 400 professional baseball players in 1996 to measure their visual acuity (clarity of vision, the one measured by the eye chart), distance stereoacuity (fine detail depth perception), and sight contrast sensitivity. The study's conclusion was that their eyesight was significantly better than that of the general population for their age group. We can conclude from this, not surprisingly, that vision is an important element of playing baseball well.

Just as vision is critical to baseball performance, so can vision aging affect our capabilities as senior players. While some of the aging issues are correctable with glasses, contacts, or surgical techniques, we still need to be sensitive enough as the changes to take some corrective action. By the way, if you need to wear glasses, make sure they have unbreakable lenses. I have been wearing glasses to play baseball for more than 45 years. Over that time, I've broken them three times, each on a bad hop. Luckily, the worst thing to happen was that the frames broke and cut me without affecting my eyes.

The vision aging effects we can expect are:

- The lens of the eye becomes less flexible, thereby decreasing our sharpness of vision and our focusing capability.
- The lens yellows with age, filters out colors at the blue end of the spectrum, making it harder to pick out some shades.
- The pupils become less able to take in light and less able to adapt to changes in light. Does a game at dusk before the lights come on come to mind? Does a night game with typical recreational-park lighting come to mind?
- The eye becomes increasingly sensitive to glare. Do those same less-than-adequate lights come to mind? How about a bright sunny day at a Florida tournament with a high sky and poor hitting or fielding backgrounds?

Apparently vision and concentration can be trained. There is a hitting drill being used by some major league players and the Women's Team USA fast pitch team. Tennis balls are marked with a different single digit number in either black or red. The balls are then propelled by a pitching machine at ever-increasing speeds. At each speed, the batter attempts to call out the color of the ball marking. Once proficient at the color, the batter is asked to call out the number on the ball. Think about the level of vision and concentration it takes to do that!

As we age, we will deal with visual acuity issues, as well as an increased potential for a number of eye diseases; cataracts, glaucoma, and macular degeneration. Whether because of minor changes in eye performance or the possible onset of diseases, it is clear that an annual visit to an ophthalmologist or optometrist makes a lot of sense. We do have to see the ball to hit the ball.

Injuries—They Hurt

Attention to fitness and training helps offset the effects of aging and prevent injuries. Injuries can keep us from playing for a game or two or for a career. They can have longer-term effects on our performance. Injuries have an economic effect both on overall health care costs and to the economic well being of the injured party. And—they hurt!

There is a helpful model for better understanding why injuries happen and what we can do to prevent them. The gist of the model is that there is more to what causes an injury than the event that takes place when the injury happens. For example, if someone twists an ankle while sliding, the cause of the injury is much more complicated than the act of sliding. The runner may have also come to the game with some intrinsic risk factors that predisposed him to injury.

- Age
- Body composition (e.g. body weight, fat mass)
- Health (e.g. history of previous injury, joint instability)
- Physical fitness (e.g. muscle strength, flexibility, aerobic capacity)
- Anatomy (e.g. alignment, body structure)
- Skill level (e.g. baseball-specific technique capability)
- Psychological factors (e.g. competitiveness, motivation, perception of risk)

In addition to being predisposed to injury at some level, the runner in our example was also at some level of susceptibility to the injury because of a range of external risk factors.

- Sports factors (e.g. applicable rules, level of umpiring, coaching decisions, skill level of opposition)
- Protective equipment (e.g. helmet, ankle brace)
- Sports equipment (e.g. shoes, bases)
- Environmental (e.g. weather, field condition)

Even the incident itself then has variable factors that may have contributed at some level.

- Playing situation
- Player/opponent behavior
- Position of the whole body
- Position of the affected joint

So, now ask the question, "How was he injured?" The answer is not a simple as, "He twisted his ankle while sliding." The reason for the injury is a complex set of factors, which, if understood more deeply, could be leveraged to prevent similar and other injuries in the future.

- What if the runner's lower body were stronger or more flexible?
- What if the field conditions were better?
- What if he had been wearing an ankle brace to protect him given that he had a previous ankle injury?
- What if the runner had better sliding skills?

Fortunately, many of the factors, whether they are associated with predisposition or susceptibility to injuries, are, at some level, within our control. Earlier in the inning, we addressed some of them by valuing the importance of strength, aerobic, and flexibility training. Our best efforts to prevent injuries start with being sensitive to factors that can help cause them. Then, to the extent that there are steps within our control, we have the choice to take those steps to make a difference. If we are never injured, we will never know which preventative steps made the difference. If we are injured, we may also never know which factors contributed. But we can make a difference in our injury risk profile. And why would we not take those steps?

The model above deals with acute injuries, those which occur as a result of an event (e.g. fracture, bruise, strain, sprain, or cut). There are also chronic injuries that are derived from overuse (e.g. stress fractures, tendonitis, and pitcher's elbow).

The model for understanding chronic injuries considers two factors. Intrinsic factors are biomechanical abnormalities (like misalignments), muscle imbalance, inflexibility, weakness, and instability. Extrinsic factors include poor technique, improper equipment, and improper changes in duration or frequency of the activity.

When I experienced my back injury in November 2005, there was no single incident. Rather, over the course of playing two consecutive weeks of tournaments I played 17 games over 13 days. In the second week, I pitched in three games—the second two were extra-inning complete games. I am convinced it was, in part, the repetitive rotational motion of pitching that helped cause the back problem.

We might conclude that we can prevent chronic injuries in the same way we can reduce the risk of acute injuries. Most literature about chronic injuries highlights the mistake that we tend to treat them as being less critical than acute injuries because they "sneak up on us" instead of resulting from a known incident. The universal guidance is to treat chronic injuries seriously and urgently to prevent them from getting worse themselves, and from causing other injuries that can happen when we alter our body mechanics to compensate for the soreness. Whether they be acute or chronic, injuries hurt.

Ice is Good

While we can and should do all that we can to prevent injuries, there are factors we cannot control, and, odds are, we will be confronted with an injury or two or more during our senior baseball experience. How can we recover from the injury so that we can quickly return to playing in a way that does not jeopardize our long-term safety?

Whether an acute or chronic injury, there is a process to minimize the time lost and maximize the potential for returning safely to the playing field. While maintaining its basic intent, I have taken some liberties with the recommended recovery sequence of the American Academy of Orthopaedic Surgeons. Here is the preferred process.

1. Recognize that you are injured.
2. Visit the appropriate physician for a physical examination and diagnosis, and to understand the corrective course of action. Make sure you are prepared before the appointment with any information you think the physician may need about you and your injury and with any questions you want answered during the visit.
3. Complete the corrective action.
4. Rehabilitate the injury with the appropriate rebuilding of strength and flexibility in the injured area.
5. Throughout rehabilitation, assess progress to ensure the schedule to return to playing is appropriate.
6. Get final clearance from the physician that you are ready to return safely.

We may believe there are times when it is appropriate to skip one or more of these steps, but there is going to be some risk in doing so. We may choose to skip the physician's examination because we had the injury before and know what we will need to do to rehabilitate it. But, what if we are wrong? Is it worth the risk? We may complete the corrective action prescribed but are confident that we can get back to playing without going through any kind of rehabilitation. But what if we are wrong? Is it worth the risk?

If an injury is severe, it is readily recognizable. But for some injuries it may be difficult to determine whether the issue is major or minor. During the period when we are figuring this out, there are things that we can do that are likely to be helpful regardless of the eventual answer. These steps are RICE (rest, ice, compression, elevation), heat, and over-the-counter anti-inflammatories.

As players and coaches, one of the first things we learn about injury first-aid management is RICE. We are taught, depending on the injury, one or more of these four steps can help relieve pain, protect against further injury, and speed the return to playing. Whether we are hit by a fastball, sprain an ankle sliding, pitch a complete game, or any number of other things, one of the first things we can do is apply ice. Does this really help? Is there a best way to apply it? Are there risks?

At the end of my first day at Reds Baseball Heaven, I noticed a long line going into the training room. Most of the campers coming out of the room were covered with Ace bandages holding iced towels on shoulders, elbows, knees, and seemingly anywhere else that could be wrapped. When the line shortened, I made my way to the training room and asked Mark Mann if I should be icing. The next thing I knew, he had my throwing shoulder and elbow wrapped in frozen towels and those wrapped with Ace bandages to hold everything in place. Mark explained that the ice would help me recover more quickly from a long day of throwing by keeping any swelling down.

My impression at the time was that the trainers used the towel method because it was easier and quicker to deal with a lot of players by draping near-frozen towels over body parts instead of using bags of ice that would be hard to get placed properly. As it turns out, there is actually evidence that melting ice water applied through a wet towel is the most effective icing procedure.

By camp time the following year, I had been playing more games and tournaments, had lost some weight, and was in generally better shape. Also, being a camp veteran, I had a better appreciation of how to use the training room. At the end of day one of my second camp, I was feeling the soreness already coming on. I went into the training room and asked Mark, "Do you have anything for old, tired feet, legs, and back?"

Mark said, "Follow me." He led me to a whirlpool tub, which I had used as a hot tub once the year before. I was surprised when he went over to the ice machine and proceeded to dump several loads of ice into what had already been converted into a cold tub. With the body shock of my life, I immersed myself into the ice cold bath and stayed there for 20 minutes. My belief in the value of icing was magnified. I spent my 20 minutes in that cold bath every day after camp and am convinced it helped throughout the week.

Iced down in the Reds Baseball Heaven training room

While I could not find a definitive evidence-based study that provided the best ice application procedures, there is conventional wisdom.

- Apply ice to the injured area but not directly to the skin. The only apparent risk of icing is damage to the skin from prolonged application. While iced wet towels are best, they are not always available. Ice in a bag, a frozen bag of peas, or something similar will work.

- Apply the ice as soon after the injury as possible, preferably in the first five to ten minutes, to help manage the swelling.
- Apply the ice for two to three repeated periods of ten minutes each. Removing the ice for a brief period does not substantially reduce the temperature achieved in muscle or joint, but helps protect the skin.
- Application over 30 minutes at a time will not provide further advantage.
- Application can be repeated two to three times per day for the first two to three days. Beyond that, icing will not be helpful in that all of the swelling that is to occur has already taken place.

The data that do exist on icing indicate that faster injury recovery may be a benefit. The belief is that recovery time is lessened for two reasons: 1) the ice reduces pain, allowing the player to start rehabilitation earlier; and 2) the ice prevents tissue damage secondary to the original injury, which could lengthen recovery time. Said another way, all of the evidence indicates that ice, quickly applied, is good.

Heat is Good Too

Is heat also a helpful tool for injury recovery? There are research data, conventional wisdom, and personal experience that, yes, heat is good—when applied properly. The speculation for why heat works is three-fold.

1. Heat therapy dilates the blood vessels of the muscles, thereby increasing the flow of oxygen and nutrients to the injured area, helping to heal damaged tissue.
2. The heat stimulates sensory receptors in the skin, decreasing transmissions of pain signals to the brain, partially relieving discomfort.
3. Heat facilitates stretching of soft tissues, including muscles, connective tissue, and adhesions, thereby reducing stiffness, increasing flexibility, and causing an overall feeling of comfort.

Heat application can be accomplished with, among other techniques, a heating pad, hot-water bottle, microwaveable gel pack, salves (e.g. Flexall), one of the newer products that generate low-level heat and can be worn when out of the house (e.g. ThermaCare Heat Wraps), ultrasound, and my psychological favorite, the hot tub.

It is not uncommon for tournament lodging selections to be based on whether the motel has a good hot tub area. When a game is over, there are frequently simultaneous calls for food, beer, and hot tub. While it is not clear whether it helps in the long run, there is no doubt that a long hot tub session at least attends to the psyche if not the soreness.

Direct heat applications are more common, but, as with the application of ice, there are some risks. The primary issue, again, is damage to skin. For this reason, whichever heat source is being used, it is best to have a buffer between source and skin. For example, a towel wrapped around a heat gel pack helps protect the skin. Pay attention to duration as well. Applications of extreme heating should be limited to 30 minutes unless instructions for the product indicate differently.

The best combination treatment of ice and heat is to use icing immediately and then periodically through the first two to three days, after which the ice has done its job minimizing swelling. At that point, begin heating. Be cautious about direct application of either ice or heat to the skin and manage exposure times to minimize the risk of skin damage. Ice and heat are both beneficial when used correctly.

The Perfect Storm

On a brutally hot and humid summer day in August 1990, at the age of 44, I experienced my personal analogy to Sebatian Junger's *The Perfect Storm*. The weather prediction that day was for temperatures in the mid-90s with humidity to match. My MSBL team had a doubleheader scheduled starting at 1:00 pm in Dayton, and my outdoor soccer team had begun its fall season with a 10:00 am game scheduled in Cincinnati. I was to be catching the first of the baseball games. The good news was there was not a schedule conflict, so I could play in all three games. As it turned out, the bad news was the same as the good news.

Added to the confluence of storm factors was the fact that I inherited my father's sweat glands—I perspire heavily. In anticipation of a full, fun, but difficult day, I loaded my cooler with gallons of water, a lunch to eat on the ride from Cincinnati to Dayton, and extra snacks, including bananas, for during and between doubleheader games.

The temperature during the morning soccer game was "only" in the mid-80s. I drank water heavily before, during, and after the game, and felt fine as I ate lunch in the car on the way to the baseball games. I got to the baseball field just in time, donned the tools of ignorance, and went into battle in the steam bath.

Toward the end of the game, my legs were clearly getting tired, but there were no signs of trouble. I figured that I could withstand the second game at shortstop. We had some time between games, so I found some shade and guzzled more water, ate a banana and some snacks, and thought how proud I was of myself. I was in my mid-40s and handling playing a soccer game, catching a baseball game, and finishing a doubleheader in the heat and humidity.

In mid-reverie, I felt my first cramp starting. I did not panic but merely drank more water and got up to get ready for game two. The minor spasms that precede cramps continued but I stretched, drank, and hoped I would make it through the game. To my surprise, I finished the game and got into the car for my ride home, which was to be about 45 minutes.

I was just beginning to feel the air conditioning in the car when the first serious cramp started in my left leg. Pulling my toes back toward me, I was able to reduce the tightness and keep driving, knowing that I should probably pull over but wanting to get home. Over the last 15 minutes of the drive, I fought off both leg cramps and the beginning of cramps all over my body, including my stomach.

By the time I limped into the house, got upstairs, and climbed into bed, I knew this was not going to go away. Ann sprung into action bringing me water, Gatorade, and a banana. We found out quickly that my stomach cramping was not allowing me to keep anything down. Within the next 15 minutes the cramps worsened and became more painful—we were on the phone with my doctor, in the car, and, with Ann driving, on the way to the emergency room. Two hours later, I had been given sufficient intravenous fluids to return my body to normal, as if none of it had ever happened.

So, what did I learn about dehydration that day and what should all of us think about whether it is a hot humid August day full of activity, a single night game in September, or just living on a day-to-day basis? While I had a serious experience from which to learn, managing fluids is also important to our basic health and our baseball performance.

Fluid management for general well being is important because water makes up more than 70% of our solid body tissue, helps regulate body temperature, carries nutrients and oxygen to our cells, removes body wastes, cushions joints, and protects organs and tissues. Symptoms of a lack of adequate water can be headaches, grogginess, and dry, itchy skin. Severe dehydration can affect blood pressure, circulation, digestion, and kidney function.

Fluid management is also important as it directly relates to playing senior baseball. Baseball is a warm-weather game. So whether we are playing a league game in July or a tournament game in Florida in January, the heat and humidity can combine with the normal loss of fluids to require us to replace more than normal amounts of water. If we fall behind replacement, a range of issues could occur, ranging from an imperceptible loss of speed and strength, to light-headedness, to cramping, to other heat-related illnesses.

There are a number of helpful signals we can get from our bodies that indicate our fluid level is low. Thirst is one, but the sensation is a late indicator that fluids are low. Once we are thirsty, it is difficult to catch up quickly. Also, as we age, the sensation of thirst weakens, making it an even poorer indicator.

Another indicator is the color of our urine. When it is clear, our fluid level is likely adequate. When the color is dark yellow, the level is likely low. But this is not a good signal as when we are dehydrated, we urinate less frequently.

Yet another signal is the inflexibility of skin. Hold your hand out with the palm down. Pinch the skin on the top of your hand and let go. If it recovers quickly, your fluid level is likely adequate. If the skin remains pinched or recovers slowly, your fluids may be low. A significant weight loss can be an indicator of low fluids. In my senior year of high school, I caught a doubleheader in the heat bath that is a St. Louis summer. I recall losing more than ten pounds of water weight that day. It took me three days to recover it all.

But each of these methods is a lagging indicator in that it tells us what has already happened—we have allowed our fluid intake to fall behind our output. The best way to manage fluids is to stay ahead of the anticipated losses, never getting into a serious deficiency range. While there are general rules of thumb about fluid management and exercise, each of us needs to be cognizant of our hydration needs as requirements are individualized based on things such as age, size, physical condition, position played, and rate of perspiration. We must also pay close attention to the weather conditions to round out our determination of the timing and amount of fluids we may need. For guidelines regarding fluid management, see "Fitness Guidelines" in "Extra Innings."

Strong Men Beat Arthritis

Why should I include a section about arthritis? Here are the facts, according to the Center of Disease Control and the National Institute of Arthritis and Musculoskeletal and Skin Diseases.

- Arthritis is the leading cause of disability in the United States.
- 49 million people have self-reported, doctor-diagnosed arthritis.
- Osteoarthritis, the most common form, develops as we age. It is a condition where the cartilage covering the bone end wears away.
- Younger people tend to get osteoarthritis from joint injuries resulting from sports or accidents.
- Men are more likely to get osteoarthritis than women before the age of 45.

So, the bad news is that as we get older, we are more likely to develop arthritis. The good news is that the recommended approach to prevent and treat the disease is to stay active. Both of these statements are relevant for senior baseball players.

Mid-week at Reds Baseball Heaven in 2003, I began feeling some soreness on both sides of my groin area. I had experienced groin pulls before, and this did not feel as severe. At the time, the soreness did not seem to be meaningfully affecting my play but it was bothersome. I asked Mark Mann what I could best do to relieve the soreness. He had me lie on my back on the training table, manipulated my legs, and told me, as evidenced by limitations in my range of motion, that I likely had some arthritis in my hips. I later confirmed the diagnosis with my personal physician.

Since then, while the arthritis has not substantially progressed, I am convinced that it is affecting my play. My objective has been to keep the disease from progressing. To help guide me, I read two books on the subject. The first was *Strong Women and Men Beat Arthritis* by Miriam E. Nelson, Ph.D. et al. The second was *The Kalamazoo Arthritis Book* by Alan A. Halpern, M.D. Each has an extensive description of arthritis and of the approaches for prevention and treatment. And they provided very consistent guidance on the steps to take.

Strong Women and Men Beat Arthritis dispel the myths that the best thing for arthritis is to rest, and that once we get arthritis, it is too late to make a difference. With those myths busted, their approach is encouraging because it is exactly what we should already be doing to enhance our quality of life and our senior baseball experience. The foundation of the approach to mitigating the effects of arthritis is exercise, strength training, aerobic training, and stretching. Sound familiar? I will not go into the details of their recommended exercise program design, but rather recommend *Strong Women and Men Beat Arthritis* for their guidance.

Exercise is not the only element of a full frontal attack on arthritis. Certainly, as with any disease, it is important to work out the best plan for you with your physician. There are other options for consideration.

- Nutrition improvement
- Weight loss
- Medication, like anti-inflammatories
- Physical therapy
- Surgery
- Shoes with adequate cushioning if the lower body is affected

Arthritis is just another of the realities that go along with the senior baseball experience, especially for those who are playing at older ages. Like the other realities we have discussed, arthritis does not need to be debilitating to the point of keeping us from playing or playing the way we would like.

Your Future; My Future

As I began writing this inning, I was reflecting on the walking wounded with whom I had just played at the 2005 Roy Hobbs World Series. As I end the inning, my name has been added to the roster of injured senior players. Toward the end of that tournament, I was experiencing more than the normal amount of soreness, especially in my right hip. I had, at the time, attributed it to the arthritis flaring up and assumed that, with a short rest and a return to my normal exercise routine, the soreness would subside.

Ann and I joined family in St. Louis for Thanksgiving, and I took advantage of the week to lay off any exercise. When back home in Cincinnati, I returned to the gym and went through a light workout to get back into the routine. My plan was to end the workout on the treadmill for 30 minutes of walking and running. Less than ten minutes into that session, I knew I could not continue. The soreness in my hip had returned and transitioned more to pain. I stopped, went home, and over the next several hours, the pain radiated down my right leg. Knowing this was more than the arthritis and having had a similar sensation from a football injury in high school, I knew it was my back that was the problem.

Not unexpectedly, the pain did not subside overnight, and I was in the doctor's office the next day. Based on symptoms and an examination, he diagnosed the likely cause as one or more herniated discs. He verified the diagnosis with an MRI (magnetic resonance imaging) and prescribed a short dose of oral corticosteroids, which helped a little until I twisted the wrong way one day and returned to my original condition.

It had reached the point where I could neither stand nor walk for more than a minute or two without having to sit down to relieve the pain. Fortunately, I could sit comfortably and find, with the help of codeine, a reasonable sleeping position.

During an early December discussion, I told my doctor that my objective was to play in the two weeks of tournaments I had scheduled in January, the Bob Wagner Wooden Bat Classic in Fort Myers and the Baseball International Spring Training tournament in Sarasota. He told me my objective was very aggressive, but, to give me the best chance, he prescribed spinal corticosteroid shots to relieve the pain. Depending on the success of each shot, I could, if needed, have a series of three, each separated by two weeks.

Two notable things happened during that month. Thankfully my pain was substantially relieved through the series of three shots, to about 10% of its original level. Second, my primary objective changed. After struggling to stand and walk, after recognizing how my quality of life was affected, and after not being able to pick up my two young grandsons, baseball, as meaningful as it is to me, became a secondary objective. Objective one became to return to normal life.

Three months of physical therapy and personal time in the gym made a big difference. I could move through step four of the injury recovery process I shared with you earlier. The final two steps are to assess progress to ensure the schedule to return to playing is appropriate and get final clearance from my physician that I am ready to return safely. Only a few weeks ago, I was convinced that I would not play at all during 2006. But on an April morning on the way home from the gym, I asked Ann if, tomorrow, she would play some light catch with me. I feel well enough to take that tiny next step. And I have now returned to playing in league games.

My future in baseball is still uncertain, albeit more optimistic than earlier. What does your baseball future look like? Whether you have lost a step or two, lost some speed on your fastball, lost bat speed, or are injured, you can work to resolve any of those issues to benefit from the joy of playing the game you love. Despite everything, you are never too old to play the game.

References:

Maharam LG, Bauman PA, Kalman D, Skolnick, H, Perle SM, Master Athletes-Factors Affecting Performance. *Sports Medicine* 1999, October 28 (4): 273-285

Menard D, Stanish W, The aging athlete. *Am J Sports Med* 1989; 17 (2): 187-96

Laby DM, Rosenbaum AL, Kirshcen DG, Davidson JL, Rosenbaum LJ, Strasser C, Mellman MF, The visual function of professional baseball players. *Am J Ophthalmol* 1996 Oct; 122 (4): 476-85

Yoshida T, Nakai S, Yorimoto A, Kawabata T, Morimoto T, Effect of aerobic capacity on sweat rate and fluid intake during outdoor exercise in the heat. *Eur J Appl Physiol Occup Physiol* 1995;71(2-3):235-9

Hart L, Effect of stretching on sport injury risk: a review. *Clin J Sport Med.* 2005 Mar; 15(2):113

Bahr R, Krosshaug T, Understanding injury mechanisms: a key component of preventing injuries in sport. *Br J Sports Med.* 2005; 39(6):324-9

Mac Auley DC, Ice Therapy: how good is the evidence? *Int J Sports Med.* 2001 Jul; 22(5):379-84

Hubbard TJ, Aronson SL, Denegar CR, Does Cryotherapy hasten return to participation? A systemic review. *J of Athletic Training* 2004; 39(1):88-94

FUTURE OF SENIOR BASEBALL

"Baseball's future? Bigger and bigger, better and better!
No question about it, it's the greatest game there is."
Ted Williams

"Every day is a new opportunity.
You can build on yesterday's success
or put its failures behind and start over again.
That's the way life is, with a new game every day,
and that's the way baseball is."
Bob Feller

Ken: *"OK, we each got one that inning, so all we need to do is hold 'em. A couple of runs wouldn't hurt here"*

Jack: *"Then three outs and it's hot tub time. I'm sore, but I really think I can play this game well into my 60s if the wheels stay on. I wonder if it will look and feel the same to me then."*

Al: *"Remember I told you about George Goodall; he was playing in his 90s. I think we'll all be at this for awhile."*

JR: *"I wonder if the game will change. It seems they add another older division to the World Series every couple of years. And every tournament we play in is getting bigger. Well, we'll definitely see what happens, 'cause we'll all be a part of it."*

Al: "Yep, it just doesn't get any better than this. Or maybe it will."

Read this Book; Play Senior Ball

Senior baseball is alive and well. Its growth, both in participation and quality, since its infancy only a couple decades ago, has been consistent and geographically widespread. From a few guys looking for a place to play the game they love, from others who wanted to play with their boyhood heroes at the first fantasy camp, to national organizations, to tournaments being run nationwide, to international trips, to as many as 125,000 players suiting up at one time or another throughout each year, senior baseball has matured.

Anybody over 30, regardless of skill level or age, assuming he is sufficiently healthy and fit and can muster the resources and family support, can find a place to play where he can compete and enjoy the game. The game is now so well organized, the continuing health of senior baseball for the foreseeable future is not in doubt. The remaining question is how the senior game will change in the future.

Will it grow? While senior baseball has grown significantly in the past 25 years, I believe its growth will be much more conservative in the future. Growth to date has come from the birth of the three major national organizations and their geographic expansion and from the addition of a fantasy camp for virtually every major league team. Growth has come from entrepreneurs running tournaments in Cooperstown, Florida, Arizona, Las Vegas, and many other sites. And growth has come from the creation of independent leagues to fill in the geographic gaps left by the national organizations.

Certainly, individual leagues can grow and, hopefully, they will. The MSBL web site, for example, says, "Within a few short years, membership is projected to exceed 50,000." That translates to a growth rate of a little over 3% per year. But opportunities for further geographical growth are limited because the current organizations have already done such a good job of expanding. Fantasy camps may find ways to increase the number of campers. Some already run two sessions each year to accommodate those who want to play. But with the saturation and cost of fantasy camps, growth is likely limited there as well.

While I hope it is not true, there is even one argument that fantasy camps will decline in popularity. At a Reds Baseball Heaven closing banquet one year, Ann and I had the pleasure of having dinner with Don Gullett and Denis Menke. Gullett had had an injury-shortened, but successful, pitching career, primarily for Cincinnati. His career winning percentage was .686 with, in three of his nine years, an earned run average under 3.00. At the time of the fantasy camp, Gullett was the pitching coach for the Reds. Menke, who played for a number of teams, was a versatile infielder and a two-time All-Star. He had recently been a member of the Reds coaching staff, but, by the time of this camp, had retired.

We talked about a lot of baseball topics that evening. Ann and I were surprised how open these two major league baseball insiders were. Gullett's and Menke's point of view was that today's baseball players had much less respect for the game than did players of previous generations. They speculated that the lesser level of respect, coupled with the amount of money paid to today's players, makes is much less likely that current players, as a group, would be as willing to participate as ex-professionals at future fantasy camps. Were this to be the case, fantasy camps could deteriorate over time. That would be a shame, not only for the camps themselves, but because they have been a feeder system to reintroduce many senior players to the game.

Will growth come from tournament play? It is possible that there will be more tournaments run each year, but it is unlikely this phenomenon will contribute to a meaningful growth in the number of senior players. During the last several years, Scott Green has built Play at the Plate from nothing to four well-attended events each year. However, most of the players attending Green's events also play in other leagues or tournaments. More playing opportunities will bring more players to the game, but at a much-reduced rate of growth than previously experienced, as current players merely play at more events.

Despite my conservative growth prediction, there are three things that could trigger significant growth. One is if today's younger players are attracted to the game in numbers higher than those who have already turned 30 and are playing now. Let us hope that tomorrow's 30-years-olds continue to play the game because senior baseball is so readily available, which was not the case when many of us were in our

30s. Secondly, if today's senior players who are in their 30s stay in longer and play into their 40s, 50s, 60s, and beyond while 30-year-olds are joining the ranks, growth could accelerate. And finally, if everyone who reads this book and loves the game, but is not currently playing, decides to, there would be huge growth potential.

It is hard to be totally accurate about the size of the senior baseball community. I believe, however many players there are, the growth will be in the low single digits as a percentage each year over the next decades, unlike the double-digit growth in many years of the last decades.

Higher Age Divisions

While the total number of players may grow more slowly, it is becoming evident that the number of players in the upper age divisions will increase more rapidly. It will not be based on new players starting when they are 50, 60, or 70—although that may happen as well. The growth will come from the current players who are playing in the mid and higher age divisions today.

For many of these players, senior baseball has become a way of life. Even now they are playing in leagues and attending multiple tournaments each year. Many of these players are still working and will hopefully have even more time flexibility when they retire. As I noted earlier, I only half-jokingly tell people that I retired at the age of 55 because work was getting in the way of playing baseball.

I have been fortunate enough to be able to continue to compete in my 30-and-over league and in both 38- and 48-and-over tournaments. At 60, I am not sure how much longer this will be possible. But I am encouraged by increasingly older age divisions at the national tournaments. Based on the likely growth of numbers of players at the older ages, there are two things I project will occur. One is that there will be additional older age brackets at the national tournaments. Tom Giffen is convinced that there will be a 70-and-older division in his Roy Hobbs World Series some time in the next five years.

Secondly, there will be baseball tournaments specifically for older players. Today, virtually all tournaments not associated with the national organizations are run for all senior players, 30 and older. The increase in the number of older players, combined with their time and, perhaps, financial flexibility, opens the door for the businesses that are running tournaments to cater to players in their 50s, 60s, 70s, and beyond.

Other Tournament Changes

I would suggest that older age divisions will not be the only change evident in senior baseball in the years to come. Earlier, I discussed in depth my preference for and the growing trend of using wooden bats in senior baseball leagues and tournaments. Based on the analysis we did in the fourth inning, I would expect this trend to continue. Will senior baseball ever be entirely wooden bat? I am not sure, but it should be.

I also advocated for my preference to play full baseball rules to keep the intended role of the catcher in the game. There is no current move to reduce the number of tournaments that play Cooperstown rules, so I am not optimistic. Hopefully, in the future, Cooperstown rules will be limited to only the highest of age groups, which may be appropriate. As age division limits increase, finding enough catchers capable of playing full rules for a week's event may be too difficult.

One way to think about this is that there will be more tournaments overall, some with full rules, some with Cooperstown rules. I already mentioned the likelihood of more tournaments run just for older age groups. Hopefully the economy will allow more players who want to participate in their later years to have the means to do so. While Play at the Plate added four tournaments each year, the other "East Coast" tournaments continue to be played. In the future, there should be room for even more tournaments.

One final change that I predict will take place in tournaments and, I would argue, should have taken place already, is the addition of medical professionals to tournament staffs. Currently, medical attention for injuries, whether they are minor or severe, is managed about the same at each tournament. Help is typically available from two sources. The first is the happenstance that there are doctors or other medically trained players on your field or on one nearby. I happen to be fortunate to have a number of medical professionals on my teams. I have been playing with trauma-room physicians, emergency medical technicians, and other specialists. And one of the spouses is an experienced trauma-room nurse. The problem is that we are just lucky to have them readily available to us.

The second mode of medical support for serious injuries is the local emergency services. This will always be the case. But the decision making to call for these services needs to be more coordinated. Time can be important for some injuries, and it takes too long by current procedures.

I would suggest the future of senior baseball tournaments includes having the appropriate medical professional and decision maker at the tournament complex and readily available. The professional training staff at fantasy camps serves this purpose today. With the exception of the large national organizations' tournaments, most are played at a single site, thereby allowing the tournament director to hire a single person to get the job done. The person would be responsible for first aid of minor injuries and making the decision on what is needed to address serious issues. In addition, this person would have done prework with the local services and established a direct line to make sure no time is lost for any reason.

There is no doubt that this service would add to the cost of running a tournament. But spread over the number of players, the cost would be reasonable and likely acceptable to the participants. Senior baseball needs a medical professional at its tournaments.

Women's Baseball: Catch-22

Does senior baseball have the opportunity to grow through the growth of the women's game? Today, relatively few women are playing baseball, and only a few of them are senior women. While the Roy Hobbs World Series hosts a Women's division, it is typically only six to eight teams and is an unlimited age group, the vast majority being young players, under 30. There are women's leagues, but they are few. Women's baseball has not grown recently the way men's senior ball has.

There is also little promise of the future growth of women's baseball in general or senior women's baseball, specifically. How can women's baseball grow if there is little likelihood of the growth of girls youth baseball? Or, how can it grow if there are not likely to be significantly more leagues or tournaments where women can play? It is a catch-22 situation. Because there are no places for women to play, young girls cannot see a future in the sport. Because young girl baseball players are not coming up through the system and demanding places to play, there is no compelling reason for the opportunities to exist.

Consider a hypothetical nine-year-old female athlete, Mary Carlson. She has been an avid baseball fan since her father and uncles began taking her to professional games and to her older brothers' Little League games. She began playing catch at age three and could hit line drives from both sides of the plate by age four. By age seven, she was hanging out at her brothers' practices and getting involved whenever she could. She is a baseball player, knows it, and has visions of playing major league baseball and following in the footsteps of her shortstop heroes, Derek Jeter, David Eckstein, and Miguel Tejada.

The local Little League coaches now know about her and are positioning themselves to have her play for them. But it is not only the baseball coaches that know about her. The local fast pitch softball coaches are also aware. Our future superstar is now about to turn nine, and is ready to play Little League baseball. Her whole family is supportive, and, as is not always the case, so is the youth baseball organization in her community.

Mary's extended family traditionally comes together on Thanksgiving. This holiday before her first Little League season, everyone is at Mary's grandparents' home, including her cousin, Louise Hofmann, who is a sophomore in college. Louise had been a highly recruited fast pitch softball player during her high school years, received a college scholarship, and has now been through one season of college ball. With Mary and Louise both in the room, the conversation always turns to sports, and this holiday get-together is to be no exception.

Mary excitedly tells everyone that she is looking forward to Little League. Given that her father, uncles, and brothers had been an integral part of her development as a player, they are likewise excited and cannot wait to see her play. Louise, who is being unusually quiet, finally clears her throat, gets everyone's attention, and, with some hesitation, says, "Mary, why do you want to play baseball?"

Mary, not really understanding what Louise means by her question, begins rambling about how much she loves to play, about how good she is (no brag, just fact), and how she wants to play major league baseball someday. Everyone in the room is beaming. While they know in their heart of hearts that she will never play major league ball or, for that matter, minor league ball, it is great that she is so passionate about the game they all love as well.

Louise, hesitant again, then says, "Mary, that's all great. I'm glad you're so excited, but, I think you're making a big mistake."

The family gathering freezes in time and gapes at Louise as she goes on to explain, "What I am about to say is not what you want to hear, but here goes. I know you're excited about playing baseball and you are really good at it, but after Little League, then what? While you may want to play through high school and even beyond, sad to say, realistically that will be highly unlikely. There are examples of girls who have played high school baseball, but they are very few. And even if you do play in high school, then what? What are the odds that you will get a chance to play college baseball, let alone get a scholarship?"

Mary, who is mature for nine, is beginning to get the picture. And her parents are paying close attention because they had never thought of the scholarship angle.

Louise goes on, "Think about the alternative. You have great skills that could easily reapply to fast pitch softball. You have a quick bat, great hand-eye coordination, speed on the bases, soft hands and a great glove, the strongest arm in town, and an intellect for the game. You could be a top tier fast pitch softball player. What that means is certainty that you will play on a competitive sports team in high school. And playing in college is a lock, as is likely a full scholarship. I'm not telling you this because I play college softball. I'm telling you this because it is reality, and I want you to think about this now instead of being disappointed later on."

It is not important what our hypothetical Mary Carlson chose to do. What is important is that the decision she had to make is real for girls her age. If they are to be successful fast pitch softball players, they need to dedicate themselves to it early. The need to make this decision early precludes there being a critical mass of youth girl baseball players coming through the system to force the issue on having places to play.

I found this issue to be consistently articulated by Jean Ardell, author of *Breaking into Baseball: Women and the National Pastime* and Tom Giffen, president of Roy Hobbs Baseball, who supports women's baseball by fielding a division at his World Series each year. Young girls must make the decision because there are limited playing opportunities. For example, I asked Steve Sigler, the MSBL President and a cornerstone of senior baseball, what his plans were to include women's baseball in MSBL. His response was a blunt but not surprising, "I have no plans for women's baseball."

There are women's baseball leagues, albeit few of them. An example is the Colorado Women's Baseball League, which typically has four teams and about 60 players. At least half of the players are over 30, some over 40, and a few over 50. Many of the women over 35 are playing because when they were growing up, girls' softball had not yet developed, so they played Little League baseball. Until the current league was formed, they had no outlet for the game they love other than softball, which they found less than fully satisfying. There are some of these small women's leagues around the country.

It seems, however, that many women's leagues had a difficult time sustaining team participation. The internet is replete with web sites describing the beginning of teams in the mid-90s and their demise several years later. For example, at one point there was a Florida Women's Baseball League, which failed in the mid-90s. One team from that league, the Ocala Lightning, was able to maintain funding and now recruits from around the country to put together an elite team to play in tournaments.

While the odds that women's baseball will grow are slim, Jean Ardell shares interesting points of view from two prominent baseball men. Ardell writes, "C. C. Johnson Spink, the publisher of the *Sporting News*, predicted (in 1977), 'If women eventually invade the domain of pro sports, the pioneers will come in baseball.' Henry Aaron feels the same way. Aaron, then a vice president with the Atlanta Braves, was quoted as saying, 'Girls excel at basketball, golf, and tennis and there is no logical reason why they shouldn't play baseball. It's not that tough. Baseball is not a game of strength; hitting is not strength. The game needs a special kind of talent, thinking and timing. Some women, as well as some men, qualify in that respect....People can't be put in categories.'"

Whether Spink and Aaron were right or not, the system is stacked against the likelihood that women's baseball will grow substantially at youth, adult, or senior amateur levels or at the professional level. For women's baseball, it is catch-22.

Minority Driven Growth

While I do not have the broad statistics, my personal experience is that there are an inordinately small number of blacks involved in senior baseball.

There was one exception. When I was playing MSBL ball in the early to mid-1990s, there was an all-black team in my league centered around Dave Parker, the seven-time All Star slugger, who hit almost 340 home runs in his 19-year career. Parker, at the time, was about 40 years old and out of major league baseball for only a couple years. I was catching one day when we were playing his team. He came up for his first at bat, dwarfing the umpire and me with his 6'5", 230-pound frame. What do you throw to Dave Parker? How about throwing a fastball six inches outside and three inches low, hoping that he would reach for it and drive it into the ground?

I signaled for the fastball and settled into my target outside and down. My pitcher threw the ball, but it was neither outside nor low enough. Parker went down to get the pitch, which against a mere mortal senior player, would have still been a good pitch, outside corner at the knees. Parker hit a ball that exploded off his bat toward left center. The ball rose from the height of his knees to about eight feet, leveled out, and stayed on that line until it hit the outfield wall almost 400 feet away. It was inspiring to see a ball hit that hard and see it disappear that quickly. I do not remember what he did in the rest of the game, but I will never forget that line drive.

Other than Parker's team, however, the black senior players have been scattered across my experience. It is not evident to me that there is an increasing trend of black participation. In fact, there are some data that there may even be less participation in the future.

In a recently televised game on ESPN, commentator and Hall of Famer Joe Morgan was talking about blacks in baseball. The day before had been Jackie Robinson Day in major league baseball, and Morgan was musing with his fellow announcer, Jon Miller, about Robinson's impact on the game. Morgan stated that after Robinson broke the color barrier, black participation increased in the majors to reach an impressive level of 27% of players. That number has now declined to where less than one player in ten is black today. In addition, Commissioner Bud Selig reports that only 6% of fans attending Major League baseball games are black. These data would indicate that black interest in baseball may be declining. Recognizing this issue, Major League baseball committed to and has now opened the first of hopefully many urban youth baseball academies.

By any available measure, minority participation in senior baseball is not likely to be a source of growth unless some positive steps are taken to change that situation. Doing so could help lead the overall senior baseball community to a higher growth rate than would be reached otherwise.

Baseball and the Olympic Movement

Baseball has fluctuated in and out as an Olympic sport over the years, having been a demonstration sport eight times since 1904. In 1992 it became an official Olympic sport at the Barcelona games. But in July 2005, the International Olympic Committee voted by a narrow margin to drop baseball beginning with the 2012 games. This occurred despite there being 122 baseball-playing nations around the world, up from 60 in 1990. Fourteen of these countries consider baseball a prominent national sport. There is a lobbying effort to force another vote to reinstate the sport for the 2016 games.

While the decision whether baseball will again be an Olympic sport is important in many ways, it is not fundamentally meaningful to senior baseball. Certainly, senior players care deeply about baseball, and we would like to see our game widely valued and recognized. But I believe there is an even more important Olympic movement as it relates to senior baseball—the Senior Olympics.

States have been running senior games for some time. But only recently, in 1985, did the National Senior Games Association get together in St. Louis to consolidate into a countrywide organization and run the first National Senior Olympic Games. About 12,000 athletes are now expected every two years when the national games are run compared to 2,500 that participated in the 1985 games.

The National Senior Olympics Games are comprised of the following sports: archery, badminton, basketball, bowling, cycling, golf, horseshoes, race walking, racquetball, road racing, shuffleboard, softball, swimming, table tennis, tennis, track & field, triathlon, and volleyball. Depending on the sport, there are varying numbers of age divisions, starting at 50-plus and going up to 95-plus (men's doubles tennis). In addition to the summer Senior Olympics, the organization has also run a Winter Games with competition in seven sports and a Senior Olympic Hockey Championship. In the planning stage is a National Senior Games Championship Festival for golf and tennis.

Have you noticed any sport that you might be interested in missing from the list? Given that there are already senior baseball tournaments that have age divisions up to 65 plus, baseball would be an ideal Senior Olympic sport.

According to Gregory S. Moore, the Director of National Games & Athlete Relations, there are a number of factors that determine if a sport is included at the national level. Primary among them is whether there are sufficient state-run Senior Olympics that have included the sport, and eventually call upon the national organization to create a national competition. While baseball was a demonstration sport at the 1997 Senior Olympics, only four teams participated.

Currently, there is very little activity to install baseball as a sport in state games, thereby ensuring, unless something changes dramatically, there will not be baseball at the national Senior Olympics level. For example, my state of Ohio, while responsive to my inquiries, has chosen to focus on other activities. They did, however, express interest and indicated that if someone were to advocate strongly and take coordinating leadership, they would be glad to consider baseball in future state games.

A good example where leadership has resulted in baseball's inclusion is the state of Delaware. John DeBenedictis is the baseball coordinator for the Delaware state games. John, who is now playing in the 65-and-over division of tournaments, was reintroduced to playing baseball when he received a trip to the Phillies Dream Week for a 50th birthday present. Following the fantasy camp, John returned to baseball in a local over-30 MSBL league. He is so passionate about baseball that, at his wife's suggestion, they were married between the games of a doubleheader at an MSBL Caribbean Classic Tournament in Puerto Rico. They walked down the "aisle" of crossed bats.

Although he enjoyed his over-30 league, John found, as he aged, that he was less competitive and sought opportunities to "play with kids his own age." Not finding any such leagues, he decided to create his own. John began the first over-50 local league, which now has an over-55 division as well. And he petitioned the Delaware Senior Olympics to begin baseball as an annual sport. At this point, John signs up 30 players for each of the state games, and has an over-50 team play against an over-55 team. John has been a pioneer who has demonstrated that baseball and the Senior Olympics can go together if someone takes a leadership role.

There are more than 70 teams from around the country that are playing in the Senior Olympic age range each year at the Roy Hobbs World Series. And Roy Hobbs is the smallest of the three major national senior baseball organizations. The match between the Senior Olympics and baseball is obvious. The magic will occur when someone steps up to advocate for and lead the coordination of Senior Olympic baseball. Other than leadership, the only barrier I can envision is a concern by current national senior baseball organizations and tournament directors that a Senior Olympics baseball tournament would be competition for them. They should be persuaded, however, by an argument that baseball in the Senior Olympics would add national awareness and help grow our sport to the benefit of all.

Baseball: Life Sport

Those currently playing senior baseball, especially those playing into their 50s, 60s, 70s, and beyond, know it is a life sport. We played it in their youth, perhaps through high school or college. Whether we continued to play without interruption or were reintroduced to the game after a hiatus, we can consider ourselves as having a life-long baseball career. I know I do.

But when most people think about life sports and consider what games they may be playing at more advanced ages, they probably think more about golf or tennis. There is certainly nothing wrong with these sports. I enjoy them both. It is not uncommon for senior baseball players to bring their clubs to tournaments and try to get in a couple of rounds during a week. Frequent teammates of mine, Charlie Cooper, who is 65, and Tony Styons, a young pup at age 36, seldom join us for after-game drinks or dinner. They leave the game as soon as it is over, drive to the golf course, change in the car if need be, and get in as many holes as possible before it gets dark.

Many of my former work colleagues, when talking about retirement, include golf in their plans. Occasionally, the plans include tennis, with an added caveat, "I only play doubles now." I enjoyed the look on their faces when I said that my retirement plans included baseball as a primary activity.

For a couple of years in my mid-50s, my Cincinnati Colts baseball team decided to use basketball as a way to get together and help stay in shape over the winter. We played in a 50-and-over league organized by the Cincinnati Recreation Commission. There were only four teams in the league and no sign of it growing. The level of play was pretty good, in fact, too good for us. We dropped out after two seasons and stayed with indoor baseball practices in the winter. It is difficult to envision basketball as a late-life sport, but I am sure that it is for some.

Recently, Ann and I ran into the father of Mike Godar, who played on the youth baseball team that I coached. Mike was a strong pitcher and hitter. But the first love for the whole Godar family was hockey. His father, Dave, told us he was still playing in an over-30 league. Although much of his team is over 50, they continue to be competitive. There are hockey leagues around the country with older age brackets. To the credit of those players, they have chosen a non-traditional late-life sport.

Whenever Ann and I are driving and pass a soccer game or football game, whether tackle or flag, we have a little ritual we go through. I sigh and say, "Wow, I would love to get back into that sport." She sighs and says something to the effect of, "Fat chance." I played soccer, indoor and outdoor, into my mid-40s but needed to drop out because of some foot problems. My football days ended in my mid-30s, playing for a Procter & Gamble team in a local flag football league. But, regardless of the risk, I would love to get behind center, having been a high school quarterback, once more in a tackle football game, hoping that it was a 60-and-over game. But that is not going to happen as football, in any form, is not a likely late-life sport.

Go through the list. I know friends who ski in later years and, while it is a great sport and recreation, they are not competing except against themselves. Bowling, like tennis and golf, can be a late-life sport. But the choices are few. Perhaps I am biased, but my conclusion is that baseball is the most compelling competitive late-life sport and, importantly, a team sport.

For those of you who are reading this book who are playing senior baseball but are only in your 30s and early 40s, consider the possibility that you could and, perhaps, should still be playing 30 years from now. It is possible. Just look around, and you will see those who have made the choice to do that. They can be your role models. If you love the game, why not continue?

For those of you who have played baseball and love the game but are not playing now, why not? There may certainly be some good reasons. But some of the reasons you have may not be good enough. If you like to compete, enjoy team sports, and love baseball, you can include the game in your choice of late-life activities. Hopefully, this book has helped you consider reentering the game. The opportunities are available, and you can join the many that have already made baseball their life-sport.

No One Ages in Baseball

This book has been about the game of baseball from the perspective of the senior player. It has been about why we still play the game, about the people who play, about organizations that make the game available, and about how we are continuing to play even after losing a step or two or more. While it applies to anyone playing senior baseball, typically thought of as 30 years old or older, this book has been mostly about senior players growing older into their 40s, 50s, 60s, and beyond.

Ted Simendinger loves the game of baseball as evidenced by his founding of the No Bats Baseball Club, which "views itself as a global advocate of the game of baseball and goodwill, encouraging and supporting programs and individuals that in turn encourage and support baseball and friendship." Since it began in 1991, the club has raised and contributed nearly $400,000 for charities related to baseball or sponsored by baseball players (e.g. the Randy Johnson Homeless Foundation, the Jim "Catfish" Hunter ALS Foundation).

As noted earlier, Simendinger is also an author of the hilarious and sometimes poignant book, *Critters, Fish & Other Troublemakers.* In his essay, "Play On, Cal—The Night Ripken Broke Lou Gehrig's Record," Simendinger writes, "Men like me, of course, wish Cal could play forever. Forty, fifty, sixty, a hundred more years. No one ages in baseball. And if you can play well enough to avoid making 27 outs, you can play the game forever."

Baseball is a game for the ages played by those of all ages. Increasingly, those ages are 40 and 50 and 60 and beyond. The reason playing beyond 40 years old is most impressive is that up to that age, one could argue that baseball players, whether professional or amateur, are still in their prime. Professionals continue to train to maintain their fitness and form while recreational players may not. But it is useful to look at age demographics in the major leagues to see that 40 may be more likely the cutoff between prime and past prime.

Many major league baseball players are in their prime in their 30s. As evidence, on June 10, 2005, of the 750 active major leaguers, 363 were 30 years old or older with 17 active and still-productive players 40 years old or older, among them Roger Clemens, Randy Johnson, Kevin Brown, David Wells, Jamie Moyers, Pat Borders, Steve Finley, and Julio Franco. Also, on June 10, 2005, a significant percentage of the top ten league leaders in the most vital major league statistics were 30 or older.

	National League		American League	
	Avg Age	% >30	Avg Age	% >30
Batting Avg	29	50%	31	60%
Home Runs	29	50%	30	50%
RBI's	32	70%	30	70%
ERA	30	50%	31	50%
Saves	31	60%	32	90%
Strikeouts	29	30%	29	30%

If those are the major league demographics, it would be understandable that many men in their 30s would be and should be playing amateur baseball as well. They are still in their baseball prime. While these men are to be commended and are an integral part of senior men's baseball, this book has largely been describing their futures as they both grow older and continue to play.

For those senior players ages 30 to 40, the challenge is to continue to play the game as long as you can. Hopefully, you can take your love of the game, your fitness, and your resources to become the 40, 50, 60, and beyond players of the future. Many of us left the game and returned to it. Players in the 30 to 40 range have the opportunity never to leave it. It can truly be your life-long and late-life sport.

Top Ten Reasons to Play

Many players in their 40s, 50s, 60s, and beyond have chosen to make baseball their life sport, many younger senior players have yet to make that decision, but have the opportunity to do so, and many who are not yet playing senior baseball can still make the choice. While covered throughout this book, here are, consolidated into one place, my top ten reasons why we choose to play baseball as we get older.

10. *Fathers and Sons*: Baseball is a game of intergenerational relationships. We played catch with our fathers and then with our sons and daughters. The game was passed on to us and we are passing it along to others. Continuing to play evokes the most pleasant memories of those relationships.

9. *Comfort*: Baseball provides us with certainty in a world filled with uncertainty. The field dimensions and rules are constant. Regardless of where we are playing, there are three outs, three strikes, four balls, 90-foot bases, a batting order, and more. While we do not know going into a game who will win or lose, we know with certainty after the game how we did as a team and as an individual. Baseball is a game of black and white, not one of gray. Playing baseball is a comfortable and certain place to be.

8. *Community*: Playing makes us active members of the baseball family. We belong to leagues and teams; we play in tournaments and fantasy camps; we socialize with life-long friends and make new ones. We are tied together by a common love for the game, its culture, and the role it plays in our lives. Our human need for a sense of belonging is well met by the family that is the senior baseball community.

7. *Respect*: Playing baseball as we get older helps us gain others' respect, both those we play with and those who know we play. Perhaps more importantly, playing senior ball helps us build and maintain our self-respect. "The hard is what makes it great."

6. *Tradition*: Continuity is important to our well-being. While surprise and spontaneity have their place, predictability leads to a certain level of contentment. What is more predictable

than baseball's rituals, its sights, its smells? Each season, each game, each at bat, each pitch has a predictable and comforting rhythm. And it is baseball's traditions that are the foundation of this predictability.

5. *Passion*: We learned to love baseball in our youth. We played it with "boundless enthusiasm." We were old enough to make choices about what we really wanted to do yet were not yet burdened by peer pressure and life's conflicting priorities. Playing as we get older allows us to return to the passion of our youth, making time for the game just because we love it and to play it.

4. *Opportunity*: Without the opportunities made available to us, it would be difficult to play the game. Those who have turned local pickup games into teams, leagues, and national organizations and those who have initiated and run fantasy camps and tournaments have given us the chance to play.

3. *Support*: The amount of time and financial commitment needed to play senior baseball varies greatly from player to player and family to family. But regardless of the size of the commitment, the support we need from our families is not trivial. We can play because of that support.

2. *Health and Fitness*: The physiological realities of aging can affect how and how often we play. Yet within our control is the ability to mitigate these aging effects. We play because we have done what it takes to be sufficiently healthy and fit to do so, or we have found ways to compensate for our limitations. Some of us even use baseball as one way to help overcome those limitations.

1. *Never Too Old*: Age in and of itself is not a determining factor in whether we can continue to play. In fact, age can be worn as a badge of honor on the field. So the number one reason we choose to play ball as we grow older is simply, "Because we can."

Baseball: Never Too Old to Play "The" Game

Perhaps there is only one really important question to answer regarding the future of senior baseball. What, for each of us, is our personal future? How do we personally relate to the ten reasons for continuing to play? These are the questions that each of us will be asking before each league season, tournament, or fantasy camp.

There is not a question about age, which is irrelevant in and of itself. Certainly age affects the answers to the other questions whether we are 30 or 70. For up to 125,000 players, so far, the overall answer to whether we will continue to play is, "Yes." What is the answer for you?

As I complete the editing of this book, I am completing my seventh month of rehabilitation for the bulging lumbar disks I experienced in late November 2005. As I noted in the eighth inning, during my recovery, I had altered my primary goal from returning to baseball as quickly as possible to returning to normal life as quickly as possible.

Once I achieved my primary goal, only then would I set my sights on returning to the field. During those first four most difficult weeks of the injury, I had also noticed a significant weakness in the quadriceps muscles and hip of my right leg. Apparently, the disk issues that were causing the pain had also affected a nerve sufficiently to cause the significant residual weakness.

When I started rehabilitation, the weakness in my right quad and right hip combined to cause that leg to be measured at 60% of the strength of the other. The weakness, which made it difficult to walk stairs, became another barrier to normal life functioning as well as to returning to baseball. Happily, the weakness has improved such that my legs' strengths are virtually equal. Unfortunately, the long layoff due to the injury allowed all my muscles to atrophy. In the first three months, I lost almost ten pounds, all of it muscle mass.

Through epidural corticosteroid injections, physical therapy, and a corticosteroid shot in my right hip to address an unrelated bursitis issue, I have reached my primary goal of returning to normal life functioning. I am regularly back in the gym, doing the full battery of weight lifting, aerobics, and stretching that I was doing before the injury, albeit at not nearly the intensity. Importantly, physical therapists have helped me modify my techniques to minimize the risk of recurring injury.

The league season for my team was in progress, and, until recently, I had already concluded that I would sit out the 2006 season. My plan was that later this year, I would decide if I were confident enough to return to the game without a substantial risk of a serious recurrence. Would I need to limit the positions I play? Would I ever catch or pitch again? Would I be able to play without overcompensating for the potential of back injury? Would I shy away from difficult defensive plays or slides? Could I play the game the way I want to?

My heart and soul always told me to get back on the field. My mind was to be the final decision maker. My mind and I had been having a thorough conversation, trying to figure it out. Happily, in mid-July 2006, I returned to playing the game. I have completed my league season and am looking forward to returning to tournament play. Though the return was in doubt, it is no longer.

What I knew throughout the ordeal is that baseball is a great game, which is being made available to us to play as long as we are willing and able. Realistically, I knew that there would come a time when I could no longer play or it would not be prudent for me to do so. I also knew that when you love the game and the people who play it as much as many of us do, you owe it the game, your fellow players, and yourself to play as long as you can. George Goodall played when he was in his 90s. Others play regularly into their 60s and 70s. I made it to 60 before I faced the tough question of whether it would be right for me to continue.

I recently came across an article that was written for the *Tunkhannock New Age* newspaper in July 1976. Ann, Dana, Kevin, and I were transferring from Procter & Gamble's manufacturing facility in Northeastern Pennsylvania to its headquarters in Cincinnati. We had lived and played in Tunkhannock, the small town near the plant, for eight years. While there, I joined up with a number of locals to play softball, basketball, and touch football— we were playing something five to seven days per week all year long. When I was about to leave, I was pleasantly surprised by the emotional sendoff my local friends and teammates gave me. One of them, Roger Shupp, was kind enough to write the article for the weekly local paper.

He wrote many nice things about me, and thanked Ann for being so understanding about how much we played and for being at so many games. But it was the last paragraph that got to me, and did so again when I recently reread it. The article was entitled, "Midnight

Train is Pulling Out." My nickname was Train or Big Train, reflecting how I sounded as I ran the bases. Roger concluded the article by writing the following.

"Best wishes in your new home and on your job...and may God allow you to don a pair of spikes and sneakers until you can no longer bend over to tie them. We love you ' Train,' Goodbye!"

I was 30 at the time and thinking not at all about returning to the game of baseball or playing to 60 or beyond. Yet Roger was prophetic. Although he was referring to softball, basketball, and football, he was really saying that any of us can stay with our sports as long as we are able and willing. Thank you, Roger and all of my Tunkhannock teammates, for sending me on my way and setting the stage for my baseball playing career longevity.

While the question for some months was whether I could bend over to tie my spikes and, therefore, whether I would choose to continue to play or not, that is on longer the question. As of July 2006, I have returned to baseball and plan to play for a long time.

Regardless of what my choice was going to be, I am convinced of the following. I may be too injured to play or I may not be healthy enough to play, but I will never be too old to play "the" game.

Ken: *"Nice job shutting them down, JR. Chalk up another W."*

JR: *"It didn't hurt to turn that double play with the bases loaded to end the game."*

Jack: *"It's time for a beer and the hot tub."*

JR: *"By the way, Al, I forgot to ask, how's that book coming along?"*

Al: *"Well, the manuscript is complete and I'm working with a publisher. My hope now is that the book is meaningful for senior players and motivates some who are not yet playing to join us. But most of all, I hope Yoke would have liked it."*

FITNESS GUIDELINES

Strength Training

1. **Do strength training for all three body areas**, the upper body, the lower body, and the trunk or core. Strength is not about big biceps. It is about building balance as you train and improve. For example, there is consensus that bat speed is enhanced by increasing lower body and core strength to get more rotational power. While arm strength is a factor, it is less critical. One of Albert Pujols' three cardinal rules is "a strong core will keep you in any game longer than big biceps will."

2. **Warm up before strength training**. Light aerobic exercise for five to ten minutes will get the blood flowing to muscles and help prevent injuries.

3. **Train hard but do not over train**. The proper weight-training program should involve two to three sessions per week for each muscle group with at least a day in between to allow the muscles to recover. Increased strength comes from challenging the targeted muscles to the point where they experience micro tears. As the body repairs these tears, the muscles become stronger.

4. **Use the proper form for each exercise** to get the maximum benefit and to help prevent injuries. There are many reputable books that are available if you want to learn about form on your own. If you think you need help figuring it out, you may want to consider an investment in a personal trainer.

5. **Choose the right exercises** for each muscle group you are working, the **right number of sets**, and the right **number of repetitions**. Typically, two sets are appropriate, a warm up set at 50% to 60% of the weight you will lift on your second set, which is your target weight for that day. Based on the consistency

I have found in my reading, I suggest each set have 12 repetitions with about one minute between sets. Your target weight should be that which you find to be very difficult to complete with good form on the last repetition of the second set. More repetitions per set, while good for muscle endurance, will not sufficiently challenge the muscles to build strength. Fewer repetitions per set are more for bodybuilding versus balanced strength gain.

6. **Gain advantage from both the concentric (lifting) and eccentric (lowering) motions**. Frequently, lifters focus on only the lifting motion of the exercise (e.g. bringing the weights toward your chest in a biceps curl), but then allow the weights to "fall" back to the exercise's starting position. By allowing gravity to help in the eccentric part of the lift, you lose strength-building potential. The University of Kentucky's baseball team strength training coach spoke at a clinic to which I took my 12-year-old boys team in the mid-1980s. He said that he prescribed a two-second lift and a four-second return for each repetition to ensure his athletes were not letting gravity do their work.

7. **Work the muscle through the full range of motion.** Our bodies experience a wide range of motion during any baseball game. During throwing, running, sliding, reaching, bending, or crouching, our muscles need to protect us from injury by being able to take the stresses applied. If we do lifting in only a limited range, the muscles will not be adequately trained to deal with real game situations.

8. **Periodically change exercises** to target the same muscle group to help manage boredom and keep your body challenged. Changing your routines about every eight weeks should help.

9. **Expect soreness, but respond to injury**. Strength training can be safe and effective. But you should expect soreness both during (the burn) and after (DOMS-delayed onset muscle soreness) lifting. You will quickly learn to recognize and value these sensations as your body helping you know that you are making a positive difference. You will also learn to know if you have gone beyond these helpful sensations into the realm of injury. If you do, address the issue quickly without trying to work your way through it.

Aerobic Training

1. If you are just starting, **choose an aerobic exercise that you will most enjoy**. Among those to pick from are walking, jogging/running, swimming, rowing, stair climbing, bicycling, hiking, cross-country skiing, step and dance exercise classes, roller skating, and the more continuous forms of tennis, racquetball, and squash. The intent is to exercise using large-muscle groups rhythmically and continuously to elevate your heartbeat and breathing for a sustained period.

2. **Choose your exercise based on goals, physical condition, and any injury or illness history.** For example, if you are just starting, you may want to walk versus jog. If you have a history of knee or back problems, swimming may best for you versus running.

3. As you progress, **alternate among types of exercise**. This "cross training" will help reduce the chances of overuse injuries, provide more balanced conditioning, and maintain an enjoyment level by staving off boredom.

4. **Use proper techniques** to prevent injuries and optimize efficiency. There are many resources that you can read to help you here. But, like strength training, technique can also be learned from a personal trainer if that is what might help you most.

5. **Gradually increase your frequency, duration, and intensity** guided by your progress, available time, and any other personal factors. Increasing too fast risks injury or discouragement. Increasing too slowly will reduce the pace of your progress.

6. **Train three to four days per week** to improve your fitness. Training two days per week will help maintain fitness. More than four days per week will positively affect fat loss, a goal for many.

7. **Sixty minutes total per exercise session is optimal** for many people. However, if you have less time, use it. The most recent government recommendations indicate that exercise times can provide benefit by accumulating them throughout the day if you do not have time for one longer session. If you can extend your session, there is additional benefit to be gained, especially in body fat reduction.

8. **Train at the optimum target heart rate.** Target heart rate is calculated as a percentage of your maximum heart rate, which is 220 minus your age. At 50–60% of maximum, you will gain benefit from decreased body fat, blood pressure, and cholesterol at a low risk of injury. At 60–70% of maximum, you will get the same benefits but will burn more calories. Between 70–80% of maximum heart rate is the zone (the aerobic zone) which best improves your cardiovascular and respiratory system health. You will burn even more calories than at the previous two training zones. Training at higher heart-rate levels has benefits more associated with those striving for significant endurance gains that are not relevant directly to baseball.

9. **Warm up and cool down for each training session.** Warm up for about five minutes by doing your exercise at a lower intensity. This reduces your chance of injuries. Stopping abruptly and standing around increases the risk of getting dizzy. Cool down by either reducing the intensity of the exercise for a few minutes or use the period for stretching.

Stretching

1. **Involve all of the muscle groups and joints.** Select the stretches that will complement your strength-training program to include upper body, lower body, and core areas.

2. **Stretch when the body has warmed up.** If you have just finished a workout in your strength or aerobic training program, the body is already warmed up and it is an excellent time to stretch. As noted before, using the stretching period after such a workout can also serve as the cool down portion of your exercise. If you are only stretching, do some form of light aerobic activity for five to ten minutes to get the body warmed up and help prevent injuries.

3. **Stretch at least three days per week.** I have found the best way to ensure that the stretching regimen is adequate is to tie it to the strength and aerobic training schedule. Stretch at least those muscles targeted during the workout session. If you do this and your strength and aerobic program is well designed, the stretching will be adequate.

4. **Take each stretch to a position of mild discomfort.** This

will ensure an adequate stretch but keep you from straining by stretching too far. Always work into the stretch slowly and smoothly, and do not bounce. A concept that has helped me says, "Breathe into each stretch."

5. **Hold each stretch for at least ten seconds.** You can then work your way up to 30 seconds. The research shows that stretching beyond 30 seconds provides no additional benefit. Perform two to three repetitions for each stretch.

6. **Stretch the right amount for your body.** Do not observe others and try to stretch as far as they do. Everyone's body is different genetically and at a different level of fitness. The training is about making your body more flexible, not trying to be as flexible as someone else. This principle applies to strength and aerobic training as well. Your goal is continual improvement for you.

7. **Use proper form**, which can be gleaned from any number of books or from a professional. I learned, for example, from my physical therapist during rehab for my back that I had been doing some stretches improperly, thereby exacerbating my back issues. As an example, I was stretching my hamstrings by standing and elevating my leg on a bench, then bending over toward my toes. This was stressing my back. I now stand, elevate my leg, keep my torso erect, and push my stomach forward into the stretch.

Fluid Management

1. Our total fluid intake should be 125 ounces per day. About 80% comes from drinking, and the other 20% comes from extracting liquid from foods. **Drink six to eight glasses of water per day** as a basis for consumption for a day of normal activity. Fluids like milk, juice, and decaffeinated soft drinks are also hydrating beverages that can help maintain body fluids. Caffeine and alcohol-containing drinks act as diuretics, causing the body to lose water though increased urination.

2. On game days and especially at tournaments when you are playing multiple days in a row and perhaps multiple games per day, basic intake is not sufficient. **Drink ten to 12 ounces of water about 20 minutes before starting to warm up**. If you are playing a tournament and the weather is hot and humid or if you had significant fluid deficiencies from the previous day,

you should start over-hydrating earlier in the day to get the level to a good point prior to your first game.

3. During a game, I **take six to 12 ounces of fluids during every offensive half inning**. I base the amount on the weather conditions and which position I am playing. If pitching or catching, I am likely to be sweating more and I will increase intake.

4. When I had my serious dehydration problem, my physician told me that water is generally sufficient for replacing fluids, but **on a challenging day, using sports drinks helps replace the electrolytes**, like sodium, potassium, and chloride, which can be lost beyond those stored through nutritional intake.

5. After a game or tournament day, assess whether you have lost more fluid than you have taken in. The indicators of thirst, urine color, skin flexibility, or weight can help. You may find other symptoms that work for you. For example, my voice gets raspy when my fluids are low. **Drink consistently** at the rate and quantity comfortable to you **to replace the needed fluids so that you can start the next day at a good level.**

BIBLIOGRAPHY

Ardell, Jean Hastings. *Breaking into Baseball: Women and the National Pastime*, Southern Illinois University, 2005.

Coleman, Gene. *52-Week Baseball Training*, Human Kinetics, 2000.

Elfers, James E. *The Tour to End All Tours; The Story of Major League Baseball's 1913-1914 World Tour*, University of Nebraska Press, 2003.

Garagiola, Joe. *Baseball is a Funny Game*, J.B. Lippincott, Inc., 1960.

Garagiola, Joe. *It's Anybody's Ballgame*, Contemporary Books, Inc., 2001.

Gennaro, Vince. *Field of Dreamers; Tales from Baseball Fantasy Camp*, 1st Books Library, 2003.

Goodwin, Doris Kearns. *Wait Till Next Year, A Memoir*, Simon & Schuster, 1998.

Gordon, Peter H. *Diamonds are Forever; Artists and Writers on Baseball*, Edited, Chronicle Books, 1987.

Hall, Donald. *Fathers Playing Catch with Sons; Essays on Sport (Mostly Baseball)*, Dell Publishing Co, Inc., 1985.

Halpern, Alan A. M.D. *The Kalamazoo Arthritis Book*, 1984.

Malamud, Bernard. *The Natural*, Harcourt & Brace, 1952.

Maslow, Abraham. H. *Motivation and Personality*, Harper & Row, 1954.

Nelson, Miriam E. Ph. D. et al. *Strong Women and Men Beat Arthritis*, G. P. Putnam's Sons, 2002.

Shannon, Mike. *Baseball: The Writer's Game* by Mike Shannon, Brassey's, Inc., 2002.

Shannon, Mike. *Coming Back to Baseball: The Cincinnati Astros and the Joys of Over-30 Play*, McFarland & Co Inc Publishing, 2005.

Simendinger, Ted. *Critters, Fish & Other Troublemakers*, Airplane Reader Publishing, 2000.

Smith, Curt (Editor). *What Baseball Means to Me; A Celebration of our National Pastime*, Warner Books, Inc., 2002.

Sullivan, George. *Baseball's Boneheads, Bad Boys, & Just Plain Crazy Guys*, The Millbrook Press, 2003.

Whitford, David. *Extra Innings; A Season in the Senior League*, Harper Collins, 1991.

Wolfe, Rich. *For Cardinal Fans Only!*, Lone Wolfe Press, 2003.

Wolff, Nelson W. *Baseball for Real Men; Seven Spiritual Laws for Senior Players*, Eakin Press, 2000.

WEB SITE RESOURCES

Baseball: Never Too Old To Play "The" Game
www.aaspector.com

Topic	Web Site
American Women's Baseball Federation	www.awbf.org
Barnstable Bat Company	www.barnstablebat.com
Baseball International	www.baseballinternational.com
Baseball Reliquary	www.baseballreliquary.org
Bob Wagner Wooden Bat Classic	www.woodenbatclassic.com
Cape Cod League	www.capecodbaseball.org
Challenger Baseball	www.littleleague.org
Colorado Women's Baseball League	www.coloradowomensbaseball.com
Dusseldorfs on the Beach	www.dusseldorfs.com
ESPN Magazine on-line	www.espn.go.com
Friends of Doubleday	www.friendsofdoubleday.org
Gray Iron Fitness	www.grayironfitness.com
Legends of Baseball	www.legendsofbaseball.com
The Longfellow Clubs	www.longfellowclubs.com
Men's Senior Baseball League	www.msblnational.com
National Adult Baseball Association	www.dugoout.org
No Bats Baseball Club	www.nobats.com
Play at the Plate	www.playattheplate.org
Ponce De Leon Baseball League	www.poncedeleonbaseball.com
Reds Baseball Heaven	www.redsbaseballheaven.com
Roy Hobbs	www.royhobbs.com
U. S. Over Thirty Baseball League	www.usotb.com
Ultimate Experience Baseball Tour	www.majorleagueexperience.com
Vintage Baseball Association	www.vbba.org

ABOUT THE AUTHOR

Herman Spector put a bat and ball in his son's hands as soon as he could hold them, and Al has not let go for 60 years.

Al grew up in the back alleys, on the sandlots, and on the baseball fields of St. Louis, where he played youth, high school, American Legion, and college baseball. While he left the game from time to time because of conflicting life priorities and a temporary infatuation with softball, Al returned to playing baseball beginning in his early 40s and then again in his early 50s.

Retiring from a 33-year career as an executive with the Procter & Gamble Company gave Al the time to play more and to write *Baseball: Never Too Old the Play "The" Game*. As he only half-jokingly says, "I retired because work was getting in the way of playing baseball."

Al plays about 75 baseball games a year. He and his wife, Ann, travel extensively, nationally and internationally, for baseball tournaments, to visit family (including two grandsons), and for other recreation. Al has begun work on several new book ideas, is researching his family tree, is addicted to crossword puzzles, and works out at the gym daily to fend off the reality of aging.

When at home, Al volunteers as a management and quality assurance consultant with Every Child Succeeds, a prominent Cincinnati social services program. He also consults with for-profit companies and with other non-profit organizations.

For Additional Copies of

Baseball: NEVER TOO OLD TO PLAY "THE" GAME

Use the form below
Or
Go to www.aaspector.com

Reply to: Cincinnati Book Publishers
              2449 Fairview Avenue
              Cincinnati OH 45219

PLEASE SEND ME _____COPIES
of Baseball: Never Too Old To Play "The" Game

MY CHECK FOR _____IS ENCLOSED.
PLEASE MAKE CHECK PAYABLE TO: Cincinnati Book Publishers

1-9 COPIES $18.95 + $1.23 TAX(STATE Ohio) + $2.82 S&H= $23.00 EA.

10-50 COPIES $17.00 + $1.11 TAX(STATE Ohio) + $1.89 S&H= $20.00 EA.

50+ COPIES- email BballNever2old@aol.com

NAME _____

ADDRESS _____

_____

_____

_____

CITY _____ STATE _____

ZIP _____

PHONE _____

EMAIL _____
              Thank you!